DIARY OF A SIT-IN

Blacks in the New World

August Meier, Series Editor

A list of books in the series appears at the end of this volume.

DIARY OF A SIT-IN

MERRILL PROUDFOOT

Second Edition

With an Introduction by
MICHAEL S. MAYER

University of Illinois Press

Urbana and Chicago

To

THE STUDENTS OF KNOXVILLE COLLEGE

whose vision and courage

shamed the rest of us into making ourselves expendable also

in the struggle for the rights of man

© 1962, 1990 by Merrill Proudfoot
Introduction © 1990 by the Board of Trustees
of the University of Illinois
Manufactured in the United States of America
P 5 4 3 2 1

This book is printed on acid-free paper.

Library of Congress Cataloging-in-Publication Data

Proudfoot, Merrill.
    Diary of a sit-in / Merrill Proudfoot. — 2nd ed. / with an
introduction by Michael S. Mayer.
      p.   cm. — (Blacks in the New World)
    ISBN 0-252-06062-8 (alk. paper)
    1. Afro-Americans—Civil rights—Tennessee—Knoxville—
History—20th century. 2. Civil rights demonstrations—Tennessee—
Knoxville—History—20th century. 3. Proudfoot, Merrill.
4. Knoxville (Tenn.)—Race relations. I. Title. II. Series.
F444.K7P95 1990
976.8'85053—dc20
                                     89-77561
                                       CIP

Contents

Introduction

Michael S. Mayer

THE events recorded in Merrill Proudfoot's *Diary of a Sit-In* were part of an extraordinary sequence of events that began with the bold action of four courageous, young black men in Greensboro, North Carolina. The sit-in movement marked an extraordinary moment in history. Long-standing grievances merged with a tradition of nonviolent direct action to express the discontent of black Americans and their demands for change. At the same time, however, what happened in 1960 was not simply a culmination of past protest; it also represented a break with the past and the beginning of something new. The tactic of sitting in ideally suited the goals of the students; they wanted access to American society, and their method of protest dramatically symbolized the injustice of denying them that access. Although usually associated with Greensboro and the subsequent protests in 1960, the tactic was not new. The Congress of Racial Equality (CORE) and the NAACP Youth Councils had employed the techniques of nonviolent direct action in the past. Indeed, they had even protested by sitting in. However, something different began in Greensboro. The events in Greensboro unleashed a tide of protest that swept across the South. The sit-ins expanded and changed the civil rights movement. They also exerted a powerful influence on the white student movement. Ultimately, the sit-in movement had a profound impact on American society in the 1960s.

On Monday, February 1, 1960, four freshmen from North Caro-

ix

lina Agricultural and Technical College, Joseph McNeill, Ezell Blair, Franklin McCain, and David Richmond, walked into the Woolworth's store in Greensboro, bought some school supplies, took seats at the segregated lunch counter, and ordered coffee and donuts. When they were told "We don't serve colored here," Blair politely responded that they had already been served at another counter and showed the receipts for their school supplies. The dumbfounded waitress got the manager, to whom the students explained their protest. Although they never received service, the students remained seated at the lunch counter until closing. That evening, they met with other students, formed the Student Executive Committee for Justice, and decided to continue the sit-ins until they were served. They also committed themselves to the tactics employed by Martin Luther King, Jr., during the Montgomery bus boycott. Whatever they encountered, the protesters would remain nonviolent; they would not return insults, threats, or physical violence.

Blacks had practiced the tactic of nonviolent direct action for a century before the four students from North Carolina A&T took their seats at Woolworth's, though the term *nonviolent direct action* seems to have been used first by CORE, an organization established by a group of pacifists in the early 1940s. Direct action emerged as a prominent form of black protest in the 1930s, exemplified by "Don't-Buy-Where-You-Can't-Work" campaigns in various cities. After World War II, campaigns got under way, primarily in the North, against segregated public accommodations. However, these demonstrations never equaled the level of activity in the thirties. CORE played a central role in many of these protests, yet few of the participants shared the organization's pacifist commitment; rather, most regarded nonviolent tactics as a useful strategy.

Direct action protests declined in the early fifties, partly because blacks were gaining access to public accommodations in the North, partly because of the conservative tenor of the times, and partly because of the difficulty of applying direct action against other forms of discrimination. When direct action revived in the later part of the decade, the principal area of activity shifted from the North to the

South, and access to public accommodations was again the focus. Decisions of the United States Supreme Court and the recalcitrant southern response combined to heighten black militance. Blacks boycotted buses in Baton Rouge in 1953 and Montgomery in 1955, the latter of which brought Martin Luther King, Jr., to national attention. Blacks also undertook direct action protests in places such as Miami, Tallahassee, Lexington, Nashville, Tulsa, Oklahoma City, Atlanta, and Petersburg. Rarely, however, did direct action alone achieve its purpose; the success of protests in Montgomery and Tuskegee, for example, came about because of decisions by federal courts.

Nevertheless, the inspirational impact of nonviolent direct action far exceeded any immediate concrete results. Despite the skepticism of adult leaders, the NAACP Youth Council in Wichita, Kansas, began sitting in at lunch counters as early as 1953. Demonstrations led by the NAACP Youth Council also took place in Oklahoma City in 1958. Encouraged by the protests elsewhere, the local branch of the NAACP sat in at drugstores in downtown Louisville in 1959. In Durham, Floyd McKissick, a young attorney and an adult advisor to the NAACP Youth Council, and Rev. Douglas Moore of the Southern Christian Leadership Conference (SCLC) conducted sit-ins at local bus stations, parks, hotels, and ice cream parlors. By 1959, CORE affiliates sponsored sit-ins in Lexington and Miami, and some even began occasional sit-ins in South Carolina.

With a decade of increasing activity behind them, fueled by the rising expectations generated by decisions of the Supreme Court and enactments of the Congress, yet frustrated by the slow pace of change, students began the sit-ins of 1960. The day after the original four students took their seats at Woolworth's lunch counter, twenty-five students from North Carolina A&T, joined by four black women from Bennett College, returned to Woolworth's. To emphasize the reasonableness of their demands, the men wore coats and ties; some wore ROTC uniforms. The women wore dresses. When refused service, they continued to sit. By Wednesday, students occupied sixty-three of the sixty-six seats at the lunch counter. For the first time, blacks who were not students joined the sit-in. On Thursday, scores of black students were joined by three white students from Women's College of the University of North Carolina, and the demonstrations spilled over to the S. H. Kress store down the street. Over three hundred blacks demonstrated on Friday, and even larger protests took place on Saturday. With tensions rising, city officials finally decided to negotiate; after which, at a mass rally on Saturday night, the protesters agreed to stop demonstrating to allow negotiations to proceed.

Over the weekend, while the students in Greensboro decided to suspend their sit-ins, news of the protest spread to other black campuses. Over one hundred students met in Winston-Salem to plan a demonstration. Their sit-in began on Monday, February 8. On the same day, seventeen students from North Carolina College and four from Duke University sat in at the lunch counter of the Woolworth's in Durham, where McKissick had been organizing similar protests for several years. The next day, about one hundred fifty black students from Johnson C. Smith University began sit-ins in Charlotte, and students from Shaw University and St. Augustine's College, spurred on by a radio report assuring its listeners that there would be no disturbances in their city, initiated sit-ins in Raleigh. By the end of the week, the protests had spread to Fayetteville, High Point, Elizabeth City, and Concord. The demonstrations were often met with arrests, and black communities responded with campaigns urging blacks: "Don't buy where you can't eat." As was the case with the direct action campaigns of the 1930s, economic pressure proved to be a most effective weapon.

On February 11, Hampton, Virginia, became the first city outside of North Carolina to be engulfed by the wave of sit-ins. Norfolk and Portsmouth, where CORE had been active, quickly followed. By the end of February, Nashville, Chattanooga, Richmond, Baltimore, Lexington, and Montgomery had all been hit by the wave of student protest. The arrest of thirty-three blacks at Thalhimer's department store in Richmond sparked demonstrations in Petersburg, Newport News, and Arlington. Throughout the South, students were inspired by news of sit-ins elsewhere and decided to do something themselves. In this way, the sit-ins spread throughout the entire South.

Sit-ins organized by college students tended to be characterized by strict discipline; however, outbreaks of violence occurred at several protests in which high school students participated. The first such incident took place in Portsmouth, Virginia, where high school students staged an unplanned and unorganized sit-in on February 11. Their protest was met with police dogs, but the demonstrations continued. After a sit-in on the 16th, hundreds of black and white high school students fought each other. Chattanooga experienced a more extensive outbreak. Two days of rioting broke out after a protest on February 23. In High Point, which had no black college, high school students followed the example set by college students elsewhere. In the course of their demonstrations, black protesters responded with retaliatory violence. Worried that such incidents might discredit the whole movement, civil rights leaders, particularly those in CORE, attempted to inculcate the precepts of nonviolence. In Portsmouth, CORE organized a workshop to teach black high school students nonviolent tactics.

The sit-ins spread to Tallahassee, another city where CORE had been actively organizing, on February 14, when students from Florida A&M and local high schools sat in at Woolworth's. The following week, eleven protesters were arrested. Subsequent demonstrations attracted the participation of white students from Florida State University. After a group of demonstrators was arrested at Woolworth's on March 12, a large number of blacks marched on Woolworth's and McCrory's intending to "fill the jails if necessary." When arrested and found guilty, the students chose to go to jail rather than pay their fines. The black community reacted to the jailings with a boycott of the downtown stores.

Meanwhile, in Greensboro, the store managers proved unwilling to compromise, so the sit-ins resumed on April 1. The students expanded the protests to other stores that served blacks at merchandise counters but not at lunch counters. Faced with the determined students, the merchants switched tactics. Forty-five students were arrested for trespass on April 21. The arrests served only to enrage the black community, which responded with a boycott of the variety stores. To the surprise of many, the administration of North Carolina A&T resisted pressure to restrain the students, as did that of Bennett College. With profits off by more than one third, Greensboro's white leaders grudgingly gave in. Woolworth's, S. H. Kress, and Meyer's department store opened their lunch counters to blacks.

By the end of February, thirty-two cities in North Carolina, South Carolina, Virginia, Tennessee, Florida, Maryland, Kentucky, and Alabama had experienced sit-ins. A month later, the total climbed to forty-two cities, and Georgia, Texas, Louisiana, and Arkansas joined the list of states hit by the sit-ins. By April, the demonstrations had spread to seventy-eight communities across the South, and not even Mississippi was exempt. Before a year had passed, over seventy thousand people had participated. Most were black, but they were joined by a significant number of whites.

Nashville ranked among the most significant centers of protest. In early February, blacks from Fisk University, the American Baptist Theological Seminary, Tennessee State College, and Meharry Medical School, along with a few whites from Vanderbilt University, began a massive campaign of nonviolent direct action. Nashville had a well-developed protest movement; a group of students had been training in the techniques of nonviolent direct action and was ready to act when they learned of the sit-ins in Greensboro. They had conducted "test sit-ins" at two large downtown department stores before the Christmas holidays in 1959 and had plans to begin a campaign of sit-ins in 1960.

James Lawson, a black student at Vanderbilt's Divinity School and a pacifist, was the group's mentor and informal leader. He established ground rules for the protest, which reflected his own religious commitment to nonviolent protest: "Do show yourself friendly on the counter at all times. Do sit straight and always face the counter. Don't strike back, or curse back if attacked. Don't laugh out. Don't hold conversation. Don't block entrances." Lawson cautioned each protester to "remember the teachings of Jesus, Gandhi, Martin Luther King."

The Nashville sit-ins began on February 12 at Woolworth's. Each day brought a greater number of students to protest and increasing tension. On the fourth day of the sit-ins, white hecklers taunted the protesters, spat on them, pelted them with food and chewing gum, and pushed lit cigarettes against their backs. A white sit-inner, who refused to respond to taunts of "nigger-lover," was pulled off his stool, thrown to the floor, and kicked. At McClellan's, a variety store, whites beat a black student from Fisk. None of these demonstrators fought back, but when police arrived they arrested only the protesters. When more students rushed to McClellan's to protest, police arrested them, too. However, as Diane Nash, one of the student leaders from Fisk, recalled, "No matter what they did and how many they arrested, there was still a lunch counter full of students there." At their trial, the students chose jail over paying their fines. Nash explained, "We feel that if we pay these fines we would be contributing to and supporting the injustice and immoral practices that have been performed in the arrest and conviction of the defendants." As was frequently the case elsewhere, Nashville's black community organized a boycott of the downtown stores, which contributed significantly to the eventual desegregation of a number of private establishments. From Nashville, the sit-ins spread to Knoxville (the location of the events described by Proudfoot), Chattanooga, Memphis, and Oak Ridge, Kentucky.

In the Deep South, South Carolina experienced sit-ins at Rock Hill, Orangeburg, Columbia, and Sumter. In Orangeburg, where CORE had conducted classes in nonviolent tactics even before the Greensboro sit-ins, four hundred students from Claflin College and South Carolina State College, led by Chuck McDew, marched downtown to sit in at the city's segregated lunch counters. Police armed with tear gas and fire hoses intercepted them and arrested 388 protesters. At Rock Hill, sit-ins and picketing followed by a jail-in failed to desegregate lunch counters.

Black students who sat in risked not only violence from the white community, but also reprisals from their own colleges. Thirty-five students from Alabama State College in Montgomery, Alabama, walked into the cafeteria at the state capitol building and asked for service; when refused, they left. However, Governor John Paterson ordered the president of the college, H. Councill Trenholm, to expel any students engaged in the protests. When Trenholm expelled some of the protesters, students at the college responded with a mass rally. Although the students wanted to continue the sit-ins, many of their elders feared for the survival of Alabama State. As a compromise, the students agreed to hold a prayer service on the steps of the capitol, which over half the student body attended. Almost one thousand students pledged not to register for spring classes unless the expelled students were reinstated. Under pressure from the state government, the school's administration helped to keep the student movement in check, at least temporarily.

Other black colleges also took action against student protesters. In Baton Rouge, Louisiana, students at Southern University initiated demonstrations shortly after the sit-ins began in Greensboro. On March 29, a number of Southern students were arrested after a sit-in at S. H. Kress. The State Board of Education warned of "stern disciplinary action" against any further demonstrations. The president of Southern, Dr. Felton Smith, was reported as saying that he had "no alternative." Further demonstrations resulted in the expulsion of eighteen students. At Albany State College in Georgia, the school's president dismissed forty students who participated in the demonstrations in that city. Florida A&M also expelled students for protesting.

Faced with the new form of protest, white southerners sometimes responded violently. In Houston, a white youth slashed a black protester with a knife, and three white men flogged a black man with a chain and carved the initials KKK on his chest. In Jacksonville, Florida, a white student demonstrator was attacked in jail and suffered a broken jaw, and the KKK pistol-whipped another demonstrator. Yet another student protester was stabbed by an unknown assailant in Columbia, South Carolina.

The sit-ins touched off a massive nonviolent struggle in Atlanta, Georgia. Two students at Morehouse College, Julian Bond and Lonnie King, met with student leaders of other black schools in the city and planned a protest to begin on Abraham Lincoln's birthday. The presidents of Atlanta's black colleges and other adult leaders urged caution and suggested that the students draw up a list of grievances. Accordingly, the students took out full-page advertisements in the *Journal, Constitution,* and *Daily World* explaining their purpose. Entitled "An Appeal for Human Rights," the document demanded an end to segregation in restaurants, movie theaters, concert halls, and other public facilities; the enfranchisement of blacks; equitable law enforcement; jobs for blacks; equal expenditure on education; and equal access to housing. The students also met with Mayor William B. Hartsfield, who maintained cordial relations with the city's black leaders. Hartsfield encouraged the students to negotiate with white business leaders before undertaking demonstrations. Nevertheless, two hundred students staged coordinated protests at several locations on March 15, and police arrested twenty-seven of them who tried to get service at the cafeteria at city hall. Negotiations failed, largely because civic leaders counted on summer vacation to end the wave of protest and therefore refused to compromise. When fall came, however, the campaign resumed. Martin Luther King, Jr., and thirty-six students were arrested for trespass when they sat down at the Magnolia Room of Rich's department store. Larger protests were followed by more arrests, and once again negotiations failed. By this time, however, the black community had lined up solidly behind the sit-ins, and a boycott of downtown establishments had begun to take effect. Arrests began again in February 1961, but Atlanta's established black leaders worked out a compromise with the business community. Many students objected to the terms of the agreement, but an impassioned appeal from Martin Luther King, Jr., rallied support for the pact, in which the business community pledged to end segregated eating facilities no later than October 15.

As the protest movement spread throughout the South, some

demonstrations took on new forms. People staged "kneel-ins" at segregated churches, "swim-ins" at segregated pools, and "read-ins" at public libraries. By the end of 1961, nearly two hundred cities had begun to desegregate places of public accommodation. Most sit-ins, and a vast majority of the successes, took place in the upper South. Victories in the Deep South remained rare.

A wide variety of elements sparked specific sit-ins. A charismatic student or an especially galling local incident accounted for many; others appeared, at least on the surface, to be spontaneous. Recently, several historians and sociologists have traced the roots of black protest to the internal dynamics of black communities. Whether or not one accepts theoretical constructs such as Aldon Morris's "movement centers," this scholarship has focused attention on black institutions and the internal structures of black communities. It provides a useful addition to earlier scholarship, which tended to focus on national civil rights organizations. However, a great variety of factors account for why the protests took place when they did, and the fact remains that the protest in Greensboro touched off a national wave of protest. Demonstrations took place in cities without a well-organized black community as well as those with one. In focusing on a vertical analysis of the sit-ins, Morris and others have paid too little attention to the horizontal aspect. The sit-ins created a dynamic of their own. Something happened in the South in 1960, and it happened all over the region. At the same time, each local sit-in was distinctive. No general theory yet proposed applies to all locations at which protests took place.

Individual students had an almost endless number of reasons for participating. Perhaps there were as many reasons as there were protesters. Some cited inspiration from parents or teachers; others recalled personal experiences of humiliation or degradation. At least some of the participants had served in the armed forces or lived in the North and therefore had experienced alternative possibilities to the rigid segregation of the South. College freshmen of 1960 had been twelve or thirteen years old at the time of the *Brown* decision. Thus, college students of 1960 had come of age, at least politically, since that landmark. Frustration with the failure to realize the promise of *Brown* and the Civil Rights Act of 1957 played a large role in the growth of the sit-in movement. Moreover, young people could not help but identify with and be inspired by the black high school students who heroically faced the angry white mobs in Little Rock. Other students were influenced by the independence movements in Africa; perhaps some felt shame for being less aggressive than African blacks in demanding their freedom. Many black students were inspired by Martin Luther King, Jr.

The movement was undoubtedly imbued with King's teachings of nonviolence, though King was certainly not the only such influence. CORE had employed such tactics for years, and it provided instruction for some of the sit-inners on how to engage in nonviolent direct action and how to cover up to prevent injuries when assaulted. In Greensboro, Dr. George Simkins, a black dentist and the head of the local chapter of the NAACP, contacted CORE for advice and help after the original sit-inners called on him for assistance. Gordon Carey of CORE arrived in North Carolina a few days after the sit-ins began, and other CORE organizers went elsewhere.

That the protests originated in black colleges surprised many who considered them to be bastions of conservatism. For example, North Carolina A&T, in its early years, adhered to Booker T. Washington's ideals of education. The college had only two presidents from 1896 to 1955, Dr. James B. Dudley and Dr. F. D. Bluford, both of whom were conservative and accommodationist. Dr. Warmoth T. Gibbs, Bluford's successor and protégé, was president during the sit-ins. Moreover, as a state-supported school, A&T was particularly vulnerable to pressure from the state government. Yet beneath the placid surface ran an undercurrent of protest. When Governor Luther Hodges addressed students at an assembly in 1955, he pronounced "Negro" as "Nigra." Students responded by booing the governor. Not long before, students had booed a trustee, Julian Price, for a similar transgression in diction. Moreover, Gibbs, who was chosen to succeed Bluford in part because of his deferential manner, did nothing to halt the sit-ins. Even Gibbs was less content with the status quo than his outward demeanor indicated, and he lent clandestine support to the sit-ins.

If the black colleges were not so conservative as they might have appeared, neither were the demonstrators so radical as some at the time feared. The student protesters of 1960 were not economic radicals or marxists; they did not demand fundamental alterations in the political or economic system of the United States. Far from a rejection of mainstream America, their protest represented a desire by young blacks who aspired to middle-class status for further assimilation. The students who participated in the lunch counter sit-ins were not alienated from America; they wanted to share in its dreams and rewards. Indeed, the student protesters justified their actions in terms of the dominant political values of the United States, much as did Martin Luther King, Jr. Leaders of the sit-in movement in Atlanta, for instance, cited the supremacy of federal law and proposed to use every "legal and non-violent" means to achieve their aims. The sit-inners were radical only in their demands that America live up to its promise of equality and that it do so immediately. To be sure, the changes they demanded constituted a profound change in the racial and social arrangements of the South, and in that sense they were radical indeed. However, their radicalism drew on Jefferson and Paine, not Marx. Students who sat in sincerely believed that the changes they demanded would benefit the nation by making it live up to its stated ideals. Many argued that ending segregation would place the United States on firmer ground in the cold war, especially in the competition for the loyalty of emerging African nations and the third world in general.

The right of a well-dressed, polite, young person to eat a hamburger or drink a soda at a lunch counter became a potent symbol for the black struggle against the inhuman degradation of segregation. Young blacks outside the South profoundly felt the movement's impact. James Forman, a former schoolteacher in Chicago then doing graduate work in French, and Robert Moses, a twenty-six-year-old math teacher with a master's degree in philosophy from Harvard, were just two of those deeply moved by accounts of the lunch counter sit-ins. Moses recalled that "the students in that picture had a certain look on their faces, sort of sullen, angry determined. Before, the Negro of the south had always looked on the defensive, cringing. This time they were taking the initiative. They were kids my age, and I knew this had something to do with my life."

The student protests also served to energize and inspire many adults in black communities. Parents, relatives, friends, and strangers raised bail, provided legal counsel, organized boycotts, and gave moral support. Harvard Sitkoff has written that "the behavior of the students taught their elders that the way it used to be did not have to be."

The courage, dignity, and determination of the students won many white supporters. Not long after the sit-ins began in Greensboro, the student newspaper at the all-white University of North Carolina, the *Daily Tar Heel*, ran an editorial proclaiming, "We hope they win. We hope they win BIG and we hope they win SOON." Frank Porter Graham, a former president of the University of North Carolina and a former United States senator who lost his senate seat in the racist campaign of 1950, said that the protesters were "in their day and generation renewing springs of American democracy. . . . In sitting down they are standing up for the American dream."

The University of North Carolina had a reputation for liberalism, and Graham was a maverick on racial issues. However, the reasonableness of the students' demands and the dignity of their bearing won grudging respect from southern moderates. According to an editorial in the Greensboro *Daily News*, "There are many white people in the South who recognize the injustice of the lunch counter system. It is based on circumstances which may have made sense 100 years ago; today it has a touch of medievalism. It smacks of Indian 'untouchables' or Hitlerian Germany's Master Race theories." Governor LeRoy Collins of Florida admitted that, whatever the legalities, it was unjust to open a store to the public and accept the patronage of blacks in all departments except one.

Even the conservative Richmond *News Leader* could not help but be impressed. "Here were the colored students, in coats, white shirts, ties, and one of them was reading Goethe and one was taking notes from a biology text. And here, on the sidewalk outside, was a gang of white boys come to heckle, a ragtail rabble, slack-jawed, black-jacketed, grinning fit to kill, and some of them, God save the mark, were waving the proud and honored flag of the Southern States in the last war fought by gentlemen. Eheu! It gives one pause."

If nothing else, once the sit-ins got under way, southern whites could no longer remain unaware of the depth of black discontent. No longer could whites delude themselves that blacks were content with things as they were. The risks the students had taken testified to their commitment to bring about change. Entire communities rallied to their cause, making it virtually impossible to attribute the demonstrations to a handful of agitators from the North.

The sit-in movement won support all over the country. CORE organized supportive actions in the North, and a wide variety of groups staged demonstrations against the variety store chains. People picketed national headquarters and integrated stores in the North, hoping to force a change in policy. Woolworth's reported that sales for March 1960 were down 8.9 percent from March 1959. Unions, student groups, and Jewish organizations joined groups committed to the advancement of blacks in the protests. Campuses all over the country formed support groups, raised money for the sit-ins, and demonstrated at local branches of the chain stores.

The sit-ins marked a profound change in the struggle for black equality. Students revolted not only against segregation, but against the more cautious legalism of the NAACP. Judicial and legislative change came slowly, and neither had produced the results promised. Reporting on the sit-ins, Michael Walzer observed that "none of the leaders I spoke to were [sic] interested in test cases; nor was there any general agreement to stop the sitdowns or the picketing once the question of integration at the lunch counters was taken up by the courts. The legal work of the NAACP was important, everyone agreed; but this . . . was more important."

Sitting in overcame the frustration of delay; it could be carried out immediately, and it was something students could do themselves. In fact, students were ideally situated to undertake such a protest. Most did not yet have families. Full-time employment and careers remained something for the future. Thus, they had time to protest and were less vulnerable to reprisals than many potential leaders. These factors contributed to the distinctive nature of the groundswell of protest in 1960. The sit-ins of the 1950s had been organized by adults, often by people of standing in the black communities. From Greensboro on, however, students assumed the lead, often pushing ahead of traditional black leaders. For example, some local branches of the NAACP and several conservative ministers initially refused to back the sit-ins in Greensboro.

Mass participation was essential to the success of the protests, and the sit-ins involved the masses—that was part of the beauty of sitting in. The students were ordinary people, and their protest could be joined by other ordinary people—ordinary people with extraordinary fortitude and commitment. The impression that common people had effected an uncommon change pervaded the movement. One black student said: "I myself desegregated a lunch counter, not somebody else, not some big man, not some powerful man, but little me. I walked the picket line and I sat in and the walls of segregation toppled."

This sense of taking part in, and helping to create, a profoundly important moment in history made sitting in an exhilarating experience for many. A spirit of millenarianism infused the movement. One student from North Carolina A&T remembered that "It was like a fever. Everyone wanted to go. We were so happy." Participation in the protests produced a sense of euphoria. When police arrested some protesters at a shopping center in Raleigh, students, in a determined but celebratory mood, flocked to the site. Everyone wanted to be arrested. It was indeed like a fever, and the fever fired the movement.

Jack Bloom has observed that "the demands of the civil rights movement have often been called middle-class demands." In one sense, equal access to places of public accommodation was relevant only to those who could afford to eat in restaurants or shop in department stores. However, even if many blacks were not in an economic position to take advantage of such access, these demands generated widespread support in the black community because a general consensus held that they worked to the benefit of everyone. "The common denominator," wrote Bloom, "was human dignity."

Many of the leaders of the sit-in movement came from middle-class backgrounds, although by no means all did. Most students in black colleges in 1960, however, must have considered themselves bound for a middle-class existence, whatever their parents' economic circumstances. A good number of leaders also came from backgrounds that exposed them in one way or another to alternatives to the South's caste system. Some were from the North, or had lived or visited there. Others had served in the military. Chuck McDew, a leader in Orangeburg, came from Massilon, Ohio, and "never adjusted to South Carolina." One of the student leaders in Durham was a veteran who had spent two years in Japan, which he recalled as the only time in his life he had lived like a free man. Bernard Lee, a student leader at Alabama State, had served in the Air Force, which stationed him in Montana, and was a father of three. Diane Nash, one of the leaders of the Nashville movement, came from Chicago and went to Howard University in Washington, D.C., before transferring to Fisk. Julian Bond attended a white private boarding school in Pennsylvania. These students knew that things did not have to be the way they were in the South, and the degrading restrictions of segregation did not mesh with the future they envisioned for themselves.

On the other hand, not all participants in the protests, or even all leaders, shared such backgrounds. John Lewis, another prominent figure in the Nashville movement, which produced so many leaders, came from a small farm deep in the countryside of Alabama. However, it does seem that experience outside the South formed the ideas of at least some participants. Similarly, while a good number of leaders came from middle-class backgrounds, students at North Carolina A&T were not children of the middle class. Neither did most students at Knoxville College come from even moderately affluent families. The only firm conclusion that can be drawn is that no generalization about the backgrounds of the participants in the sit-in movement, or even the movement's leaders, will hold. For every generality, one can find numerous exceptions.

One thing does seem fairly consistent. Many leaders of the sit-in movement were already student leaders. A significant number held elected positions in student government or other positions of leadership on campus.

The sit-ins caught traditional black organizations by surprise. No one could have predicted that Greensboro would touch off similar protests all over the South. Representatives of the NAACP, CORE, and SCLC rushed from city to city as demonstrations sprung up, but there was no central planning or organization. Students in each town learned of sit-ins elsewhere and decided to do something themselves. Local leaders emerged from the sit-in movement itself, and, despite attempts by the NAACP, SCLC, and CORE to impose their influence, students displayed a strong desire to control their own movement.

This independence manifested itself when Ella Baker, the executive director of SCLC, organized, under the auspices of SCLC, a meeting of students involved in the sit-in movement. Three hundred students met in Raleigh and agreed to form a coordinating body, which became the Student Nonviolent Coordinating Committee, or SNCC. The conference might have led to an assertion of control by King and the ministers, but, for a variety of reasons, this did not happen. The sit-inners were proud of what they had accomplished, and they did not intend to surrender control of their own movement. King, who would have liked the student organization to function as a branch of SCLC, did not want to appear to appropriate the student movement for his own benefit. In addition, Baker, who was already on her way out as executive director of SCLC, functioned as an adult advisor to the students, and she strongly supported their independence. Moreover, the sit-in movement was inherently decentralized, with many local organizations, and the students distrusted centralized control and hierarchies of leadership. Finally, by the time of the conference in Raleigh, the students had developed a sense of themselves as an independent and potent force.

The student movement rejected tokenism; participants in it wanted an immediate end to Jim Crow, and they believed that nonviolent direct action was most likely to bring about that result. The organization that grew out of the sit-in movement would become the shock troops of the civil rights movement. When CORE organized a group to test a Supreme Court decision extending the Court's earlier prohibition against segregated vehicles in interstate travel to include terminal facilities and their protest encountered violent opposition, SNCC stepped in and finished the "Freedom Rides." SNCC took a leading role in voter registration and in organizing black communities in the Deep South. The key to the sit-ins was direct action, which provided a model for the phase of the civil rights movement they initiated. Participants in the sit-ins did not simply demand, they acted. They asserted their right to sit at a lunch counter by doing so. They denied the legitimacy of segregation by acting as if it did not exist.

More than just activism or militancy, the sit-in movement bred a "culture as well as a politics." The students who formed SNCC distrusted organizational structure; many questioned the very concept of leadership. Their attitudes would have a momentous impact on the struggle for black equality in the 1960s. Moreover, the sit-in movement and SNCC exerted a strong influence on the developing white student movement. Thus, in more ways than one, the sit-ins would do much to shape politics in the 1960s.

Merrill Proudfoot was a white minister teaching at Knoxville College, a Presbyterian black college in Knoxville, Tennessee, when the sit-ins in that city began. Relatively few whites and very few faculty members, black or white, became actively involved in the sit-in movement. All of this makes Proudfoot's diary an extraordinary document. However unusual Proudfoot's participation may have been, his diary nevertheless reveals much about the sit-in movement and what it meant to be involved. It gives its readers a first-hand account of what it felt like to participate in a sit-in and to be caught up in the sit-in movement. However, the impressions and emotions it records are not only those of a participant, but those of a white participant. As such, it offers readers a particular insight into the sit-ins in Knoxville and the broader sit-in movement. Proudfoot's diary cannot speak for everyone who participated in the sit-ins, and it does not claim to. It is the intensely personal record of one man's involvement. On the other hand, it expresses feelings and records impressions shared by many who joined the sit-in movement, and the light it sheds on the Knoxville sit-ins reflects on events elsewhere.

Many of the major issues of the sit-in movement emerged in Proudfoot's account. Proudfoot had a deep religious and moral commitment to nonviolence, but, he also reflected upon its effectiveness as a tactic. Beyond that, however, he recorded in his diary the physical and emotional cost of the tactic to those who employed it. At times, the tactic placed protesters in uncomfortable moral positions. The fine line between nonviolent resistance and civil disobedience caused anguish for some, including Proudfoot. Proudfoot's story also documented the importance of economic pressure to the success of the protest movement. To be successful, such pressure required support from the adult black community. After some initial hesitancy, Knoxville's black community rallied behind the protests. Finally, the diary raised issues of relations between blacks and whites within the movement for black equality as well as in the society at large.

The protests in Knoxville were, in many ways, typical of the first wave of sit-ins. The city was about 15 percent black and located in the upper South. Knoxville College was a private school, which offered a good education to blacks from a variety of backgrounds. Most students did not come from middle-class families. Like Greensboro, Knoxville had a history of civil race relations. Segregation in Knoxville wore a polite face, which made it no less bitter and perhaps even more difficult to address. When Proudfoot and Robert Booker, a student leader, first sat down at Rich's lunch counter, the waitress politely told Booker, "I'm sorry, we can't serve you here, but we can serve you at our other counter if you would care to step over there" (p. 2). Knoxville's blacks had to surmount such "civility" to gain their civil rights.

Booker, the student through whom Proudfoot became involved in the protests, fit the mold of the student leaders discussed above. Booker had served in the military and lived outside of the South. He was four years older than traditional entering freshmen when he came to Knoxville College. Moreover, Booker was articulate, charismatic, and held an elected position of leadership; he was president of the student government when the sit-ins began.

Black students at Knoxville were inspired by the sit-ins in Greensboro, and their actions reflected their dissatisfaction with older black leadership (p. 2). Knoxville had no preexisting movement such as Nashville's. The students learned of the sit-ins in Greensboro and were moved to act. Adults in the black community urged the students to negotiate rather than to demonstrate. Finally, with negotiations at a standstill, the students forced the issue. At the same time, the sit-inners accepted the culture, ideals, and values of the larger society. Indeed, they were acting out values they had learned in school: "that 'all men are created equal,' [and] that America is 'the land of the free'" (p. 185).

Knoxville's students and their supporters believed that their protests worked for the benefit of the larger society. They would make a better America by compelling it to live up to its promise of equality. In his first diary entry, Proudfoot remarked that, following the teachings of King and Lawson, the demonstrators sought "not simply to grasp privileges for a single group, but to create a society in which freedom and dignity are the heritage of every man regardless of race or group. As a consequence, the benefit of their work is accruing, I am convinced, to our entire culture, including those who oppose them most bitterly" (p. 5). Proudfoot told a meeting at the Tabernacle Baptist Church that "we are not working *against* America; rather we are working *as Americans* to secure that which the American ideal has always claimed—and to serve a *better* America" [emphasis in the original] (p. 175). Proudfoot was firmly convinced that "the rights we seek are not for ourselves alone, but for all Americans" (p. 195). A coordinate belief was the conviction that they acted in the spirit of Christian selfless love. Proudfoot sincerely believed that "We're doing this as much for Rich's [department store] and Walgreen's [drugstore] as for ourselves" (p. 152). Religion was central to Knoxville's sit-in movement. Local black ministers, such as Robert Jones and W. T. Crutcher, played important roles in the movement. At a more fundamental level, however, the commitment to nonviolence and the sense of social justice that permeated Knoxville's sit-ins had deep religious roots. The church was central, and the influence of Martin Luther King, Jr., pervaded the movement. Yet, attesting to the local nature of the movement, Proudfoot's account mentioned King only twice (pp. 5, 176). Another powerful influence, and one closer to home, was James Lawson.

At the same time, it should be pointed out that not all black clergy, and only a small minority of white clergy, actively supported desegregation, much less the sit-ins. Many white clergymen functioned as spokesmen for segregation. In Knoxville, none of the black churches ultimately failed to line up behind the sit-ins, nevertheless, some were reluctant. Although more insulated than many black institutions, black churches could also be subject to pressures from the white community. Ultimately, however, all black ministers felt that they had to support the sit-ins; their parishioners pushed them in that direction. In contrast, very few white ministers lent their support to the sit-ins. Proudfoot frequently bemoaned the failure of the churches to take the lead in advocating racial equality.

One way in which those who participated in the sit-ins hoped to make America better, perhaps in spite of itself, was to improve its moral position in the cold war. The cold war provided a backdrop for the sit-ins, one from which the sit-inners did not yet dissent. One protester in Knoxville carried a sign reminding passersby that "Khruschev Could Eat Here—I Can't" (p. 85).

Sitting in proved to be a marvelous tactic. It offered a graphic demonstration of the injustice of the southern lunch counter system. As a means of protest, it provided more drama and excitement than, say, a court battle. In fact, many participants felt a kind of euphoria. Aside from the "freedom high," the commitment to nonviolence, the conviction that they were struggling to make America a better place by making it live up to its promise, and the belief that they were helping even their opponents imbued the participants with a sense of moral superiority. In addition, the discipline and courage required by nonviolent protest, along with the explicit rejection of inferior status, destroyed racial stereotypes. Thus, sitting in instilled a sense of pride in participants. Finally, integrating lunch counters did not interfere with any vested interest in the black community, as did, for example, desegregating schools; many black teachers, with good reason, feared losing their jobs if schools desegregated.

As a demonstration of disciplined, nonviolent direct action, the sit-ins won grudging admiration from opponents. During the Knoxville sit-ins, a waitress at Grant's variety store was heard to say, "I think they should be served. You know, you really have to admire their courage!" (p. 48). Perhaps even more important, the tactic won the support of "neutrals." At Cole's drugstore, when a young black woman took a seat at the lunch counter and the person who had occupied the next seat got up and left, an older white woman sitting at the counter was moved to slide over and sit next to the black woman (p. 58).

The pattern repeated itself throughout the demonstrations. The bravery and dignity of nonviolent protest, coupled with sometimes savage assaults on the protesters, caused neutrals to take a stand, if not for the demonstrators, at least for decency and order. When hecklers poured a Coke over Proudfoot and then struck him, a customer at the lunch counter, a young white man, intervened. "You fellows have gone far enough," he said, "and now you'd better get out of here! Look, I'm neutral in this, but this fellow was just sitting here" (pp. 93–94).

At times, the heroism displayed in this kind of protest had an impact even on those who perpetrated violence against the sit-inners.

Harry Wiersema, Jr., a young white whose entire family supported the sit-ins, was attacked by a duck-tailed tough as he left a sit-in. The assailant punched him first in the face and then in the midsection. The tall, athletic Wiersema regained his composure, folded his arms, and turned quietly to face his attacker. The young thug was stunned, confused, and disarmed by Wiersema's unexpected response and did not press his attack. When the police arrived, Wiersema refused to press charges (pp. 107–8). Whatever the young tough thought about blacks, integration, or sit-ins, Wiersema's actions gave him something to ponder.

Further testimony to the effectiveness of the sit-in as a tactic was that store owners could come up with no better response than the self-defeating action of closing down the lunch counters. Grant's, Sears, Rich's, and Todd & Armistead (a drugstore) all closed their counters during Knoxville's sit-ins.

In Knoxville, like so many other places, economic pressure proved more successful than demonstrations alone. "Selective buying" (buying only from stores that did not discriminate at their lunch counters), returning credit cards to stores that refused to desegregate, and other tactics proved ultimately to be the deciding factors. In the early stages of negotiations, the manager of Rich's told Proudfoot that he was in business to make money, not to do good. Some managers who were not unsympathetic were afraid to desegregate without the other stores for fear of losing customers. As Proudfoot came to realize, "the store managers respected economic power more than moral power" (p. 192)—hence, the necessity and justification for resorting to economic pressure.

Still, this realization caused several crises of conscience. Sit-inners had to ask themselves what their purpose in demonstrating was. Did they intend to demonstrate that desegregation would not hurt business? Or was the sit-in an instrument precisely for hurting business? Proudfoot, a white adult, and Booker, a black student, arrived at different answers to these questions (pp. 6, 20–21). Could a boycott be morally justified? Proudfoot struggled over whether it was "Christian" to harm another—for any purpose—and whether he had a right to coerce another person to do what was right. Was the economic pressure segregationists employed against blacks any different from the black boycott of downtown stores? Proudfoot finally settled this for himself by making the distinction that "the Negro is saying, 'I want this right *too!*' while his white opponent is saying, 'I want this right *exclusively!*'" (p. 194).

Nonviolent protesters also had to consider when their protest became civil disobedience. In the early stages of the protests, Rich's decided to keep its lunch counter open and to admit whites, while excluding black demonstrators. The protesters gathered around the gate to block the entry of other customers. A white woman who had come to get something to eat hesitated when she saw the situation. As the guard prepared to escort her past the demonstrators, Proudfoot stepped in front of the woman and declared that he had been there first. The woman left, but Proudfoot had to confront the realization that he had crossed the line between protest and civil disobedience; preventing customers from entering a place of business violated a Tennessee law prohibiting persons from "conspiring to interfere with the lawful conduct of business" (p. 24–27). Acutely aware of this issue, Proudfoot raised it at a meeting of organizers of the sit-ins. While not necessarily opposed to adopting civil disobedience should the need arise, he wanted to make sure that the demonstrators did not take such a step without due consideration. The protesters again faced this dilemma when Todd & Armistead obtained an injunction against the sit-ins.

Among the most significant observations in Proudfoot's diary were those about the difficulty of nonviolence and the toll such protests took on the demonstrators. This simple truth would have much to do with shaping the course of the civil rights struggle in the 1960s. Nonviolent protest was not an easy thing. One could be subject to brutal beatings. Fear of physical injury could never have been far from the demonstrators' thoughts, but concern for personal safety was hardly the only problem they had to face. When Proudfoot stepped in front of the woman at Rich's lunch counter, he was shocked by his own vehemence. It was with some discomfort that he realized he was "not as nonviolent as [he] had thought" (p. 32). When the tough attacked him at Walgreen's, Proudfoot discovered that "it is a mortifying experience to be attacked in public by another person and not be able to do anything in your own defense" (p. 93). He felt as if everyone in the place were looking at him—in this case, not an unreasonable assumption.

Proudfoot found that sitting in placed a "terrific strain" on his nerves (p. 28). He did not eat or sleep well (p. 67); he lost weight, developed nervous indigestion, and found it difficult to concentrate (p. 100), as did many long-term participants. Psychologists observed similar symptoms, magnified by the longer periods of time to which they were subject to stress and the even greater danger and isolation, in SNCC workers involved with voter registration and community organizing in the Deep South.

Proudfoot was also subject to terrible agonies of conscience. When a heckler threw a saltshaker at a demonstrator and it struck a baby, Proudfoot agonized, "if we had left immediately when we were first asked, none of this would have happened" (p. 96).

Proudfoot and the demonstrators found themselves harassed by their friends and colleagues. Letters from hatemongers did not disturb Proudfoot nearly so much as a negative letter from a friend who belonged to Proudfoot's former church.

Other dangers could befall participants in sit-ins. The white pastor of the Euclid Avenue Baptist Church was asked to leave his pulpit. Black teachers risked their jobs, for which they were dependent upon the white power structure. Virtually any black who worked for whites stood a chance of losing his or her job for protesting.

Proudfoot's strikingly honest account also revealed attitudes that foreshadowed divisions between blacks and whites in the movement that only later became obvious. He admitted to having to overcome his own racist feelings when he began teaching at a predominantly black school. The occasion for his reflection was the compassion Proudfoot felt for a white woman who left her food when blacks sat down at Grant's lunch counter. She told a waitress that she could not eat it. Proudfoot recalled that "when I first came to the South seventeen years ago, the thought of eating food that had been *prepared* by Negroes turned my stomach" (p. 33). Typically, he found hope for the woman in the fact that he had grown beyond his own prejudice.

Several of Proudfoot's remarks might seem condescending from the perspective of the 1990s—perhaps even from that of the late 1960s. He commented on a "permissive atmosphere about lateness at almost all group gatherings of Negroes" (pp. 79–80). At that, Proudfoot characteristically looked for a positive approach ("I appreciate this relaxation when I am a member of the audience, but it exasperates me when I am presiding at a meeting," p. 82). However intended, the remark reverberates with racial stereotypes.

Similarly, Proudfoot's reflection on black culture might be taken as offensive today. After commenting on "the lower degree of intensity in Negro culture as compared to Anglo-Saxon culture," he observed: "I use the term 'Negro culture' with considerable reservation, recognizing that the culture of Negro Americans is by and large simply the culture of America, learned from and shared with white Americans" (p. 115). This observation calls to mind a similarly well-intentioned statement found in the introduction to Kenneth Stampp's important book on slavery, *The Peculiar Institution:* "innately Negroes *are*, after all, only white men with black skins." While some later took offense at Stampp's assertion, few, if any, found it objectionable when it was written. Like Proudfoot, Stampp argued for the commonality of blacks and whites and for the brotherhood of all people; both reflected liberal doctrine of the day. Even if one sees grounds for offense in such comments, it is ahistorical to hold people of one era accountable to the standards of another. One need not accept, or even condone, such attitudes to note that they were common in their day and that they were not considered offensive.

Along the same lines, Proudfoot commented that the distinctive elements blacks contributed enriched "the cultural pattern of our nation. . . . They help to compensate for our prevailing Anglo-Saxon depreciation of emotion and beauty; our reticence they make up for by their genuine appreciation of personality; our puritanism they correct with their frank enjoyment of life; and yet they compensate for our materialism with their almost innate feel for the spiritual" (p. 115). Once again, one might argue that references to blacks' "innate feel for the spiritual" could be seen as racialist, and some would undoubtedly find it racist. Such judgments inevitably call to mind the notion that blacks have rhythm, an idea that one could run across at liberal gatherings in the 1950s and early 1960s as well as in the company of avowed racists. As the sixties progressed and blacks became less willing to accept such notions, the expression of such attitudes became one source of friction between blacks and white liberals. On the other hand, it is only fair to note that blacks did not take offense at the time. Indeed, Booker recalls that black students at Knoxville College regarded Proudfoot as a "great person" and that his involvement in the sit-in movement greatly "boosted the effect" of the protests. So few whites took part that any white sympathy, much less participation, was warmly welcomed.

Moreover, few faculty members, black or white, were deeply involved in the sit-in movement. Proudfoot's involvement, if not unique, was extremely uncommon. Even where one or two white professors became actively involved, as at Morgan State and Spelman College, their commitment came out of a secular consciousness, not a religious one. Thus, while he was in many ways typical of participants in the sit-ins, Proudfoot was, in other respects, quite unusual.

No one could doubt the sincerity of Proudfoot's commitment to the sit-ins or to his students. Booker recalls that Proudfoot wanted to "feel the black experience." Such aspirations may seem naive when looking back through the prism of the late sixties, but Proudfoot's desire to "feel the black experience" and his belief that he could do so relates back to his belief in the commonality of all people, a basic tenet of the civil rights movement in the early 1960s.

Merrill Proudfoot's diary invites the reader into the inner world of the sit-ins. It offers insights into the movement and raises issues confronting the movement. The journey on which Proudfoot invites us is exciting, inspiring, and at times horrifying. It is always worthwhile. As he points out in his afterword, the events of 1960 made history, and the echoes of those events are with us today.

For Further Reading

THE proliferation of studies of the civil rights movement in recent years has greatly increased our knowledge of virtually all aspects of the movement. Juan Williams, *Eyes on the Prize: America's Civil Rights Years, 1954–1965* (New York: Penguin, 1987–88), and Harvard Sitkoff, *The Struggle for Black Equality, 1954–1980* (New York: Hill and Wang, 1981), are two general overviews. Slightly more narrow is Allen J. Matusow, "From Civil Rights to Black Power: The Case of SNCC, 1960–1966," in Barton J. Bernstein and Allen J. Matusow, eds., 2d ed., *Twentieth Century America: Recent Interpretations* (New York: Harcourt Brace Jovanovich, 1972). Aldon Morris, *The Origins of the Civil Rights Movement: Black Communities Organizing for Change* (New York: Free Press, 1984), attempts to shift focus away from national civil rights organizations and to examine the internal dynamics of black communities. Doug McAdam, *Political Process and the Development of Black Insurgency, 1930–1970* (Chicago: University of Chicago Press, 1982), uses the political process model to examine institutions within black communities as sources of protest. Jack M. Bloom, *Class, Race, and the Civil Rights Movement* (Bloomington: Indiana University Press, 1987), employs a class analysis to study the birth and development of the civil rights movement. William Chafe, *Unfinished Journey: America since World War II* (New York: Oxford University Press, 1986), contains some useful information on the development of the struggle for black equality.

In addition to these studies, there are some helpful anthologies.

Charles Eagles, ed., *The Civil Rights Movement in America* (Jackson: University Press of Mississippi, 1986), contains a significant debate over the future of scholarship in the area of civil rights. Of particular interest is the article by Clayborne Carson, "Civil Rights Reform and the Black Freedom Struggle," and the comment on it by Steven F. Lawson. August Meier and Elliott Rudwick have added considerably to our knowledge of the struggle for black equality. A collection of their essays, *Along the Color Line: Explorations in the Black Experience* (Urbana: University of Illinois Press, 1976), contains an important essay, "The Origins of Nonviolent Direct Action in Afro-American Protest: A Note on Historical Discontinuities." In that essay, Meier and Rudwick argue for discontinuities between earlier protests, including sit-ins and other nonviolent direct actions taken in the late 1950s, and the sit-ins that began in Greensboro in 1960. Also of interest is the essay "Attorneys Black and White: A Case Study of Race Relations within the NAACP," which contains some important observations on tensions between blacks and whites in the movement. Other anthologies include: Meier and Rudwick, eds., *Black Protest in the Sixties* (Chicago: Quadrangle, 1970), and Francis Broderick and August Meier, eds., *Negro Protest Thought in the Twentieth Century* (Indianapolis: Bobbs-Merrill, 1965).

There are several good studies of civil rights organizations, including: August Meier and Elliott Rudwick, *CORE: A Study in the Civil Rights Movement* (Urbana: University of Illinois Press, 1975); Clayborne Carson, *In Struggle: SNCC and the Awakening of the 1960s* (Cambridge: Harvard University Press, 1981); Howard Zinn, *SNCC: The New Abolitionists* (Boston: Beacon, 1965); and Adam Fairclough, *To Redeem the Soul of America: The Southern Christian Leadership Conference and Martin Luther King, Jr.* (Athens: University of Georgia Press, 1987).

Martin Luther King, Jr., was a central figure in the civil rights movement, if not in the sit-ins. His role is discussed in Taylor Branch, *Parting the Waters: America in the King Years, 1953–63* (New York: Simon and Schuster, 1988); David Garrow, *Bearing the Cross: Martin Luther King, Jr., and the Southern Christian Leadership Conference*

(New York: Vintage, 1986); Stephen Oates, *Let the Trumpet Sound: The Life of Martin Luther King, Jr.* (New York: New American Library, 1982); and David L. Lewis, *King: A Critical Biography* (New York: Praeger, 1970).

Two fine books tell the story of the Greensboro sit-ins. William H. Chafe, *Civilities and Civil Rights: Greensboro, North Carolina and the Black Struggle for Freedom* (New York: Oxford University Press, 1980), stresses the role of civility in maintaining segregation. More anecdotal is Miles Wolff, *Lunch at the Five and Ten* (New York: Stein and Day, 1970).

Two important early analyses of the sit-in movement are August Meier, "New Currents in the Civil Rights Movement," *New Politics* 2 (Summer 1963), and Charles U. Smith, "The Sit-Ins and the New Negro Student," *Journal of Intergroup Relations* 2 (1961). August Meier, "The Successful Sit-Ins in a Border City: A Study in Social Causation," *Journal of Intergroup Relations* 2 (1961), deals with the sit-ins in Baltimore.

Contemporary accounts of the sit-ins include Michael Walzer, "A Cup of Coffee and a Seat," *Dissent* 7 (Spring 1960); Michael Walzer, "The Politics of the New Negro," *Dissent* 7 (Summer 1960); Wilma Dykeman and James Stokely, "Sit Down Chillun, Sit Down!" *The Progressive* 24 (June 1960); and Louis E. Lomax, "The Negro Revolt against 'The Negro Leaders,'" *Harper's* 220 (June 1960).

Accounts by participants include: Julian Bond, "The Movement Then and Now," *Southern Exposure* 3 (1976); Ted Dienstfrey, "A Conference on the Sit-Ins," *Commentary* 30 (June 1960); Cleveland Sellers and Robert Terrell, *The River of No Return: The Autobiography of a Black Militant and the Life and Death of SNCC* (New York: Morrow, 1973); James Forman, *The Making of Black Revolutionaries* (New York: Macmillan, 1972); and Howard Zinn, *SNCC.* Howell Raines, *My Soul Is Rested: The Story of the Civil Rights Movement in the Deep South* (New York: Putnam, 1977), contains interviews with a number of participants in the civil rights struggle. Of particular relevance to the sit-ins are the interviews with John Lewis, Franklin McCain, Julian Bond, and Lonnie King.

Several important articles analyze the backgrounds of participants in the sit-ins. John M. Orbell, "Protest Participation among Southern Negro College Students," *American Political Science Review* 61 (June 1967), contends that those most likely to protest attended good quality, private, black colleges in urban settings with relatively small black populations. As Orbell puts it, "proximity to the dominant white culture increases the likelihood of protest involvement." Anthony Orum and Amy Orum, "The Class and Status Bases of Negro Protest," *Social Science Quarterly* 49 (Dec. 1968), argues that blacks from middle-class, or at least more privileged, backgrounds were more apt to participate in the protests. Based on a study of three black colleges in North Carolina, Ruth Searles and J. Allen Williams, Jr., "College Students' Participation in the Sit-ins," *Social Forces* 40 (1962), concludes that the sit-ins were led by middle-class and upper-class blacks and that those most active in the protests were "from generally higher social status backgrounds."

Robert Coles, "Social Struggle and Awareness," *Psychiatry* 27 (Nov. 1964), deals with the psychological impact of nonviolent direct action on those who employ the tactic.

Todd Gitlin's insightful book, *The Sixties: Years of Hope, Days of Rage* (New York: Bantam, 1987), is excellent on the white student movement and contains some interesting observations on the black student movement as well. Kirkpatrick Sale, *SDS* (New York: Vintage, 1973), was the standard work on SDS until the publication of Gitlin's book.

For information on the Knoxville sit-ins, the author is deeply indebted to Rev. Merrill Proudfoot and Robert Booker, both of whom discussed the sit-ins there and answered questions at some length.

Preface

WHEN the events recorded in this diary took place, I had been for three years a professor of religion and philosophy at Knoxville College in Knoxville, Tennessee. The school is a coeducational liberal arts college operated by the United Presbyterian Church and attended primarily by Negro students; I am white by race and an ordained minister of the Presbyterian Church. During the Knoxville lunch counter sit-in demonstrations, I had the privilege of sitting at the counters daily with my Negro friends and serving as a member of the council that devised the strategy for the protest. This book tells the story of that demonstration from the first sit-in to the day of desegregation.

Although most Americans became aware of "sit-ins" only after a widely noticed demonstration of the kind in Greensboro, North Carolina, on February 1, 1960, the fact is that the sit-in technique had been used considerably earlier and with some success in desegregating eating places in such cities as Washington, Oklahoma City, and Louisville. Groups of Negroes or Negroes and whites together had gone into lunch counters, seated themselves at the counter, and waited for service. When service was denied the Negroes, the group remained at the counters as a moral protest against discrimination. This is essentially what a sit-in is. From the beginning it had been consciously allied with the philosophy of non-violence, inspired by Jesus and Gandhi, nurtured in Chris-

tian pacifist groups, and popularized among American Negroes
by the Montgomery bus boycott of 1955-56 under the leadership
of the Reverend Martin Luther King, Jr.

But for some reason that is not entirely clear, the Greensboro
sit-in captured the imagination of Southern Negroes, particularly
of the college students, as other such efforts had not, inspiring a
wave of non-violent action to end lunch counter segregation.
Sweeping over the middle and upper South and even spilling
down a little bit into the Deep South, this tide of sit-ins marked
the first time that Negroes in the South had asserted themselves
in a mass movement to end discrimination.

Within a few days after the news from Greensboro, there arose
spontaneously among our students at Knoxville College a strong
feeling that they ought to do something to show their support of
this new cause. The protracted negotiations that resulted are described later in the diary. These negotiations failed in a way that
left the Negro community resentful and determined. The next
step could only be open demonstration. This happens to be the
very point at which I became involved and is where the diary
begins.

The course taken by the lunch counter struggle in various places
was largely determined by the personalities of those who took
part in it and especially by the locale in which it occurred. For
the South is far from being "the solid South." In my own state
of Tennessee, for example, almost the whole spectrum of the
Southern problem is represented, ranging in intensity from Memphis in the cotton country along the Mississippi River in the west,
to Knoxville in the mountainous tobacco country in the east, and
finally to Oak Ridge, one of those increasingly numerous "islands"
within the South which for some special reason are oriented more
to the nation as a whole than to the surrounding region.

To understand the way it happened in Knoxville one must know
that Knoxville has never had at its base a slave-holding economy.
There was in East Tennessee strong Union sentiment during the
War Between the States and the city was within Union lines

during much of the war. These realities of the past are reflected today in the fact that East Tennessee is predominantly Republican in its politics. In addition to these economic and historical factors, Knoxville has been subject to the liberalizing forces of the University of Tennessee, the national headquarters of TVA, and nearby Oak Ridge. Thus, while the city is geographically well within the South, it is a border city in its ways of thinking. One could grow up there a true liberal or one could grow up a Dixiecrat. But this very indecision as to whether Knoxville is a "Southern" city has made Knoxvillians extremely timid about suggesting changes in the inherited racial patterns.

What is chronicled in the following pages really happened. No facts, no incidents, no names, no comments were invented by me. There really was a diary, kept while the events were transpiring. The emotions it captures are the original ones, not those of later reflection. Needless to say, I had to polish my sentences a bit before I could present them to public view, and a good many entries that proved later to have no importance were cut out. During this process I took the liberty of adding a few interpretive comments and expanding others. I hope these will add meaning to the story without obstructing it.

After the lunch counter struggle in Knoxville was all over but the shouting, another mass meeting was held on July 31 at the Rogers Memorial Baptist Church. On the principle that when a story is over, it is best to stop telling it, I did not leave the description of this meeting in the diary. But I did take the liberty of retaining a few of the items that were of interest in that meeting by inserting them into the record of two earlier Sundays—on July 10, the deacon's anecdote and the particular way in which the offering was taken; on July 24, the hymn, James's question, "How many feel better?" and his comments on the election, and some of Crutcher's comments on people who were not keeping the economic withdrawal. Unfortunately the threat to blow up Dr. Crutcher's house I failed to record in the original diary; the date given it here is our guess. I believe these minor adjustments have augmented the interest and unity of the story without endangering its essential accuracy.

My acknowledgments should begin with the loyal members of that group of demonstrators who won both my affection and my admiration during those critical days described in these pages. My debt of love to them is unbounded. To the three individuals who read this manuscript and made helpful suggestions I am deeply appreciative—the Reverend Robert West, the Reverend James Foster Reese, and the Reverend W. T. Crutcher. And finally I am grateful to The University of North Carolina Press for making available to the reading public this account which I hope will make a small contribution to the quest for human brotherhood.

MERRILL PROUDFOOT

Diary of a Sit-In

Thursday, June 9

WHEN I made that promise to Robert Booker three months ago, I did not expect that I would ever have to keep it. Yet at 11:15 this morning I found myself—a white, bespectacled college professor at the usually conservative age of thirty-six—advancing to my baptism by fire as a sit-in demonstrator! With me was Robert Booker, a tall dignified Negro youth who is president of the student body of our college. As we approached the basement lunch counter in Rich's, the city's largest department store, Booker showed no fear; I was secretly terrified.

We quickly observed that Rich's, fearing demonstrations, had built a partition around the counter so that access could be gained only through one narrow gate. A burly guard dressed in an ordinary business suit stood near this gate. I nervously fingered articles on the toy counter as Booker walked on to the gate. The guard, taken by surprise, exclaimed, "Say, Buddy, you can't go in there!"

"My name isn't Buddy!" Robert answered testily, "And why can't I go in? I'm hungry. I want something to eat."

"Well, then, you can eat over at the other counter for colored customers." He referred to a segregated facility which seated six or eight, almost hidden by the kitchen appliances display.

"But I want to eat here where these other people are eating. I'm not interested in any segregated eating place!" With that,

Booker brushed by the astonished guard and took a seat at the counter.

The seat of my personality had shifted to the solar plexus. "Could I possibly be the fellow, I who get nervous indigestion when I have to make an announcement in chapel, who has got himself involved in this situation?" I was asking myself. "Now have you got enough nerve to go through with it, or are you going to let your student understand that you are a coward?" I sauntered in after Booker, trying to look like an ordinary customer, but I could not have felt more self-conscious had my skin been coal-black.

I selected a seat next to Booker. The waitress set a glass before me; I quietly pushed it over in front of him. She gave me a menu; I handed it to Robert without looking at it. My face burned with embarrassment. The waitress hurriedly conferred with the woman who apparently was supervising the counter, who then came over and told Booker politely, "I'm sorry, we can't serve you here, but we can serve you at our other counter if you would care to step over there." Booker again made it clear that he was not interested in a segregated facility. The waitress asked for my order. I said meekly, "This gentleman was here before I was; don't you want to serve him first?" She looked hurt, said simply, "We can't serve him," and walked away.

As we sat waiting for—nothing, my mind shuttled nervously over the events of the past four months: the initial excitement of our Knoxville College students when they heard of the first lunch counter sit-ins, and how this energy had been channeled by us nervous adults, Negro and white, into "a more creative approach for Knoxville"; the three exasperating months of negotiation through the bi-racial Mayor's Committee; the feeling of Booker and the other students that they were being left out of a historic movement, that they were fighing two battles—one against the merchants, another against the adult leadership of the Negro community and the college; the day in my office when

I had tried to persuade Robert, "If we have to resort to demonstrations, it may take a long time before passions are calmed even
to the point where we are now in our race relations in Knoxville";
how concerned I was that Robert and other students not feel
that their elders were really "Uncle Toms," more concerned
to protect their personal status in the community than to achieve
full citizenship for all the members of their race; my self-conscious
feeling, deep down, that because I am white, Robert might be
suspicious of my motives; and then my fateful commitment,
"Robert, I'll make you a promise—if the negotiations fail to the
point where the Negro members of the Mayor's Committee
agree to demonstrations, I will personally sit in with you on the
very first day!"

A man who identified himself as the manager of Rich's food
services interrupted my recollections: "We can't serve your
friend here, but we would be glad to serve both of you at our
other counter." I appreciated the kindness with which he spoke
and thanked him, but declined. Actually, this offer to serve us
both at the counter reserved for Negroes was a departure from
previous practice at Rich's, but represented a moral gain too
small to settle for.

We had been watching apprehensively for the other three
demonstrators, all Negroes, who were to join us at Rich's. Finally
we saw them come up to the gate, but the guard was alerted now
and they were turned away. Booker and I were disturbed that
they did not stay to form a protest line.

Booker professed to be really hungry. I was so upset that I
could not have eaten had the management served up a lunch
"on the house." My mouth was parched from nervousness, but
on principle I refused to take a sip of the water I had shoved in
front of Robert. I was thinking regretfully how many times we
had believed the community problem almost solved, only to
have our hopes dashed by some new objection. How our mayor,
breaking all precedent for Southern cities, had even taken a

committee including Booker and another student to New York, but the variety store executives had refused to see the students and had given the Mayor little encouragement. Then the students tried out the stools a few times, and the merchants, scared, proposed (so we understood) to desegregate at the end of ten days. The end of the ten days, school out, no move by the merchants, the complete collapse of the Mayor's Committee, and after ten more days, the Negro members' decision to keep faith with the students. And so my promise, too, had to be kept.

We were carefully observing the entire lunchroom, alert for any reactions to our presence. Business was going on as usual; the employees seemed to be the only ones perturbed by our presence. They were scurrying around, making telephone calls, and conferring with one another. The ridiculousness of it struck me, that one nice person who happened to have a dark complexion could throw their whole organization into such pandemonium simply by sitting at the counter and asking to eat. A young mother with two small children took the three stools on the other side of Booker. She didn't say anything to us, but once I thought I overheard her say to the little boy, "Don't bother the nice man." As the noon hour approached, the entire counter filled and people were standing in line for seats. This certainly did not bear out the contention the managers have been making that they will lose business if they integrate!

Booker, my companion, is a young man of mature good looks. His relatively light complexion is set off by a mustache that does not appear as an intrusion among his well-ordered features. Just as he is older than most of our students by the length of a tour of duty with the army in Europe, Robert Booker is by the same measure more intensely impatient with the segregated, paternalistic society Negroes have to put up with even here in Knoxville, his home town.

We developed a little game which occupied us as we sat food-less. We had been told that there would be white observers, friendly to our cause, at each of the places we were going. There were in fact to be two such groups, because the white men and white women were organized separately. Our diversion was to guess who these secret fellow-conspirators might be. We easily spotted our male friends, two University of Tennessee professors, who are active in interracial groups in the city. But we did not see any women we recognized and our curiosity increased. I spied one woman I thought I recognized, but it soon became evident that she was a store employee working for our defeat. Booker pointed out two bluenose dowagers he said looked like Presbyterians. They really did, I agreed, but not the kind of Presbyterians who would be helping us!

Robert's gentle dig was not lost on me. We have talked about religion more than once. He claims not to be interested in it, yet he exists here at Knoxville College in an atmosphere of Presbyterianism marked not so much by piety as by the bland assumption that the religious question is settled in our favor. In his a-religiousness Robert is not typical of our students. And yet I have known other young Negroes for whom religion does not supply a meaningful way of response to racial discrimination—enough others that I am anxious both about them and about America.

Booker is one of a growing group of proud, able young Negroes who are literally bursting with aggressiveness that will find an outlet. That outlet will be either constructive or destructive depending upon the way their own hearts are turned and the response they meet with from society. The Christian way of love is finding expression in the work of leaders like Martin Luther King and James Lawson in that they are seeking not simply to grasp privileges for a single group, but to create a society in which freedom and dignity are the heritage of every man regardless of race or group. As a consequence, the benefit of their work is accruing, I am convinced, to our entire culture, including those who oppose them most bitterly. We have hardly been acquainted in this country with the other kind of Negro leader—the racist. With alarm we are beginning to see his type in Africa, while the strange

sect of Negroes who call themselves "Muslims," and who advocate the separation of Negroes from white America, remind us
that even in this country, despite the deep impression Christianity
has made upon the Negro people, it is by no means a foregone
conclusion that Negroes will continue to take the "Christian" way
of righting the wrongs that have been done them.

I could not fail to be proud to be sitting there beside a young
man like Robert Booker. He will be a leader someday; what kind
of leader, I am not sure. I yearn for him to become a more convinced Christian.

Booker was restless; he kept saying, "We are not doing any
good here!" He seemed to feel that the aim of a sit-in is to cut
down the counter's business, whereas I felt we were doing a considerable good by demonstrating to the other customers that having a Negro at the counter is not such a devastating thing as some
suppose, and by showing the management that white customers
will continue to come while a Negro is at the counter. After forty-
five minutes, however, we did leave the counter. I felt that the
completion of my mission now demanded that I visit the manager.

By this time we had learned to identify three plain-clothes
"guards." We could recognize them by the fact that they wore
straw hats in order to disguise themselves as customers (most of
whom were *not* wearing straw hats). Our original bouncer had
recently donned one that did not suit him at all, and he looked
very funny. As I went up the escalator, I saw that one of the
guards was following me, hardly three steps behind. (What do
you suppose he thought I might do?) Since he was coming along,
he might as well make himself useful, I decided, so I turned, and
striving for a pattern of respectful behavior, asked him, "Sir,
would you do me the favor of directing me to the manager's
office?" He did, but the manager was out.

Back on the basement floor we were joined by the three Negro
friends and by two white University of Tennessee students who
had come after morning classes to help us. A reporter from
WATE-TV interviewed some of us. He admitted that the various

news media have cooperated in clamping a boycott on news of lunch counter desegregation in Knoxville, but he denied that this resulted from any pressure exerted by the merchants. We know that at the beginning of negotiations through the Mayor's Committee, everyone including the Negroes agreed that we had a better chance to make a quiet transition in the community if we had a minimum of publicity. But now the quiet is hurting our cause; we have no way to tell our story to the public unless these sit-ins break the news barrier.

Suddenly Pete Bradby, who is director of public relations at the college, said, "Well, we're going to eat some lunch," and moved toward the counter. Silently, as if by pre-arranged signal, the entire group moved with him. Immediately the guards barred the gate with their bodies; we formed a line as though waiting to be admitted. The guards put a chain across the gate and moved up a sign that said, "Luncheonette Closed." I could feel for the Negroes in our group because at this moment my own cause was so completely aligned with theirs: what I felt was inferiority and resentment contradicted by a sense of new power. If the presence of four Negroes could cause a restaurant seating eighty people to close, what power was placed in our hands? I did not think at that moment of Jesus' temptation to throw himself from the pinnacle of the temple and be borne up by angels, but it would have been an appropriate analogy. The temptation that has been presented to us is to wield this power simply for the thrill of wielding power—to use it in selfish and whimsical ways.

We noted that the small counter for Negroes had been closed as well as the main counter. We waited in line until everyone who had been eating at the counter had left, and then we left too. It was 12:30, precisely in the middle of the lunch hour.

Leaving Rich's, we walked up the street to the Todd & Armistead Drug Store, where we knew another group had been sitting-in. This group had left and the counter was now reopened. Robert and a Negro girl sat down at the rather small counter. I sat down next to the young lady. Immediately a waitress put up a cardboard sign on which was scrawled in crayon, "counter closed." The counter employees went into the back room and no one said anything to us.

Robert had taken a seat next to a white youth. This young man, looking down the counter at the Negro girl, muttered to Robert, "Say, do you think they are going to serve that—" The young man, belatedly noticing Robert's complexion, broke off in embarrassment.

Robert asked him testily, "What's the matter? You don't like sitting beside a Negro?"

Huffily, the fellow said, "I'm going to move!" and took the farthest seat at the end of the counter, because, as he muttered to another customer, he was determined to finish his hamburger. (I gleefully made a mental note to the effect that anyone who is more interested in a hamburger than in a protest is really on our side!) Immediately I slipped over onto the stool next to Robert on the other side so that the man would know that not all white people felt as he did. This did not mean that I exactly approved of Robert's approach. By his sarcastic comment he had again showed that he is not quite attuned to the spirit of Christian love which is supposed to be the keynote of our movement.

Shortly, an elderly white man came in, and although there were a number of vacant seats at the counter, chose to sit next to Robert on the stool the youth had vacated. He waited a long time for service. Finally Robert told him he thought the counter was closed. The old man protested, "But these other people are eating!" Robert explained, "Yes, but they were here before we came; you see this store doesn't serve Negroes." The old man couldn't understand such a ridiculous practice. Robert and he engaged in a conversation which was still going on when I slipped off to make a one o'clock engagement.

By phone I had arranged a five o'clock appointment with Byrl Logan, assistant manager of Rich's, who I had been told was in charge of the lunch counter matter for his store. Two others had agreed to go with me—Dr. Howell, a professor of entomology at the University of Tennessee, and Lee Butler, a University student. Mr. Logan received us in his luxurious, mahogany-paneled office. He was a man of imposing stature, no more than forty years old, who was good looking without being attractive. After introductions, my companions explained that they had come to learn his attitudes and to let the store know that it has white customers sympathetic to the Negroes' cause, but that they would leave most of the talking to Mr. Logan and myself.

"I am a minister, Mr. Logan; I'm sure you will understand that my motivation in this lunch counter matter is a moral and religious one." I felt this kind of beginning would be meaningful to a man who is superintendent of the Sunday school at one of the larger Baptist churches.

Mr. Logan's disciplined face and voice revealed little of what he was feeling. "Well, this seems to be a matter on which the ministers themselves do not agree. I have talked with several about it at length." He named in addition to his own minister two others of the most prominent pastors in Knoxville, one a Baptist and one a Methodist. "Their viewpoints are as different as yours and mine. Dr. J—— admitted that he did not know what the solution is."

My heart sank, because I knew well enough the failure of Christian testimony on this point in Knoxville. It is true that one of the ministers mentioned has taken a leading role in the efforts to get the lunch counters desegregated, despite what must have been considerable opposition from within his congregation. But I remembered a little "between us fellows" talk one of the others made only two months ago to the Knoxville Ministerial Association in regard to this very matter of integrating the counters. It went something like this:

"I am pastor of a congregation which likes to take a middle-of-the-road course. Since they interviewed twenty other ministers before they called me, I take it they were convinced that I am a middle-of-the-road minister. They were right. The spirit of my congregation is, 'Let's keep our ears to the ground and find out what the sentiment of the community is before we jump.' That is my approach to this matter of integration." The man who took this position is a leader in the Ministerial Association.

I also know Dr. J——. He is a man of genial good will whose usual role in the Ministerial Association whenever a bold step in human relations is proposed is to rise and offer a substitute motion whose effect is to take the cutting-edge off the proposed action. The result of this is that every minister is able to leave the meeting feeling piously courageous, yet not in fact having risked a thing.

I frequently hear the question put as to why Knoxville, in spite of its long tradition of good will between the races, and with a Negro population of only 15 per cent, has moved less rapidly than some other cities in the South on such matters as school integration. As a concerned Christian, I have to admit that a part of the answer is that the leadership of the Christian forces in Knoxville has been hesitant, confused, and timid in interpreting to the community what "Love your neighbor" means in terms of modern intergroup relations. It was easy to see that the Church had had an influence on Mr. Logan in this matter, but a negative influence: the Church by its own indecision was giving him an excuse to continue that course in which he thought his economic self-interest lay. "A house divided against itself cannot stand." I believe it was Jesus rather than Abraham Lincoln who first said that.

Dr. Howell mentioned his association with the University. "Yes, I know all about each of you," Mr. Logan informed us. "We have been doing some investigation. In fact, I talked on the phone a long time this afternoon with Dr. Holt, the president of the University, about you, Dr. Howell."

Dr. Howell bristled, understanding this as a gloved threat. He said, "I did not come here with my president's blessing; I did not seek it. I think I am enough of a man to stand on my own two eet and say what I think about a controversial issue, and the University has always allowed me that freedom." I appreciated his courage.

In an effort to slide over the situation, I joked, "I trust in your investigation you found out that we are not Communists!" He agreed with a slight smile which relaxed the tension.

Mr. Logan confided to us that Negroes don't really want integration. "More Negroes have apologized to us for the sit-ins than have protested the fact that we have segregated lunch facilities," he contended. I was surprised that a man of Logan's intelligence would try to defend this position, and he did soon retreat from it. Meanwhile we tried to explain the difference between saying, "Virtually all Negroes want desegregation" and "Virtually all Negroes desire to eat beside whites." Negroes want restrictions removed; they want to know that they are free, although it will probably be a long time before many care to eat at the downtown lunch counters.

"I myself was born in Indiana," he continued. "I want you to know that I have nothing against Negroes." (This to me was a *non sequitur;* I have long since learned to discount place of birth as a credential in the discussion of race relations.) "Personally I would be glad to see them eating at our counter. But we do not feel that we should be called upon to make an economic sacrifice to bring this about. Like any other firm, we are in business to make money and not to 'do good.'" Logan was courteous, but hard as steel. "Rich's does not set its own policies; the public sets our policies, and unfortunately the public in Knoxville is not ready to accept integration."

This was just the point which I wished to belabor with him. "I know the merchants have been proceeding on the assumption that the white people of Knoxville will not accept integration at the counters, but it is a mystery to me how you have arrived at this conclusion. Has there been any objective study made?" He admitted there had not. "This morning a Negro sat in your lunch counter for forty-five minutes and business continued so good that people were waiting in line for seats. Nobody seemed to pay any attention to him except the employees."

"We are aware of that. We observed it very closely. You will notice that we did not close the counter until we were besieged by a large crowd." (Four Negroes, to be exact!)

We assured Mr. Logan that we were convinced Negro leaders would be willing to cooperate on some plan of controlled experiments to ascertain the attitudes of the eating public. He discounted the value of this, ridiculing the so-called "Nashville plan" by which the Negroes had agreed to restrict their patronage to certain hours of the day.

"And what have the Negroes in Nashville really accomplished? Nothing, so far as I can see, except that they can now buy a hamburger in a few places where they couldn't buy one before."

"What they have accomplished," I said quietly, "is that in Nashville a Negro can now walk into a store with a feeling of dignity, with a feeling that he is a full citizen." Mr. Logan admitted that this was a good answer. He conceded that he knows this is what the Negroes really want.

We pointed to other cities in which desegregation has been successfully carried out. The discussion revealed that the management of Rich's is at great pains to keep informed of what is going on wherever lunch counter agitation has occurred, even to the point of being in telephone contact with stores in other cities. Logan's interpretations of course were different from ours. He felt Joske's of San Antonio is being persecuted because it does not want to go along with the majority; I expressed the opinion that a huge store like Joske's ought to be leading rather than following in community advances.

The reference was obvious, and Logan responded: "Yes, people are always telling us Rich's ought to take the lead—that is, to stick our neck out and let it be chopped off. Mr. Rich in Atlanta, who is president of Rich's stores, is Jewish himself and feels strongly against discrimination of any kind. But Mr. Rich stated his position this way: 'Rich's cannot afford to make itself a guinea pig for a social experiment.' " The inconsistency of this struck me, since that is exactly what Rich's has become, as of this morning. I tried to communicate this:

"Mr. Logan, there is one thing about your position that I simply do not understand. I hope you will not misunderstand what I say as a threat, but you seem to place it all on an economic basis." He objected to this, but eventually asked me to go on. "The point is, you must surely see that you are taking an economic risk also if you do not desegregate. This would seem to leave you free to settle the question on moral grounds."

Perhaps it was at this point that Logan indicated Rich's could always free itself of the economic risk. "One of the officials of Miller's (the other leading department store) has threatened to take out their lunch counter entirely if these protests continue." Young Butler, who up to this point had been silent, handled this with a diplomacy that surprised me. He explained that he was acquainted with both stores and knew Rich's to be more sophisticated in outlook. "Miller's might close their counter, but I am sure Rich's never would do a thing like that!" Mr. Logan conceded that Rich's would not, adding with a smile, "That is the reason I quoted Miller's, rather than say that Rich's would do it." Nevertheless, it was clear to us now that we had made the right decision in choosing to use economic pressure, for this is the only language that will impress Rich's.

In explaining why Negroes feel offended by lunch counter segregation, we put it this way: "A Negro can come into your store —in fact, you urge him to come in—and buy at any other counter, but when he wants a hamburger, he cannot buy that because of his color." I had made a mistake in putting it this way, and Logan was not slow to capitalize on my slip.

"Ah, yes, but he can get a hamburger at Rich's! We have a lunch counter for Negroes, complete with every facility that the

counter for whites has, and serving food from the same kitchen."
We were back to the "separate but equal" doctrine. "In fact,
when we opened our store four years ago, we set up a colored
lunch counter almost as large as the one for whites. We were
offering a facility for them that no other store offered; we felt we
were making a very fine gesture toward the colored population.
But what has happened? It had so little business that we ultimately
turned the room over for other purposes and set up the smaller
counter for Negroes that we have now. They haven't even pa-
tronized it very well."

I couldn't resist the temptation. "And why haven't they pa-
tronized these counters?" His answer was evasive. I asked him to
use his imagination to try to picture Dr. Colston, the president
of Knoxville College, going into Rich's little segregated counter
to eat. Now Colston, whose doctorate is earned, is a man whose
consummate ability and poise gain deference from any group I
have ever seen him in, Negro or white. "Does this make a consistent picture?" The only defense Logan could think of was,
"Well, they've been doing it for a hundred years!"

He went on. "Why after all this time should there be such a fuss
over it now? Why should it be lunch counters which get all the attention? Why not restaurants, swimming pools, churches?"

One of us said, "I suppose it is because Negroes are welcomed
in every other part of your store, and it is only at the lunch
counters that the stores do not welcome them."

"Ah, but that's where you are wrong," the businessman declared. "Our beauty parlor does not serve Negro women, and
almost every day we get complaints that our nursery will not
take Negro children." This was news to us; it was just another
demonstration of the fact that white people can be heedless of
discrimination going on under their very noses. (A Negro girl
with whom I was discussing this the other day could not believe
that whites are not aware of all the discrimination that goes on.
But my conviction is that probably not even Negroes are aware

of all of it; it is carried on in such gentlemanly ways, depending heavily on the well-mannered Negro not to present himself and the comfortable white not to ask "theoretical" questions which might have the result of disturbing his own conscience.)

Logan referred to the fact that he is chairman of the United Fund for Knoxville and that it benefits many Negro agencies. "Rich's and the other stores which are being molested by sit-inners are expected to contribute heavily to the United Fund. Don't the Negroes of Knoxville appreciate what is being done for them?"

"We are sure that they do," one of us replied, "but surely you would not want them to purchase this help at the price of giving up their claim to full first-class citizenship?" Mr. Logan agreed that he would not, but his implication was not thereby removed.

"Why should the community place this bear on *our* backs?" he continued. "Retail stores are not social welfare agencies."

"Mr. Logan, this just happens to be where history is focused today in a great social revolution. In a way, you are in an enviable position. You have an opportunity to make history!" The assistant manager was more amused than impressed by this. For him, it was another instance of idealism which had no bearing on the practical situation.

He became more specific: "Where this thing ought to start is not in department stores, but in the churches. When the churches are integrated, then we can expect the stores to follow." He had hit again a very sensitive spot. I suspect that almost any white congregation in town polled on this question would vote against desegregating the lunch counters. Why this gap between what we think we ought to believe and what we really do believe? Dr. Howell and Lee Butler responded that they belonged to the Unitarian Church, which is an integrated congregation. I added that Union Presbytery, of which I am a member, is also fully and successfully integrated.

"You mean to tell me that Second Presbyterian Church has

Negro members? I attended a meeting there the other night and didn't see a single Negro!"

"No," I replied ruefully, "Second Church has no Negro members, but lots of integrated meetings are held there. The Presbytery—or 'Association' I believe would be the parallel group in the Baptist Church—the Presbytery to which it belongs is fully integrated."

"Well, I think when the time comes that Second Presbyterian Church and these other major churches in town each have a number of Negro members, then it will be time for you to talk to Rich's about desegregating our lunch counter." He was not speaking sarcastically.

We conceded, of course, that the practice of the churches is a long way behind what they preach. "All of us as church members certainly ought to be working at this problem within the churches too. What are you doing in your own church?" I asked rather brutally. He didn't really answer. I went on to contend that when anyone decides to be good, he doesn't first be good "over here," and then decide to be good "over there." He works on all fronts at the same time. Is this not what we should expect of the individual Christian and of the Church? (I refuse to abstain from appealing to Christian ideals simply because these have not been fully put into practice by the group that holds them in trust. Furthermore, I can no more say to the Church, "You must refrain from preaching against social evils until you have cleared them out of your own organizational life," than I can say to an individual minister, "You should cease preaching against sin until you become sinless yourself." Nevertheless, I recognize how the sin of both Church and preacher hurt their testimony.)

As we rose and moved toward the door, I said, "There is one last thing I want to say, and it is this: I came with the young man this morning and plan to continue participating in the sit-ins because I cannot let my Negro friends think that this is a matter of Negroes against whites."

Logan spoke more gently than at any other time during the conversation. "Well, if you feel that is what you ought to do, then you should follow your conscience." For the first time I was able to visualize him as a Sunday school superintendent. I wondered how our conversation might have gone had Mr. Logan been free to work it out with us on this level—but there were the stock-holders, the Atlanta office, the Knoxville public, and the profits. No one is really a free moral agent, I suppose, but I am far freer than he, because there are no such pressures upon me as I make my decisions. What a relief it was to me when I came to teach at a Negro college, for now I no longer had to live in the tension of trying to witness to my convictions while keeping in a work-able relationship with a congregation which was antagonistic to those convictions. I felt sympathy for this man of business in his captivity. Society cannot afford to give to many the freedom which I enjoy, any more than it can afford to let the majority become monks and nuns. Therefore it is *not* primarily the social welfare institutions nor the Church as such, but exactly men like Byrl Logan, enmeshed in the contingencies of this world, to whom it is left in their agonizing decisions to open life to the Kingdom of God.

I have reported this conversation in some detail, not because any basic attitudes were changed or because I think it will affect much the final outcome of our struggle, but because in the span of an hour we covered almost every argument that is used on both sides of this question. Those who advocate negotiation—and I still do—need to know the position they are negotiating with. When I was a little boy I fell from the tip-top of a cherry tree. On the way down, I clutched frantically at branches, twigs, and leaves—everything I could touch, hoping desperately to catch hold of something that would break my fall. That is what most of Logan's arguments were—just clutchings at twigs and leaves. This mercantile executive exhibited just one concern about which he was overwhelmingly serious, and that was his fear of being hurtled by social change onto ground that would do his firm economic injury. If we can find a way to convince the Logans that the economic ground is really quite soft beneath the tree, they will no more snatch at twigs. Negotiation without that economically convincing argument will never bring results.

I came home from this meeting all keyed-up emotionally. Today has been historically important for Knoxville. The movement begun today will succeed—of that I am convinced because I sense the urgency of the Negro's protest all over the South—in fact, all over the world. I keep thinking of Anne Morrow Lindbergh's phrase, "the wave of the future." It's too bad the term is spoiled by such unsavory associations. The movement will succeed—but how much conflict must intervene? (Mrs. Lindbergh's application of her phrase to the Nazi movement reminds us that one can bid too high for the future.) Surely if people like Mr. Logan and his superiors understood the social revolution that is going on in the world today, or knew the strength of the aspirations of the Negro people, they would understand that they are making economic sacrifices in a lost cause. Is there no way we can make them see this? I feel a sense of desperation, as when in my dreams I am trying to rescue someone from a burning building and my legs are too weak to move.

This afternoon's paper carried a brief notice of the sit-ins on page forty-three next to the obituaries. It contained only a small excerpt from the statement our group released to the press today. The original statement emphasizes the four months of patient negotiation which Negroes have engaged in without result, and says that the Council decided "with a deep sense of regret" on a resumption of peaceful sit-in demonstrations as the only alternative left to protest injustice. The statement, after paying tribute to the Mayor for his leadership, reflects the disillusionment of the Negroes and their friends in the observation, "No city in the country has been given a greater opportunity to set a pattern in race relations," but disavows any spirit of bitterness because the conferences have failed.

Later this evening I called some minister friends and the members of my Presbytery Committee on Social Education and Action to let them know what is going on. The ministers were intensely interested, but volunteered no help with the sit-ins. I suppose I should not be critical; if I had a white congregation, would I be doing this? But if the congregation had some Negro members—even a very few—the matter would be different. Then one would only be working to produce in society the pattern that already existed in the church. This is the break-through we need.

I can hardly wait to tell Robert Booker what I learned from Mrs. Spahr, my colleague on the Presbytery Committee who has worked for forty years for brotherhood in Knoxville: our "good angel" this morning was not one of the bluenose "Presbyterians," but the young mother with the two small children sitting next to Robert! Mrs. Spahr thinks she is a Catholic. She came as a representative of "The Fellowship of the Concerned," an interracial and inter-faith women's group recently organized on the initiative of Mrs. Spahr to work for better race relations.

Earlier I mentioned Booker's mustache. For a while after I came to Knoxville College, I wondered why so many of our lads prefer mustaches. The reasons were not hard to figure out. One is, of course, that a mustache goes well with a dark complexion. Then too, the natural pride of a youth in demonstrating that he has enough facial hair to make a mustache is augmented in the case of Negro boys by the fact that Negroes are as a rule less hairy than whites. ("You're further advanced on the evolutionary tree!" I sometimes tell them in jest.) But what is most important to them is the fact that the mustache minimizes the frequent racial characteristic of the prominent upper lip. Why should they wish to minimize it? Why, in order to look less like Negroes, of course—to accommodate themselves more nearly to the white man's standard of beauty. This is a part of the tragedy, that we whites should have forced our standards upon them to the extent that they strive to obliterate everything that reminds themselves or others that they are Negroes. (Even the word "Negro" comes from their lips with hesitation, although they generally prefer it to any other group designation.) This is genteel genocide. The new freedom must include the freedom to be themselves, or it will be no freedom. And this means that Negroes must first free themselves from the burden of the inferiority-feeling that our white-dominated culture has placed upon their personalities. When the ads in *Ebony* and *Sepia* picture as many dark-skinned models as nearly-white ones, and the blurb for hair-straightener and skin-bleach is no longer in evidence, when the mustache is used purely for decoration and not for camouflage, then we will know that the Negro has really won his freedom—including the inner freedom to be a Negro.

Friday, June 10

WHEN we came together at 10:00 this morning, it was not as rookies, but as campaign veterans. We had been under fire, and now felt a degree of confidence in going into battle again.

Someone from each of the groups reported on what happened in the store he went to yesterday. Both at Grant's and Sears' the counter was closed as soon as several Negroes sat down. The demonstrators then hung around to be ready to sit again should the counter reopen. There was no violence or heckling. The attitude of white customers seemed to be one of casual interest or indifference, though a few sour comments were reported.

Rich's presents a special problem. Should we try to get one or two into the counter with the aim of demonstrating that it would make no difference to the white customers, or should we send a larger group, which would undoubtedly cause the counter to be closed? This forced us to face the problem of philosophy—what is the aim of the sit-in? Robert expressed himself in favor of getting the counter closed and causing the store to lose as much business as possible. I reported that the one favorable item which came out in our conversation with Mr. Logan was that the store was impressed by the fact that the white customers didn't seem to object to the presence of one or two Negroes. I urged that we try to get one or two inside the gate about 11:00 A.M. and let them sit for forty-five minutes or so for the sake of making this particular testimony, and that later others could come, which probably would result in the counter being closed during the lunch hour. This strategy was agreed upon. It was in effect a compromise which avoided having to solve the philosophical question.

But who would we send for the delicate task of getting into the counter at Rich's? Robert and I were out, since we would be recognized before we got to the gate. Someone suggested Mrs. Perry. "Sure," I exclaimed, "Mrs. Perry could walk right in without anyone noticing the difference!" I had reference to Mrs. Perry's light complexion and impressive bearing. She took it as a compliment. Mrs. T. G. Perry was active on the Mayor's Committee until it expired. She is a rather well-to-do matron who has in times past been one of Rich's very good customers. However, her friendship for Rich's began to cool some years ago when the store bid for the opportunity to handle the services for her daughter's wedding. Mrs. Perry had replied, "We will be happy for Rich's to do it, provided you open up all your services to the wedding party, including the Laurel Room, the beauty parlor, and the rest rooms." Needless to say, Rich's withdrew its bid. It was also Mrs. Perry who protested to Rich's that no Negro choir is included in the annual Christmas tree lighting ceremony at Rich's store. So Mrs. Perry felt a special mission to go to Rich's. Selected to accompany her was Mrs. Griffin, another matron of near sixty who has a medium light complexion and red hair. It is an inspiration to me to see people like these who have secure positions in the community willing to risk them to fight alongside the kids for social justice. If the stores could just understand what this means.

Booker and I chose to go to Sears' this morning. The counter is in a separate room, but the doors were open and no one was there to prevent our entering. Dr. William McArthur, the chairman of our science division at the college, who is a Negro, was already seated at the counter. We took two seats next to McArthur because they were the only two together that were available. We spotted the two white women who must be our "good angels" over at the next section of the counter; one of them was Mrs. W. B. Hembree, a Presbyterian whom I know personally.

"At last the Presbyterians are vindicated!" I murmured to Robert. Mrs. Hembree attended the workshop on social education and action sponsored recently by our presbytery committee and expressed there a keen interest in doing something to help with lunch counter desegregation. She has been placed in charge of securing the participation of white women. I am pleased to think our workshop may have made a small contribution at this point. One always wonders.

Also quietly sipping coffee nearby was Arthur Jones, a professor of zoology at the University of Tennessee. Arthur, who is president of the congregation at the Tennessee Valley Unitarian Church and on the board of the Knoxville Area Human Relations Council, has accepted responsibility for the participation of white men in the sit-ins. Gee, we got all the brass with us this morning! With Arthur was another University professor—chemistry, I think. (The sciences seem to be doing better than the humanities!)

Quickly three more Negro boys came in. The management moved efficiently to close the counter. This was accomplished simply by closing and locking the doors that led from the sales floor to the counter. A few lights were turned off. To make it perfectly clear, the man in charge called out so everyone could hear, "The counter is closed, folks; there's been a—breakdown!" His words were more prophetic than he realized; indeed there had been a breakdown of Southern tradition. The fact that the store management could think of no other response than the closing of the counter symbolizes the bewilderment of the white South when confronted with this breakdown. They are at first unable to imagine working out some other *modus vivendi*. The only alternative is to cease to live—"we will close the schools, we will close the counters"—a form of cultural suicide.

We sat until everyone who was eating had left; then they turned off all the lights and we left too. The whole atmosphere had been more relaxed than at Rich's. No one had spoken to us; no one told us not to enter; no one told us to leave; no one told us we wouldn't be served. McArthur said one of the waitresses sitting at the far end of the room stuck out her tongue at Robert. I told Robert it was probably her way of flirting with him, and I half believe it.

As we left, I discovered which man was Mr. Brookshire, the manager, and introduced myself to him. "I just want to say that I hope Sears' will soon begin to serve all customers without discrimination, because I am convinced this is the only ultimate solution."

Mr. Brookshire is a mild mannered man who, in contrast to Mr. Logan, immediately gives one the impression of being a Sunday school teacher. He surprised me. "Yes, I agree with you, but—" And there followed a number of the same excuses we heard from Mr. Logan yesterday. But he had one other—"I just hope the Negroes will be patient and not push this too fast, because I'm convinced that after the schools are integrated in September there will be a much better atmosphere for integrating the lunch counters." This reminds me of the old Alphonse-Gaston act. It is probable that whichever happens first will help the other, but it is only the first grade which stands a chance of being integrated in September, so there can be no direct carry-over. Mr. Brookshire also contended that the churches should begin the process of integration. I am convinced that this is a just judgment that will fall upon every Christian spokesman for equal rights until the Church removes the beam from its own eye. To this store manager also I suggested working with the Negroes on a plan of controlled testing, but he indicated no special interest. I told him that even if the counter were kept open and the Negroes *not* served it would be some progress.

We left a couple of youths in the store to see whether the counter reopened and went to see what was happening at Rich's. I must admit that our curiosity was keen. The counter was still open. Mrs. Perry was seated at the counter, not being served. With her was Mrs. Rosen, a Jewish friend who is active in Fellowship House along with Mrs. Perry. So far as I could tell, Mrs. Rosen was not eating either. Waldo and Anice Banks were standing at the gate, being refused admission to the counter. They told me Rosemary Martin, who has just finished a year of graduate schooling at Meharry School of Nursing, was upstairs complaining to Mr. Carson, the manager.

Presently Rosemary came down. We asked her what the manager had said. "He said a lot of things, but it all amounted to 'We're not going to do *any*thing!' " was her droll reply.

"That is the most concise summary of the attitude of the managers that I have yet heard!" I commented.

The situation here was uglier than it had been yesterday because the guards were trying to keep the Negroes out while admitting the whites, even after a group of Negroes had collected at the gate. This had worked until Booker came, but now he was insisting on trying to push in whenever they admitted a white person. The guards had to fence him off with their bodies; this held dangerous possibilities.

Waldo muttered, "Two can play at this game," and beckoned the members of the group to cluster around the gate rather than stand in a single line. This made it difficult for anyone else to enter the counter. The guards summoned a store official, who threatened to call the police if we did not stay in line, so we did move to one side.

One guard pushed Waldo a little and Waldo exploded, "Take

your hands off me!" A guard muttered menacingly, "Buddy, you'd better go to that other counter to eat *if you want to live!*" Waldo expressed his indignation at this kind of treatment, succeeding in getting the initiative sufficiently so that they were afraid to abuse him any further.

I am apprehensive about Waldo's being in a situation like this because he shows more resentment of racial segregation than any other Negro person I know. Since he came here last summer from a Midwestern university to take a position with Knoxville College, he and Anice have felt, I know, like persons imprisoned. A way of life they took for granted there is here beyond their reach. Like children with their noses pressed longingly against the bakery window, they pass by the nice restaurants and supper clubs, read the movie marquees, are dazzled by the electric signs enticing customers into plush motels and colorful drive-ins—and know that all these things they have been taught by our culture to value are so close and yet so far from them. "For everybody but us! And what is so different about us? What is so objectionable in us?" (Sometimes I think it is not the *denial* but the *display* of our hoarded privileges that constitutes for us Caucasians our greater sin.) Who can blame Waldo for the chip on his shoulder or advise him and Anice that they should forget about these things and be entirely content with the service they can humbly give here to their fellow-man?

From time to time I have ventured to suggest to Waldo and Anice that they join those who are working, however slowly, to make Knoxville a *better* place in which to live. So at least from that standpoint I was encouraged to see them participating today. The little guy who starts rattling the bakery door is making a more positive approach than the one who simply desires through the window.

There are others with different personalities who respond to segregation in a quite different way. There is, for instance, Jim Reese, the pastor of the college church. Jim is just as restricted externally, but one cannot know Jim without being impressed that somehow he has achieved an internal freedom. Jim takes what he can get, works for the rest, and fits it all into perspective in a well-rounded life. He knows he is not inferior, and therefore he does not waste much time chafing about it. I don't give Jim personal credit for this; under the circumstances, I can see it as possible only by means of a spiritual gift. A reaction like Waldo's is the more readily understandable—that one half convinced by the persistent, hammering message of the culture should continually be trying to prove to himself his equality. Waldo's frequently expressed disdain for certain traits associated with his race reveals his longing to be free of the burden which he feels an accident of birth has placed upon him. Caucasians who never get to know individual Negroes deeply never discover how tragic this burden can be and often resist knowing individual Negroes well because they do not wish to discover it.

A white woman who had wanted to eat hesitated when she saw the situation. A guard called to her, "The counter is open, come right on in!" The other two guards fenced Robert in a corner. Still the woman hesitated, whereupon the guard stepped out about ten feet to escort the woman in. This was the baldest operation they had yet pulled. Suddenly I was enraged. They would not treat my friends like that! How could any white person even consider coming into the counter past such a protest line! I stepped squarely in front of the woman. I said with furious determination, "I'm sorry, but I was here first!" The guards hesitated a moment, as though getting ready to tell me to enter the counter. (What would I have done if they had?) Then one of them, having apparently learned my name from Logan's office, said mockingly, "Oh, you're Proud-foot! I guess you are really proud of your feet, aren't you?" I didn't mind the insult, so relieved was I to be out of that difficult situation. For by now the woman had left, and the guards had decided they had better close the counter. I was left trembling from the effects of the sudden rage that had gripped me, causing me to do something I would by no means have done if I had had time to become frightened. I realized that without deliberation I had stepped over the line into the area of civil disobedience—for surely to prevent customers from entering a place of business would come under the provisions of the Tennessee law prohibiting any persons from "conspiring to interfere with the lawful conduct of private business." I realized for the first time how difficult it is to pursue a course of non-violence in the face of provocation. I had assumed that it would come easy for me because I have never had the habit of resorting to force to attain my objectives. Even as a youngster I didn't like to fight. Because my playmates were always tougher than I, I soon learned that my best defense was no defense at all—the antagonist soon got tired of fighting an opponent who wouldn't give him any resistance. But adopting non-violence as a strategy is different from adopting it on principle; it is easier to act non-violently when you have no option than when you see a quick way to hurt your adversary. I was fearful that I might not measure up to this test.

I was also ashamed. It was painful to my ego to think of myself as a person who would step in front of a woman and say, "I was here first!" Besides that, it is certainly not the way to build good will for our cause in the white community.

As we left Rich's, we were encountered by a group of about ten students from Cornell University in Ithaca, New York, who were making an educational trip through the South under the guidance of the Director of Religious Activities there. They were thrilled to run into a live sit-in. Alert and sensitive, these young people nevertheless did not have the scrubbed and pressed look that is standard for Southern college students; the beatnik influence was apparent. I was not surprised therefore to learn that the manager of Grant's had mistaken them for a group of local hoodlums bent on tangling with the sit-inners. As the manager slipped out a side door, possibly to call the police, the leader of our sit-inners had suggested that the Cornell students leave the store. As we talked outside Rich's, we learned that these students had raised $4,000 at Cornell for defense of the sit-inners in the South. They wanted to know what more they could do. We suggested that they survey their own town to see whether there might be discrimination there which they were unaware of. We told them any effective means of protest to chain store outlets there should ultimately help us in Knoxville. They asked whether caravans of students from Northern universities could be helpful, and we advised against it. It would just provide Southern obstructionists another opportunity to ascribe the agitation to "outsiders," avoiding any searching of their own consciences.

We dropped by Todd & Armistead again. I sat there quite a long time with Bill McArthur, just because we knew they would reopen as soon as all the Negroes were gone. McArthur is an extremely intelligent person and a scholar in his field. Somehow it seemed better to sit there with my friends and not eat than to sit alone and eat.

Todd & Armistead is in an area where there are many business and professional offices. Their counter is important to the store, because as the office personnel come in for "coffee breaks" they buy other things. As we sat there, people kept coming in to eat and leaving, more disappointed that they could not get lunch than indignant over the presence of Negroes, so far as we could tell. Todd & Armistead's business is being severely hurt, not so much by our presence as by the fact that they persist in closing the counter. A young woman came up to the cashier and hesitantly asked, "Can you sell me a package of *cigarettes?*"

As Mac and I left the store together I overheard the muttered phrase "nigger lover" from one of the bystanders.

There will not be any sit-ins tomorrow. Our leaders figure that there is a tougher element in town on Saturdays which would make the danger of violence greater. Besides, we need a weekend to recuperate; I for one am finding out that daily sit-ins are a terrific strain on the nerves. We are looking forward to the mass meeting called for Sunday at 5:00 P.M. I understand an "economic withdrawal" is to be organized.

Sunday, June 12

Mt. Olive Baptist Church, which has served as the headquarters for our movement, was nearly full for our mass meeting. There was an encouraging number of whites, mostly either Unitarians or persons whose interest stems from Fellowship House, an interracial group formed about ten years ago in Knoxville for the distinct purpose of bridging the gap through fellowship and which on the white side draws its members mostly from among University people. It must be acknowledged that very few whites were there out of loyalty to a trinitarian Christian faith.

The hymns chosen for the opening devotional reflected the spirit of the occasion so far as the Negroes are concerned—"Stand Up for Jesus" and "Be Not Dismayed Whate'er Betide." Rev. James presided. Rev. Robert E. James, who is pastor of the neighboring Mt. Zion Baptist Church, was chosen chairman of the loose organization that was formed Tuesday night to direct the lunch counter movement and which was christened, after some long-dead forebear, "The Associated Council for Full Citizenship." James is a handsome, brown man who neither looks nor acts like the stereotype of the preacher, something that may very well be to his credit. With a certain resemblance to George Raft and a satin-smoothness of manner to match, he could easily be taken for a successful salesman, I once thought, or even a charming operator of the underworld. As I have come to know James better, however, I have realized that his polish is not superficial but is the deep luster of his true self. I have come to understand him as a man with a devotion to justice and a tender regard for persons.

This was our first opportunity to inform people as to what was going on and why. Briefly James explained how the merchants on May 18 had asked the students for a ten-day moratorium on demonstrations, with the implication that at the end of that period

they would desegregate on the kind of gradual plan that had
proved successful in Nashville. The ten days had expired just as
the college year closed and the students went home. After waiting
ten additional days and receiving no communication from the
merchants, and aware of the fact that the Mayor's Committee had
disbanded thinking its job done, the Negro members of the May-
or's Committee had met Tuesday night of this week to decide
what to do next. Everyone present had felt that further negotiation at this time offered no hope. All felt an obligation to the
students, who had refrained from demonstrations so long only because of the assurances of the adults that negotiation would succeed. The decision was first to test the stores and, if in fact there
had been no change in policy, then to begin sit-ins. The test was
made on Wednesday, June 8, when Negro adults went two by two
to each of the ten stores which had been involved in the negotiations
with the Mayor's Committee. They were refused service at every
store except Cole's. (When the same two returned to Cole's the
following day, the manager explained to them that the employee
who served them the day before had been uninformed as to the
owners' policy; the store could only serve them orders to take
out. The Negroes asked if they could get a take-out order and
eat it at the table; the manager replied that he had no control over
where they ate it, only the type of service the store gave them.
So they ordered cokes and hamburgers to go, took them out of
the sack, and ate them at the table!) So on Thursday large-scale
sit-ins had been begun, concentrating on the three stores which
had showed the least willingness to go along with the Mayor's
Committee on a plan for desegregation—Rich's, Grant's, and Sears'.

This was all the explanation needed, since most of the Negroes
felt demonstrations had already been too long delayed, and some
had been highly critical of President Colston and other Negro
leaders for holding the students in check. There followed a description of what had been accomplished in the sit-ins. It was
necessary that the entire Negro community become aroused about

this objective, the more so because we have no student personnel ready to throw into demonstrations in the summertime.

Then Dr. W. T. Crutcher was introduced to talk about "selective buying." Dr. Crutcher has been pastor of the Mt. Olive Baptist Church for twenty-five years. If President Colston is the outstanding personage of the Knoxville Negro community, Dr. Crutcher is its leader when it comes to community affairs. I am still very hesitant about guessing the age of a dark-skinned Negro, but I would put Crutcher's at slightly past fifty. A quiet, slow-speaking man, he never appears to get ruffled about anything. It is not unusual for white persons to seek out Crutcher in his study for personal counseling, for he is that rare individual about whom one instinctively feels, "Here is a man of God." He was the first Negro to be elected president of the Knoxville Ministerial Association, an honor that could not be denied him because of what he had done for the organization. A man wholeheartedly devoted to the cause of racial equality, Crutcher is active in almost every interracial organization in the city, a fact which sets him in contrast to most of the other Negro ministers. (Those who think that Negroes are itching to associate with whites would be surprised to know how difficult it is to get proportional representation of Negroes in interracial groups such as human relations councils.) And yet with Crutcher, race interests always seem to stem from a larger, more fundamental commitment to the Christian faith.

"Now we don't use the word 'boycott,'" Crutcher warned. "That's a dirty word around here! What we are going to do is 'selective buying.' That means that we trade with those merchants who are our friends and don't trade with those who have showed that they are not our friends. Who are our friends? Those who don't discriminate against us on the basis of race! Those who treat us as first-class citizens, into whose stores we can walk with dignity and self-respect, knowing that we are welcome at *every* department in the store. We think you are intelligent enough to know who are *not* your friends!" Then Crutcher read again with emphasis the names of the ten stores, simply stating factually that they had refused to integrate their lunch facilities. It was necessary to present the matter in this devious way in order to avoid running afoul of the state laws against conspiring to interfere with the lawful conduct of business, which would certainly cover an open boycott.

The Unitarian minister, Robert West, spoke urging us to "live more economically" by cancelling various charge accounts. The implication was clear that we might as well achieve our economy at the expense of those credit stores which are discriminating— namely Rich's, Miller's, and Sears', the three department stores.

Ralph Martin, head of our guidance and testing program at the college, appealed for more volunteers to serve as sit-inners. Crutcher added to this that those who volunteer must be wholly committed to the way of non-violence. "Anyone who feels that he could not take blows without striking back should not participate in a sit-in," he urged. "Such a person would do our cause more harm than good." To illustrate, he told the story of my experience last Friday at Rich's, repeating my comment, "I guess I'm not as non-violent as I had thought!" The audience found this very amusing. I was a little embarrassed, but more pleased, I suppose. My temptation is to participate in this movement for the increased prestige it will bring me among the people I work with.

Monday, June 13

AT our preliminary meeting this morning we again had a difference of opinion about what our policy at Rich's should be in the light of the management's apparent decision to keep the lunch counter operating during demonstrations. There is no doubt that Rich's—the store which in the beginning of negotiations we all thought was working on our behalf—has been the toughest toward us and has posed us with the most difficult decisions. I pointed out that by deliberately preventing white customers from entering the counter we are in effect moving across the line into civil disobedience without ever having made the decision to do so. I was not opposed to joining in civil disobedience if the group felt the time had arrived when we must make that kind of witness, but I did not want us to slip into it by accident. My own preference was that we take enough Negro demonstrators to form such a conspicuous protest line that its purpose could not be missed by anybody. Robert again spoke strongly in favor of closing the counter by tactics such as we had been using. My recommendation was adopted for the time being.

I had my first sit-in in a variety store today, and also my first experience as group leader. My group was sent to Grant's. The counter was closed as soon as the first Negroes sat down. This was about 11:00 A.M. One customer left a full plate of food, explaining to the waitress that she was unable to eat it; the waitress told her it would be on the house. (I remember how, when I first came to the South seventeen years ago, the thought of eating food that had been *prepared* by Negroes turned my stomach; this woman would no doubt be elated to be able to afford a Negro cook, but was nauseated by the thought of eating *with* a Negro. The fact that I have grown beyond my own prejudice gives me hope for her.) The others quietly completed their refreshments and left.

When the last of these customers had gone (about 11:45), I took most of my group over to Kress's, simply to keep the demonstrators gainfully employed, for I had no orders to do so. We scattered two persons at each of the four semi-circular sections. The store personnel never gave any indication even of having noticed us. Service went on all around us. A few times I noticed persons come down the stairs, observe the situation, and go back. It was impossible to know whether they didn't want to eat with Negroes, whether they refused to eat out of sympathy with us, or simply didn't want to become involved in a demonstration. I think the last is the most likely explanation. Booker talked with the Kress manager. He said that he was personally in favor of desegregating and wished the other stores would go along. (None dares make the move by himself.)

On the occasions when I found it necessary to go from one member of the group to another whispering instructions, I became very sensible that I was presenting to the public the image of a John Kaspar in reverse. I decided to recommend that our group leaders always be Negroes.

As I left at 1:10, I noted that Grant's had already reopened its counter.

We have a small interracial civic club which has attained sufficient respectability that we are allowed to meet in a private dining room of one of the leading restaurants. Tonight as we gathered at the table Dr. Crutcher announced, "I have only a few minutes to live! A man telephoned me early this morning that if we had another sit-in today, I would be dead by 6 o'clock." The time was 5:45 P.M. We did not *really* take it seriously; nevertheless, I surreptitiously glanced at my watch several times in the next fifteen minutes. The hour of six came and went without incident.

I learned at this meeting that Rich's stayed open today under our new policy of not blocking the gate.

Tuesday, June 14

TODAY I had to miss the sit-ins in order to attend the Police-Community Institute at the University of Tennessee. The success of this meeting may be more important to our cause than the actual sitting-in. Remember that one big day of demonstrations in Nashville when the police stood by while white hoodlums tormented the demonstrators, and then arrested the demonstrators? This is surely enough to demonstrate that the attitude of the police and of the city administration which gives them their orders is crucially important to any move toward integration. So far we have seen nothing of the police during our demonstrations, and since there has been no trouble, we couldn't ask for a better arrangement. In many Southern cities, we would have been arrested long before now. We have cooperated to the extent of informing the Mayor that sit-ins were to begin and when they were to be repeated.

I was astonished to find the burly "guard" from Rich's at the meeting. He turns out to be a city policeman. I presume he is being paid by Rich's for off-duty services, but I do not like the arrangement; it compromises the impartiality of the police department. At any rate, he has received a lot of indoctrination today on good race relations, for despite the fact that this was only one area to be considered by the Institute, it has received the major emphasis. (Community discussions in the South today either fearfully avoid mention of the integration problem, or else fascinatedly concentrate upon it—it is difficult to see it fitted comfortably into the context of all community problems. This is not because it is so much greater than other problems, such as poverty, for example, or family relations, but because like sex it is so laden with emotion.) It is a fortunate coincidence that this Institute, which has been so long in the planning, should have fallen just now during this time of tension in the community. I often wonder whether such meetings do any good; one needs to see as today the antagonists actually laying down their weapons for a day to come together to talk about their problem, in order to appreciate the long-range good done by interracial workshops and institutes. The same thing is true of estimating the contribution made to a community by organizations such as the Conference of Christians and Jews, which was the initial sponsor of this meeting, and by individuals like Neal Spahr, the frail, semi-retired attorney who has given so much of his precious life-energy to bring it about.

In the discussion group I attended, nearly all the talking was done by two articulate young Negroes—a minister from Chattanooga and a city councilman scientist from Oak Ridge. This is not because they were garrulous, but because the whites wanted to hear what they had to say. Art Levin, secretary of the Anti-Defamation League for the Southeastern area, tells me that this is increasingly the pattern in interracial discussions in the South. Whites are beginning to realize that these intelligent young Negroes are in some way the key to the future and are eager to learn from them. Suddenly we whites are waking up to the fact that we don't know much about this new social adventure; our old world is crumbling down around us, and we look to these young men to learn what the new world is to be like. So it is on the world scene; so it is becoming in the United States.

George Dempster, Knoxville's colorful, millionaire ex-mayor, who was presiding over the Institute, was called out once during the afternoon and reported on his return that the call was from a group of merchants who asked him what he thought they ought to do about the lunch counters. Dempster, who was active on the Mayor's Committee before its demise, says he answered: "I can give you my reply in three words—'Let them eat!' " I hope they follow it. Dempster furnishes a good example of the liberal attitude to be found among upper-class white Southerners, according to all the social surveys of the Southern situation.

I hear that Rich's closed its counter today. I am told that the demonstrators discussed our strategy for Rich's again at the preliminary meeting and reversed the decision we made yesterday. When they blocked the aisle, the store guards threatened to call a police cruiser to "take them in." In about a half hour two policemen came and simply asked the demonstrators to leave an aisle open. They complied, but by this time the counter had already been closed.

It was also reported to me that some white bystander offered to fight Young, one of our white demonstrators, at Grant's. When this incident occurred, our group simply left the store.

Wednesday, June 15

I AM reluctant to go back to Rich's until we clarify our strategy there, because if I'm going to get into trouble, I want to be sure of my moral grounds. Since we were short of workers this morning (for now the novelty has worn off and it has become a day-by-day grind), we economized by sending only two Negro persons and myself to Sears'. Since they are going to close when one or two Negroes come in, why bother to send more? My companions were Mrs. Harshaw, a capable red-haired housewife I would judge to be in her late thirties, and Pate, a student on vacation from Hampton Institute who reads Shakespeare during sit-ins—not to impress, but because he gets a big kick out of it. (If my designations seem abrupt, it is because we don't seem to bother getting one another's full names. This is an impersonal enterprise, since we come from many different groups and do not expect to be associated after the sit-ins are over; nevertheless there is a deep sense of comradeship among us because of our common jeopardy. In both these respects we are like an army battalion at the front lines.)

As we pulled into Sears' parking lot, we saw a large man standing at the entrance to the store. "They have a spy watching for us!" Mrs. Harshaw exclaimed, recognizing the man as an employee. As soon as he spotted us, he disappeared inside the store.

Mrs. Harshaw suggested, "Let's fool him by not going in for awhile. That will make him terribly nervous." So we sauntered around the store thinking to slip in from the opposite entrance. But when we got to the other side, there was our lookout waiting for us at that entrance! We were not surprised upon entering the store to find the counter already closed. We stood around for a long time within sight of the doors to the counter, knowing that if we left, they would probably reopen the counter. I left after an hour and a half, but I learned later today that my two associates stayed on until mid-afternoon. I stand in awe of their patience and determination.

I finally got around tonight to sending in my Charg-a-plates to Rich's and Miller's. With them went letters expressing appreciation for their services in the past, but explaining that I cannot in good conscience continue to support with my dollars their practices of discrimination which hurt my friends. I hear reports that many white friends are joining the Negroes in canceling their charge accounts. Some of the white women who are active in Fellowship House are encouraging this by telephone. An employee of Rich's reports that the credit manager there remarked, "We've got to do something soon—we are losing so many accounts!"

Thursday, June 16

I HAD my most anxious time so far today. It was at Grant's. A boy who was in my freshman Bible class last semester was our leader, but I felt a heavy responsibility as the only older person present. The counter was being kept open. During the hour between twelve and one, a group of about six white youths collected who seemed to be looking for trouble. A bit later some Negro boys whom members of our group identified as Austin High School students came in and hung around behind our younger demonstrators talking with them. The white gang gave me special attention; I could see them looking at me and talking with one another about me. Two or three of them came ominously toward me, filing behind the stools. I thought, "Oh, Lord, here it comes! Can I take it?" and prayed hard. As they passed behind me, one of them gave my coat tail a slight tug. This was all they did to me, but it was effective psychological warfare.

The gang of Negro boys, joined by one or two of our demonstrators who left their seats without permission, gravitated toward the white gang. I became very apprehensive. Would a fight start? Did they have knives? Most of all I was worried that trouble would be started by Negroes, which would put our whole cause in a bad light. John Goss, our leader, tried hard to get the Negro boys to leave, but with only partial success. I asked John to send someone for Dr. Crutcher, who I thought would be at Rich's or Todd & Armistead. Finally I spoke to one of the boys, and he said the group was planning to leave. Just then Crutcher and Rev. Patterson, pastor of the East Vine Avenue Christian Church, came in. I told them I had never been so glad to see anyone before!

Grant's counter stretches in a straight line along one entire side of the store. A conveyor belt behind the counter carries orders out from the kitchen and dirty dishes back in. As we sat at the counter today, the white male cook got an idea for a big joke. He put large slices of watermelon on three plates and sent them out on the belt. One of the waitresses he alerted to stand at the far end of the belt to catch them and send them back on the return belt. They circulated the watermelon in front of us eight or ten times. They were right—we were hungry, and for some who like watermelon better than I do, it must have been a successful torture. The implication in the choice of watermelon was obvious, but our group took it in good humor.

Negroes were present in sufficient numbers at this store today that it was difficult for customers to find two seats together without having to decide: "Should we sit beside a Negro?" This may be good or bad. We will have to say one thing for Grant's—they have learned that it is possible to keep the counter open while demonstrators are present. I feel this represents progress in their thinking. But the number of persons eating was not large compared to normal noon-time business. One trouble is that any white who sits down beside a Negro is in danger of being identified as a sit-inner whether he is or not. If the waitresses think a white is there in sympathy with the Negroes, they will not ask that person for an order. They do not wish to risk the offense of being told, "My friend was here first." The whites who come in seem to sense this; if they cannot find a seat other than beside a Negro, they will sometimes stand at the counter until their order is taken, then take any available seat.

Today's experiences show our dangers. How can we keep our "friends" from hurting us? Our own group needs more discipline. Where are the Negro leaders? James, the chairman, is out of town, and we are not told when he will be back. Some of the ministers are probably in the midst of vacation Bible schools. But the upshot of it all is that our leaders—even those who have been very active before—are not in evidence. Let's give them the benefit of the doubt, but we do need them so desperately!

Galen Martin, the staff secretary of the Knoxville Area Human Relations Council, expresses concern over still other matters. He is disturbed that we are becoming too belligerent, leaving too few stools open for customers who would continue to come, and that we are not making enough contact with the managers. He and I exchanged some hot words over the last point. It was my contention that talk has had its day and that it is now our task to change the balance of power in such a way that the managers themselves will wish to talk. I fear it would be a sign of weakness for us to try to initiate further negotiation now. However, I respect Galen's opinion; he has had wide experience in inter-group work. We ought to have a meeting of the Executive Committee to make some basic decisions.

We hear today that the manager of Sears' has given all the lunch counter employees two weeks' vacation, telling them, "This will all be blown over by that time." This is a good example of the failure of the managers to find out what kind of situation it really is that they have to deal with. He is in for a surprise!

The report of what happened at Rich's yesterday is too good to pass by! For the first time, fiery little Father Jones, the black Episcopal priest, accompanied the demonstrators. One of our friends who works at Rich's said one of the male clerks hurried up to her and exclaimed, "What do you suppose is going on down

there *now?* They've got a pope or bishop or something with them
—you know, one of those guys with his collar on backwards—and
he's down there in the basement store *praying!*" Father Jones,
whose parish knows no spiritual bounds, had discovered that the
lunch counter supervisor had just learned of her brother's death;
instinctively he assumed the role of pastor. To Jones this was not
incongruous, because he firmly believes that the demonstrations
too are on behalf of the merchants' souls. Perhaps because of Tuesday's Institute, there were two or three instances of one of the
guards getting a Negro to one side and explaining that he was not
personally against them. One guard who is a city policeman asked
Father Jones to pray for him. Jones scraps like a bulldog against
injustice, but with it all seems never to be more than a "holler"
away from God.

Friday, June 17

EACH day the tension increases. This morning Crutcher told me
privately that an unidentified man called him three times yesterday threatening that his home would be bombed last night. Suspicious cars drove by the house slowly three times late at night.
A police officer who came to investigate handed Crutcher a gun
and said, "Here, keep this to protect yourself with." Crutcher
protested, "I'm just a preacher—I wouldn't know what to do with
this! Supposing you stay *with* the gun." He did. Crutcher's wife
is in the hospital undergoing serious surgery. Crutcher meanwhile
as co-chairman of the Associated Council has the full responsibility of leadership of the sit-in during Rev. James's absence. The
pressure he is under must be terrific.

We are still vacillating on our policy for Rich's. Booker hasn't
been with us for the past two days and is leaving for his summer job
tomorrow, but Father Jones's position is as aggressive as Booker's.

The ten o'clock meeting of demonstrators is being used to make policy decisions, but the group varies from day to day and is composed increasingly of teen-agers. Crutcher agrees that the movement needs tighter control, with basic decisions made by the Executive Committee. He is calling the Committee together tomorrow at 5:00 P.M.

This morning I took a crowded carful to Todd & Armistead. I let the others out near the store and then put the car in a parking lot. The counter was still serving when I got into the store. The head waitress hesitantly asked me for my order, although I was seated next to a Negro boy. I replied timidly that I was with the young man; "Are you going to serve him too?" I asked. She replied petulantly, "You know we don't serve colored—"

I saw a white youth look at me and speak to the waitress; she nodded her head. The youth, who seemed about twenty years of age and was neatly dressed, sat down next to me. I turned and said, "Hello," in a friendly way because I thought he was going to be friendly. What he said was, "Say, mister, you're a queer, aren't you? Are you a queer, mister?"

Taken aback, I made some stand-offish answer. I noted apprehensively that there were several other youths in the company of this one.

"We're gonna get you, mister! We're gonna teach you a thing or two! Come on outside if you're not yellow! I can't do a thing to you in here, but just come out on the sidewalk and I'll take care of you!" He took off his glasses as a gesture. By this time I had turned to face straight ahead and was acting as though I heard nothing he said. "You know Pete Benson? We got his name and license number yesterday and we took care of him. We're gonna take care of you the same way today!" Pete Benson is one of the University of Tennessee students who has been sitting in with us. My threatener later said he kicked Pete yesterday.

"What's the matter—ain'tcha comin'? Are you scared? You're yellow, mister, that's what's the matter with you!" He kept hitting my arm lightly with his elbow, trying to provoke my anger.

"You damned ——— you, you dirty sonofabitch! You're just as black as all the rest of them niggers—your face is black, your arms are black, your belly is black." He went on to name other parts of the anatomy.

I was tense, but I felt that as long as I stayed put I was all right. I was tempted to answer him, to tell him that I had no quarrel with him, to ask him why he hated me, why he hated Negroes. A St. Francis could have got by with it; I had no confidence that I could. But I did feel genuinely sorry for the boy, and I prayed for him a little while he talked.

"Go on, tap your fingers! Why don't you ram them up your nose?" I quit tapping the counter; I had hardly been aware I was doing it as a nervous reflex. But I could tell that my silence left him a problem—he was casting about for something to say, something to do. "You're a Communist, that's what you are, a dirty Communist rat!"

Finally he tired and left me. Dr. Robert Harvey, chairman of the mathematics department at the college, came in and sat next to me for awhile. I was greatly relieved; Harvey is a man for whom I have the greatest respect. Suddenly Hartsell, one of the young Negro men who had gone to another store, ran in out of breath and asked Dr. Harvey to come with him, gasping out something I didn't quite understand. It sounded like, "Somebody was killed in the street." I was frantic inside, but tried to remain calm outside. It *could* happen! The necessary emotions are present! I got up and looked into the street, but could see nothing. Then I began to worry that it might be a fracas at Grant's. Why hadn't I seen to it that a Negro man had accompanied the group to Grant's? I prayed that we might get through this day without violence, so that we could get better organized before we had to take the risk again.

Somewhat later Lee Butler, the University of Tennessee student who took part in the conversation with Byrl Logan I described earlier, returned for his wife and two-year-old daughter, whom he had left sitting-in with us. (The little girl, our youngest sitter, has been with us on a number of days. The manager of Grant's one day urged the mother to take the child away because he did not wish to be responsible for a baby being involved in any violence.) From Lee I learned what the trouble had been. Some of these white toughs had ganged up on him as he left Todd & Armistead earlier, roughed him up a little, struck him a couple of light blows. He ducked into a store about the time Harvey and Hartsell came up. When the boys saw the Negroes, they left. I was so relieved that the violence was not in a store that I'm afraid I sounded unsympathetic to Lee!

Just after one o'clock, when I was thinking it would be safe to go, a short white man about sixty years of age came into the store, sat down at a table with Father Jones and two Negro youths, and began a harangue. He represented himself as an attorney; the language he used would support the claim, but I'm afraid his logic wouldn't have won many court cases. "It's evident that the Communists are behind all this," I heard him charge. "They are using you people as innocent dupes!" When the others objected, he continued: "Who sent you here? Tell me the name of the man who sent you! Well, are you afraid to say who sent you?"

Father Jones in his direct manner replied, "God sent me."

This did not satisfy our attorney. "Oh now don't tell me *God* sent you! Some *man* sent you. Who was it?"

Not getting anywhere with this line of attack, he switched to another. "Well, then, what did you people come down here for? Did you come here to eat?" Before they could answer, he raced on, "I know you didn't, because if you came here to eat and they didn't serve you, you'd have gone somewhere that you could eat. If you really wanted to eat, why didn't you go over to the counter Rich's has especially for you people? If I went in a lunch counter and they didn't serve me, I sure wouldn't stay around there long! But you didn't come in here to eat—you came in here to ruin this man's business! The man who owns this store has not hurt your people in any way. He tries to be a good citizen. He has a right to conduct a business here in the free American way and choose whom he wants for his customers. Aren't you people ashamed to come in here day after day and try to ruin this man's business? Do you call that Christian, pastor?"

The responses made by our group were so low I could not hear many of them, but the lawyer was talking loudly, playing to the audience that was rapidly collecting around him. By this time the hoodlum boys, now increased to about ten in number, had come back off the street and had encircled the table in a threatening manner. I feared they were in cahoots with the lawyer, perhaps in his employ. Just then one of the Negroes, seeing the toughs closing in around them, said to the lawyer, "I hope you haven't arranged this."

"Arranged what? Why, I never saw one of these boys before in my life! I'm sure that not a one of them would touch you or harm you in any way. They're just good American boys; they are only interested in hearing our discussion." These words were directed more to the toughs than to the Negroes. He sounded worried himself. The situation was ominous. The lawyer continued his harangue, but I sensed that now, like Scheherazade, he feared to make an end.

"If you want to make progress, why don't you see to it that your own places are cleaned up, the cafes down on Vine Street, for instance? The truth is that your own places are dirty and full of disease because your people are too lazy to take care of them, and that's why you want to come up here in the places that the white man keeps clean!"

Enough spectators had come in off the street virtually to fill the store. It was impossible to continue business. I wished desperately that someone would call the police. How would we ever get out of there?

"The tragedy of all this is that you are trying to come between me and my Negro friends! Why, I have more Negro friends than any of you, or have had at least before this agitation started." (This claim to Negro friends is a stock part of the segregationist's argument, but it must be understood that the term "friend" is defined by the context.) He then brought forth another standard argument—that the agitators are only a deluded few—"The great majority of Negroes don't want to mix with white people."

The large man who spied on us at Sears' came in, observed, wrote some things in a note pad. He is always slipping from store to store, checking. I hoped he would call the police. I saw someone who looked like a manager go into the rear office with a waitress; perhaps they were calling the police.

"Do you know the nastiest, dirtiest thing you people ever did?" the lawyer continued.

"What do you mean by 'you people'?" one of the Negroes asked.

"I mean you right here—and all nineteen million of you! Every Negro in the United States! The meanest, lowest thing you ever did was in New York City. Woolworth's store there on Thirty-fourth Street had served the colored for years, had been great friends to the Negroes in New York, and yet you people went down there and picketed Woolworth's store!"

One of our group, perhaps to protect himself against the monstrous assumption that all nineteen million Negroes are a unity, replied that he didn't think that was right either.

"Well, you ought to say so publicly then! You ought to say so *publicly!*" Just what channels of publicity he thought were open to them I don't know, or who he thought would be interested in the opinions of two college boys and an inconspicuous Episcopal priest.

Finally two policemen came in. I breathed easier. One said something quietly to the lawyer person, who expostulated, "Who's going to start any trouble? I'm sure the reverend isn't, and I know I'm not!" The policeman smiled and said nothing more. But soon the lawyer was standing, saying, "Well, pastor, it's been nice to talk to you and the boys."

Just about that time Harvey came in for a moment, and as he started to leave I told him, "Wait, I'll go with you." I was sensible of the fact that one or two Negroes had made an effective bodyguard earlier for Lee Butler. I hoped we might slip out before the hoodlums noticed, but as we walked down the street, I became aware that they were behind us. I had not had time to explain the situation to Harvey before we came to the spot where I would have to leave him to get my car. He stopped to finish the conversation. Nervously I thought, "This is no time for a white and a Negro to stop and talk on the sidewalk!" but I was determined to be as brave as he was—after all, in a way, he had more to fear. By this time they had surrounded us. The one who had threatened me in the store started up his chatter again. All of it was directed against me: "Buddy, you've got the wrong friends! You're a little mixed up, aren't you, mister? It looks like we're gonna have to teach you a thing or two yet, mister; you don't learn very fast, do you?" To get to my car, which was parked in the area at the center of the block, I had to go through a long dark passage which had once been a narrow store building. Harvey walked with me. The heckler and his gang followed closely. "Are you afraid to go through the dark, mister? Afraid you'll hear shots in the night?"

Would they jump us once we got into the obscurity of the passageway? We could only bluff it through. I tried not to act scared.

With relief I saw that the attendant was close by the little office. Yet, even here in the lot he was our only protection. The inside of a business block can be a very lonely place, even when the streets outside are crowded with people. Harvey continued trying to talk while the tough, with only a little assistance from his henchmen, kept up the chatter. "Has he got some kids he would like to live to grow up?" (I had him there—no kids!) Big hero—if talk can make one a hero. They ostentatiously took down my license number and threatened that they would now soon have my name and address. I thought of offering it to them, but saw no need to take unnecessary risks. I drove off slowly, keeping Harvey in sight as long as I could, but they did not follow him as he walked on to his car. It would seem that at this time, at least, they are interested only in the whites.

Of course the Negroes are getting some insults too. John Goss reports that one white hoodlum at Grant's said to another with the intent of being overheard, "We ought to treat those niggers like they treated that one down in Maryville!"—a reference to a lynching several years ago. The demonstrators who were at Todd & Armistead yesterday said that a white woman with a child came in and said loudly, "What are you niggers doing in here?" The leader, Mrs. Davis, sent one of our boys to sit at a table near the one at which the woman seated herself. The woman exclaimed loudly, "What is that black ape doing here?" She then told her child, "Come on, let's go back here where we can finish our food without any niggers around!" Of course people like this do our cause more good than harm.

As I drove home, I was overwrought with all that had happened. I decided I just had to stop at the church and talk with Jim Reese, who is my closest friend and confidante. "It's getting rough down there, Jim, plenty rough," I said, striving with difficulty to keep my voice from breaking. "It's not at all like it was last week when you were participating." I tried to assure him that I wasn't criticizing him; as I had told him before, I was glad that he was not a professional race-campaigner—he was making a greater contribution as a Negro by being a first-class minister. He was right in feeling responsibility to the Bible school this week. "But, Jim, we've got this bear by the tail, and we can't let go of it now without getting hurt. The leaders of the Negro community simply aren't rallying to our support. We're desperate for leadership!" The weight of the anxiety bore down upon me, and I broke into tears. It proved a great relief, and I didn't mind Jim seeing. He said simply that he would rearrange his responsibilities so he could take a more active part. I knew he meant it.

June Cascante, one of our white friends, says she overheard one waitress say to another at Grant's today, "I think they should be served. You know, you really have to admire their courage!" That is the kind of testimony we must continue to give. But unfortunately there is sometimes another type given, as there was at

Grant's even today. Both gangs were back today. One Negro boy who was not a demonstrator sat at the counter without anyone's invitation. Harvey noticed that he had a vicious looking frog-stabber secured along his leg. Harvey told a policeman who was standing by, and the policeman quietly took the knife away from the boy. "If you were a butcher or sold bananas, you might need this," he told the boy, "but you have no use for it and it will only get you into trouble. Now you don't belong with this group, you don't understand what they are trying to do, and they don't want you here. So leave right now and don't come back again tomorrow or any day!"

I tremble when I think of other ways this story might have ended! Harvey told the policeman that the gang of whites hang around every day and threaten trouble, but the law officer said there was nothing he could do unless violence broke out. June later thanked the policeman for his impartial behavior in the knife incident; his answer was that this should not be taken to mean that he was on one side or the other. "I was only doing my duty." June told him, "That is certainly all we could expect you to do." The whole incident points up the importance of close adult supervision during every sit-in as well as the crucial role played by the police.

Flash! Rich's has put up a sign in front of its counter reading: "Closed for Repairs."

Saturday, June 18

THE Executive Committee, so-called, met at five today. I say "so-called" because the group seems to consist of anybody who is particularly interested or particularly needed at the moment. Fifteen or more were present this afternoon, about half of whom were whites. We all felt the tenseness of our situation. There was a general awareness that our locomotive had attained a velocity too great for the track built for it to run on. We did some re-building of the track.

Bob West, the Unitarian minister, urged that the time has come for us to set up a planned "Stay Away from Downtown" movement. Bob is a wiry young man whose keen mind quickly pierces to the heart of a problem. I have a great deal of admiration for him—almost enough now to quit wishing he were a Presbyterian. Jim Reese volunteered to serve as chairman of a committee to put the "Stay Away" program into effect. Galen Martin pleaded for more contact with the merchants; another committee was set up to contact them individually. Galen has been as interested as any-one in this movement, but feels that his role as Staff Secretary of the Knoxville Area Human Relations Council is best served by helping quietly with counsel and some office services. He is white, youngish, a graduate of Berea College, and a Methodist layman. His confidence in personal interaction as the basic technique in human relations makes this contribution to our meeting very much in character.

Crutcher was asked to request the Mayor to re-activate the Mayor's Committee, inviting the merchants to meet with the Com-mittee, for in the entire three months of negotiation, the merchants concerned never met with the entire Mayor's Committee, and met with a sub-committee of it only once. Carroll Felton, the pastor of Logan Temple A. M. E. Zion Church, spoke eloquently with regard to this. Carroll, a man to whom the cliche "tall, dark, and handsome" may be appropriately applied, has told me that he was in jail eleven times as a result of participation in restaurant sit-ins in Washington, D. C., but he hasn't yet made himself that expendable in our sit-ins. We need him to do so now.

I spoke about some of the dangerous situations developing dur-ing our sit-ins and moved for a Sit-In Committee to draw up rules to see that the demonstrators receive instruction. As generally happens, the man who made the motion found himself chairman.

Another mass meeting was set for a week from tomorrow. A suggestion to move the meeting to one of the other churches failed to receive support. I have wondered whether the failure of some of the ministers to get interested may be because the movement appears to them as a one-church, one-minister proposition.

News of the day: Todd & Armistead now has a big sign on its counter: "Closed for Vacation and Repairs." This makes three stores which have responded to our sit-ins with a "play-dead" strategy. We speculate as to their intentions. We are told Rich's has removed its stools; could that store be planning to convert into a stand-up counter? (I thought this suggestion of Harry Golden's for "vertical integration" was a joke until a drug store near the college adopted it recently. The "farthest-gone" Southerners simply can't perceive the comical aspect of segregation. Oh well, one of these days the corns will begin to hurt more than the pride, and then we will have integration!)

Sunday, June 19

TODAY is "Juneteenth," the day Negroes in Texas made a folk holiday in commemoration of the emancipation from slavery. I remember how even the white community indulgently regarded this day as "theirs"; in some towns it was the only day Negroes were allowed to use the public parks. The Negro population of Knoxville used to have a similar day, but it seems to be no longer observed. A Negro friend explained to me that this is because Negroes no longer wish to call attention to themselves as a separate group—they want simply to be identified as Americans. Is that not a thing to be grateful for? And yet it is sad that they should feel they have to cast aside their own special history in order to be identified as Americans. Is there perhaps an embarrassment in remembering that their great-grandparents were slaves? I think I can understand this: it is the present vestiges of slavery they are rebelling against more than the slavery of their grandparents. Perhaps one day a festival like "Juneteenth" will be celebrated again, with pride for a heritage more colorful, more truly American than that of any other ethnic group in our nation. I say "more truly American" because even Horatio Alger could not have imagined an American success story equal to that of the Negroes' rise from slavery to respected citizenship in little more than a hundred years. When that success is attained—and I have faith that it will be sooner than most of the world expects—all Americans ought to join them in the reinstitution of their "Juneteenth," because to repeat their story will be to vindicate our democratic ideals. And there is no group that believes more wholeheartedly in those ideals than the Negro Americans. Even when the Negroes have been treated in a way that made mockery of our belief in liberty and equality, the hope of one day attaining those elusive ideals has made oppression endurable. As their sweat and tears have for three hundred years blended with this native soil, America has become a part of them, and they of America.

Our Sit-In Committee met after church—Robert Harvey, Galen Martin, and I, with the helpful counsel of one of our Negro attorneys—and worked out a list of suggested rules for sit-ins. We did not have anybody else's list to go by; our rules come from our own experience under fire. Two basic decisions were called for: should demonstrators prevent customers from entering a counter in a situation where demonstrators themselves are barred from entry, and should we fill so many seats at a counter as to have the effect of preventing normal business? The first decision we put off with a compromise. As for the second, we will propose to the group that shutting off a counter's business is not one of the objectives of our sit-ins.

Monday, June 20

AT the ten o'clock meeting I reported the rules drawn up by our committee. We did not mimeograph them for fear they might fall into the hands of hostile persons. Our compromise position on the question of civil disobedience appeared in these rules:

"Demonstrators should not leave an establishment at the request of the manager alone, but will leave when requested by the police.

"In situations where management tries to exclude demonstrators while admitting other customers, we will send such a large delegation of demonstrators that when they stand in line in normal fashion it will be difficult for other customers to enter; we will not deliberately try to prevent their entry."

We listed the objectives of the sit-ins in the following order of importance:

"1. To secure service on a non-discriminatory basis;

"2. To demonstrate that white customers will continue to patronize the establishment when Negroes are at the counter;

"3. To demonstrate to the management that more money would be made by serving all the people seated at his counter."

Number 3 would set the minimum number of demonstrators, number 2 the maximum. To implement both we provided:

"Normally a Negro and white demonstrator will sit together with two vacant seats on either side of them."

Several rules served to clamp a tight discipline on demonstrators:

"Each delegation must have an adult leader whose authority is recognized by every demonstrator. The leader should be a Negro.

"Demonstrators will stay in their seats facing the counter—no moving about in the store or from store to store.

"No knives or other sharp instruments, no smoking; men will not wear hats at the counters. . . ."

(We intended leaning over backward to avoid any appearance of toughness. We wanted our group to look better and behave better than anyone else at the counter.)

Two rules were designed to discourage uninvited "friends." These provided that the leader take a firm position against anyone joining the demonstration who did not understand our objectives and methods and that demonstrators not talk to persons standing around them.

Based on our experience of Friday, one rule provided that whenever a white demonstrator leaves a store, one or two Negro men should follow to protect him.

Finally, the non-violent nature of our protest was recognized in two simples rules: "Demonstrators will ignore heckling, blows, and other attempts to provoke. Demonstrators will avoid caustic remarks." The second had not been so carefully kept as the first.

We all agreed to be bound by these rules.

The number of workers was distressingly small again today—only about twenty-five in all. Since of the four counters which up to now have been our primary objective only Grant's is still operating, we now have to decide what other stores to expand our operations to. We have to make our decision without sufficient knowledge of the present attitudes of the managers. We rely heavily upon Dr. Crutcher's opinion; we know he has a contact person from whom he gets some information. The decision really should be made by the Executive Committee, not the demonstrators. Cole's Drug is a solid choice, because we do know the owner of this chain has never agreed to go along with desegregation, but the other choice is a toss-up; the other three variety stores, Walgreen's Drug, and Miller's Department Store all told the Mayor's Committee they would desegregate if seven stores would. At the beginning of our sit-ins, there were some who thought we should hit all ten stores, because so long as some were exempt, they would get part of the lunch business from the ones we hit and consequently would have a financial interest in *not* desegregating. But this has remained an academic question because we never have had enough workers to sit-in at more than three or four places on one day. By now, after a week and a half of sit-ins, with no firm indication that the merchants are taking any step even to talk with us, most of us feel we are relieved of any special obligation to those merchants who were cooperative earlier and that we might as well start making the rounds, if we can't hit them all at once. The one merchant who professes to be our great friend and serves as a channel of information (which we never know whether to trust or not) we will grant immunity for a while longer. Cole's and which other? Walgreen's? Okay.

I chose to go to Cole's, since it would be a new experience. Lorenzo, who read twenty-one chapters from his Catholic Bible one day last week, had a chemistry book today. He exchanged after a while with Pate, who was reading *Hamlet*. Somehow, I have never felt that I should read; it's right for me to sit at a man's counter and wait to be served, but not right to use it as a lounge. My position in this respect is different from that of the Negroes; I have to work harder to be identified as a demonstrator. When two seats are left between demonstrators, I observe, they are usually empty, but when three seats are left, the middle one is nearly always occupied by a customer. Why is it white people are hesitant to sit beside the Negroes? Jim Reese points out that when any one of us, Negro or white, enters a train, he always looks for a seat that is not beside anybody else; if he has to sit beside someone else, he chooses first someone of his own race and sex, next one of his own race and opposite sex, only after that one of the other race. If this is true, what we see operating is a natural reserve which would be no problem once desegregated counters became a fact.

Two young white men took seats next to Negroes. After some uncertainty, the waitress put water before one and asked for his order. I saw his lips move. She jerked the water away and tossed the glass down in evident irritation. We do not recognize all the whites participating in the demonstrations because most of them come directly to the stores without attending the preliminary meeting. Occasionally University people participate without being asked. Those whites who participate in this way and even those who are asked to be present by Mrs. Hembree or Dr. Jones are left free to choose whether they will order or refuse to order. Some seem to do it one way and some another. Those who do order have some value as observers and are in a position to make an effective testimony to managers. Then too, it is possible to take a very long time sipping a coke. I heard a white woman sitting near Bonnie remark, "Well, every step of progress somebody has to start!"

Two or three times white youths standing around made me a little nervous, but they apparently were just curious. Our sit-in was as quiet as the first days, probably because the gangs hadn't learned yet that we were in this store.

The most astonishing thing about our experience today was the number of Negroes who shopped in Cole's while we were there. How can we get the message to them? If they would stop, Cole's would feel it. One young Negro woman actually tried to get standing service at the fountain on drinks to go, which apparently she was in the habit of doing; the waitresses consulted and refused the service. The woman walked out of the store indignant.

When the time came for me to leave, I did not think it necessary to ask for protection; nevertheless, two Negro boys followed me according to our new rules. Whose eyes should I meet upon emerging from the store but those of the hoodlum who had threatened me last Friday at Todd & Armistead! He was standing in front of the store, apparently waiting for me. I was very grateful for the two boys behind me. The heckler did not say a word. Somehow, separated from his nine friends, he didn't look so big to me today.

Tuesday, June 21

It was a discouraging thing that Bob West and I were the only adult males at this morning's meeting until Jim Reese came late from Bible school. (Thank God for Jim!) Crutcher had asked

Bob to have charge of the meeting and me to review the sit-in rules. Reese reported that his committee is preparing a handbill urging a "Trade with Your Friends" movement. They have decided against an all-out "Stay Away from Downtown" movement for the present. The total turnout of sit-inners was small this morning too, but those who do come are beginning to get concerned about this, so maybe something will happen.

I elected to go again to Cole's, since it was so easy yesterday. Seven Negroes and I constituted the group, with Mrs. Davis, the pleasant but determined little housewife, as leader. I parked the car at the parking garage; it is more expensive than the lot, but I want the personal protection in case someone follows me. Arriving at the store, I was surprised to find that our group was not at the counter. The reason was evident: access to the stools was blocked by a new rope stretched behind the stools about waist high and anchored by bookracks. Fastened to the rope was a sign reading "Counter Closed," but the counter obviously was doing business. At the end of the counter nearest the front door, a male employee held the loose end of the rope in such a way as to form a gate which he could open or close by taking a step in one direction or the other. I was flustered; we had not anticipated anything like this! We had taken our opponent too much for granted.

I found Mrs. Davis in the store. We decided to follow the strategy that had been devised for Rich's—to form a protest line, not attempting today at least to go under the rope. I asked her to go first, because if I had gone first, the man might simply have let me in. So we formed in line, standing in complete silence directly in front of the gate-keeper.

For the first twenty minutes or so, the rope plus our presence kept almost all business away from the counter. The rope fence was not closed at the far end, but the situation was too complicated for most customers to figure out in a glance. Mrs. Davis pointed out to me that one of our youngsters was at the counter—little Ann, who is so light I had not even noticed her there, had deftly slipped under the rope when they first entered the store.

The man holding the rope, who I later discovered was the assistant manager, was having difficulty controlling his emotions. Finally he exploded bitterly, "Well, why don't you go home now? You've proved your point, haven't you?"

I said calmly, "Thank you, but we'd like to go on proving it a while longer."

A white woman sitting at the counter sidled over next to Ann when the person who had been eating there left. I had paid no attention to her up to this time; she was a tall distinguished-looking woman with graying hair. She spoke with Ann, smiled, accepted good-naturedly Ann's gift of a comic book, looked at it with amused curiosity. I could tell that her friendliness toward one of the demonstrators infuriated the assistant manager. The lady leaned back, touched the rope in an effort to see what the sign said. Instantly the assistant manager shouted, "You let that rope alone! I mean YOU!" and he pointed defiantly at the woman. He was spurred on by unreasoning fury: "You can come here and sit, you old—BAG, but you'd better keep your hands off that rope if you know what's good for you—TRASH!"

We were all astonished by this kind of attack against a woman, a woman old enough to be his mother, and one who gave every appearance of being a prominent citizen of the community. He could be sued for slander, the store for damages. At first the woman tried to protest that she wasn't aiming to bother the rope, but when she realized the unreasoning nature of the attack, she simply suffered it in silence. Her jaw worked a little as she pretended to go back to reading the comic book. I wanted very much to thank this stranger for her heroism, but for any of us to communicate with her now would only have brought the ire of her persecutor down upon her more bitterly.

Still smoldering, the assistant manager decided on a course that would put us in our place. He called another employee to take the rope, while he stationed himself in front of the counter alongside the rope, beckoning with a wide gesture to people as they entered the store to come and eat at the counter. Sometimes he would say, "Do you want to eat? Come right ahead, the counter's open!" He had assumed the role of a sideshow barker. When someone accepted his invitation, he lifted the rope to let him under. The implication was unmistakable that he was doing this partly to humiliate us. He made this very clear when an old tramp came shuffling in, dressed in dirt-encrusted, baggy overalls, with a dirty felt hat crushed down on his forehead. The tramp looked as out of place in this slick store as a donkey in church, but he had that one indispensible qualification—beneath several days' growth of whiskers, his skin, one could still discern, was fundamentally "white." The assistant manager welcomed this man with a special show of hospitality, virtually insisting that he eat at the counter, while all the time casting triumphant glances at us. The logic of our cause could not have been more effectively dramatized. I feel certain that many of those who saw this little comedy realized that the assistant manager was bearing testimony against himself.

Our antagonist kept trying to establish that we were interfering with customers getting into the store; several times he barked at us to move over out of the aisle, although we were hardly in it. He tried physically shoving us together with the sarcastic exhortation, "Come on, let's have some close communion now!" This told me two things about our friend—he is a churchman, and he thinks it will humiliate us whites (for Pete Benson had joined us by now) to have to stand so close to Negroes. Once he accused all of us of "standing around like apes."

He beckoned me to come over to talk with him alone. I obtained our leader's permission. The assistant manager told me, "I want you to get your group out of here. They're obstructing traffic."

I told him he was asking me to do something I didn't have the authority to do. "Well, you're their leader, aren't you? Aren't you a nigger like the rest of them?" He said this with a slight sardonic smile, expecting it to anger me.

Instead, I simply smiled a little and said, "I'm their brother." I wanted to say something more specifically Christian, but couldn't formulate it in time. My answer seemed to disarm him, and he seemed almost kind in his attitude toward me personally after that. My remark apparently convinced him that I was a minister, for later I overheard him say as he pointed at me, "There's the minister." He did not press his demand that we leave.

(This is not the first time during the sit-ins that I have been called a Negro. The other day Jim Reese expressed appreciation for the fact that I was laying myself open to insults even though I didn't have to. "Well," I replied, "there's one thing sure—I will never be insulted by being called a 'nigger,' though I may object to the man's pronunciation." I could almost wish for a little bit of African ancestry if it meant having a closer bond with persons I admire as much as Jim, Dr. Crutcher, and Dr. Colston. And yet in this present circumstance, it means more to these whom I feel to be my people for me to be white.)

The assistant manager was talking with some acquaintance whom I guessed to be a lunch counter manager from some other store. They seemed to be discussing strategy, but I could hear them only when they wanted to be heard. "This whole thing is emanating from Moscow!" the Cole's man said. I don't think he believed it at all. A man who would choose to say "emanating" is too smart to believe that. What I really think is that he's troubled by Christianity. I think he is laboring under a guilt complex. He resents being placed in such a position, and is taking it out in hostility toward us.

A muscular high-school-age boy from our group, with my collusion, slipped quickly under the rope. The assistant manager tried to catch the rope under his neck, but couldn't keep the boy from getting a seat. Indignant at being thus outwitted, he demanded the boy's name. He refused to give it, referring the man to our leader, Mrs. Davis. She said, without indicating disrespect, "I can't see how that is any concern of yours."

"Then I'll take care of this in another way!" He went away for a few moments as though calling the police. We waited apprehensively, expecting the police to arrive at any moment, but nothing happened. I was glad I hadn't known the boy's name. Perhaps it is best in an operation like this to preserve anonymity, as intelligence operatives do.

When some customers left, the lad sidled down to another seat, which had the effect of blocking one more seat to customers. Hurriedly the assistant manager sat down on the counter, virtually rubbing against the boy, in such a way that the boy could move no farther down. The spectacle of the manager sitting on the counter was so unusual that even more of his potential customers shied away.

The standing protest requires much more physical stamina than a sit-in. We tried to remain utterly motionless as much as possible. After two hours of this, my knees were ready to give way. The others chose to stay; I admire their physical endurance as well as their patient courage. One most encouraging factor today was that in the entire two hours, in sharp contrast to yesterday, we did not see a single Negro buying in the store. Maybe the word is getting around.

I called Mrs. Hembree this afternoon to find out the identity of the heroic woman who took our part today. I found Mrs. Hembree very indignant that an employee at Walgreen's this morning sprayed her and two others directly in the face with something that gave off obnoxious fumes which nearly drove them from the store and made Mrs. Hembree ill. Mrs. Hembree was able to tell me that the woman at Cole's was Mrs. Harry Wiersema; she has joined the sit-inners on several occasions and her husband, who works for T.V.A., has been at one of the stores almost every day. (He was one of those who got sprayed.) They are Unitarians.

The *News-Sentinel* finally came out tonight, after being prodded in a sermon of Bob West's widely distributed by the Associated Council, with a small article reporting that Rich's, Sears' and Todd & Armistead have closed their counters. But this is the payoff: the article carried a statement from Rich's that its counter is *per-*

manently closed and the space is being turned over to other merchandise! And this only a week after the assistant manager told us that Rich's would never close its counter! Jim Reese expresses a bitterness widespread among the Negroes when he says this is more insulting than keeping segregated counters. It in effect announces: "We would rather close our counters than serve Negroes at them!" The article reported that Miller's has a sign up, "Employees Only, Please," but that many non-employees were eating there.

At the meeting of the Human Relations Council tonight I learned some things about Cole's assistant manager which confirmed my "psychoanalysis" of him. He is an active member of one of the downtown churches. Recently in his Sunday school class he took a stand against all the others in which he spoke up for the rights of Negroes to conduct sit-ins. And yet, his friend confessed, he is known to harbor deep hostility feelings—not toward Negroes in particular, but toward the world at large.

While the Human Relations Council has no part in sponsoring the sit-ins, it is interested in all attempts to eliminate segregation. Members of the Council feel more contact with merchants is needed. Four of our members agreed to visit with management personnel of four different stores this week.

As we continued informal conversation about the sit-in situation, Bob West, who is the Wiersema's pastor, related that Mrs. Wiersema overheard the conversation of the two managers in Cole's today and reported to Bob that one of them remarked skeptically, "If this thing is right, why aren't there more ministers in it?" It is a devastating criticism. Bob and I deserve little credit for our participation; everything I do in this cause simply increases my prestige among the people I work with, and Bob has a liberal, racially integrated congregation which expects him to take the kind of position he does. But isn't there in this city one white minister with an ordinary congregation who has sufficient conviction about the justice of our cause to risk offending some members of his congregation? In my discouraged moments—and this is one of them—I become convinced that the theme, "After all, I've got to maintain contact with my congregation!" has ruined the prophetic function of the ministry. It is the same rationalization by which any coward escapes martyrdom: "After all, I've got to stay alive to do any good for anyone!" It is the attitude of Pétain rather than De Gaulle.

Yet, as disappointed as I am about the white ministers, it is the absence of the Negro ministers which weighs heaviest on me. James, our chairman, has been out of town for a week; I understand it is unavoidable, having to do with the health of a member of his family. Crutcher, the co-chairman, who has given up a scholarship for summer study at the theological school of Virginia Union University in order to stay with the movement here, is at present in Nashville attending a Human Relations meeting which may have an important bearing on our crusade here. But I am thinking of the others—strong leaders in the Negro community, active in other causes affecting their race—many of whom I know to feel deeply about segregation. Each day I look for them and am disappointed. It is difficult for me not to be resentful. I have to remind myself that not everyone is in the fortunate position I am, with a whole summer to spend as he chooses. Each of these men has a sense of vocation to the leadership of his congregation; it is not easy to leave daily responsibilities to flock to the banner of a special cause. Yet as Bob West and I talk about it, we know this is exactly what must happen. "If we can only arouse and enlist the Negro leadership, we will win this struggle," I say to Bob, and we are both much aware of what a ridiculous thing it is for two whites to be in the position where we need to say this to one another.

The emotional drain of the sit-ins and the anxiety of feeling that we are left without support overcomes me momentarily, and I rest my head on folded arms at the table while the meeting goes on around me. "Maybe I should just quit if the Negroes aren't interested enough to support the movement with leadership!" I say to myself, as I have many times before, and then I realize as always that this is a false estimate of the situation. Negroes began the movement and have largely carried it on so far; it is only about the future that there is question. "Besides," I remind myself, "this is not just a battle for the rights of Negroes, but for the dignity and freedom of all of us."

Perhaps there is something we can do. Jim Reese is secretary of the Knoxville Ministerial Association. He and Bob and I decide to send a letter to each man on the mailing list inviting him to a meeting Friday morning. The purpose of the meeting will be to inform the ministers of what is going on and suggest ways they can help. I stop at Jim's on the way home; it is 10:30 P.M., but we must work out the draft for the letter.

Wednesday, June 22

THE writing I had planned to do this summer isn't getting done very rapidly! There was no private work for me this morning as I hastened to shape up the draft of the letter to the ministers and rushed over to Mt. Olive Church early to type the stencil.

As the time for convening the meeting passed and I was still the only adult male present, a sort of spontaneous murmur arose among the workers, "Where are our ministers?" I was glad to see that I am not the only one noticing this. I should not be surprised if the ministers begin to feel some pressure from members of their congregations. Finally at 10:30 I reluctantly took charge of the meeting.

We had a few more workers this morning and could have returned to Walgreen's, but in view of the tough reception there yesterday, I was reluctant to try it without more adult leadership.

Besides, some of our friends last night raised the question again of whether we were not moving in reverse when we demonstrate against stores which have already indicated their readiness to go along with a group move to desegregate; I prefer our regular leaders to participate in this decision. Therefore we limited our field to Cole's and Grant's for today.

Two possible strategies were suggested for Cole's. One we referred to simply as "going under the ropes"; the other was to stand alongside the rope so that others would find it difficult to get under it. But the second plan would raise the bugaboo again of "conspiring to interfere with . . . business"; it is infuriating to management and, I think, morally questionable. We decided to wait until the management let one white person under the rope, then make a bee-line to scramble under it ourselves. This would secure our legal position that, in spite of the sign, the counter was not in fact closed, and we would only be accepting the same courtesy offered to other customers. Jim Reese was put in charge of this group. I turned "sissy" and asked to go to Grant's on the plea that it was too rough for me yesterday at Cole's.

As the white women had agreed to have personnel at all three stores, I had to stop by Walgreen's and ask the women there to go to other stores. Here I encountered Mrs. Wiersema and at last had my chance to thank her for enduring the insults at Cole's so bravely yesterday. She said to me, "I didn't mind. I just thought, why should I complain, when these people have taken the same kind of thing every day of their lives?"

Mrs. Wiersema told me that her son, Harry, Jr., had come down this morning to participate in the sit-ins for the first time. She and Mr. Wiersema had always been concerned that Harry have the right attitude toward persons of other races. "But I will admit I am worried about his taking part in a sit-in, because Harry is not the non-violent sort. If someone insults him or strikes him, it would be in Harry's nature to strike back without stopping to think." Mrs. Wiersema asked me to look out for him and help him as much as I could.

We walked down to Grant's together, and there Mrs. Wiersema pointed out her son to me. He is a tall blond youth of about twenty with carefully chiseled features and an athlete's body. He was absorbed in conversation with a Negro youth of about the same age sitting beside him at the counter. They were poring over a book, *Teach Yourself Radio*, which the Negro youth has been bringing with him every day. Harry's mother told me that Harry has just completed the fourth year of the five-year engineering curriculum at the University. His new friend told me the other day that he would have entered the Engineering School if the University admitted Negroes.

Mrs. Hembree came in and sat beside me. She had just come from Mayor Duncan's office, where she had expressed her indignation at the spraying incident in Walgreen's yesterday. I don't know what he could do about it, but it is good for the Mayor to know that prominent citizens like Mrs. Hembree (a former president of both the League of Women Voters and the United Church Women) are involved in this movement. She reports that the Mayor is deeply concerned over the whole situation. He says Knoxville hasn't got an important new industry in fourteen years; he is anxious to sell industry on Knoxville and up to now has been able to boast that we have good race relations. The Mayor himself had just come from talking with Byrl Logan of Rich's; the Mayor seems to feel Rich's is the key to the situation in Knoxville. (But they have put themselves now in a position from which it will be very difficult to move in our direction without losing face.)

There were so many demonstrators in Grant's that I felt I could do more good by working on the mailing, so I went back to Mt. Olive. Some of the Negro ministers were there. The ladies who are serving as our volunteer office crew had called them to a meeting to plan ways of enlisting more personnel for the sit-ins. I feel we are beginning to roll when the lay people ask the ministers for their leadership. I had an opportunity to talk with Carroll Felton; I believe he has come to understand the critical nature of our need.

I felt guilty about not staying through the sit-in today, but for the first time on a sit-in day I was able today to enjoy my lunch. Despite my attempts to control my thinking, I begin to get nervous over the approaching sit-in as far ahead of time as the preceding afternoon. I am not sleeping well nor eating well. My agony increases as we draw nearer to the time of actually entering the store. Strangely enough, the most peaceful moments come while I am seated at the counter.

From Jim Reese I have got the story of what happened today at Cole's. A different employee was in charge today. As we had planned, our group waited for him to admit a white customer under the rope. He invited a white woman to enter, she hesitated, saying, "But the sign says the counter is closed!"

"Oh that is only to Negroes; it is open to everyone else." The woman refused to enter under these conditions. Unwittingly the manager had approached one of our "friends." But our group had heard enough; they dived under the rope. Since there were ten of them, there was nothing the manager could do to stop them. About 12:30 he turned off the lights, took down the rope, and requested Jim please to take his workers away. Jim complied. Jim said the man was so nervous he had difficulty operating the light switch.

One humorous note Jim reports from Cole's today—the end of the rope near the door was formed into a noose, tied with a hangman's knot! Another note not so humorous—yesterday when the group started to leave, the assistant manager took hold of the girl Ann to "help" her up from the counter. The Negro boy sitting near her exclaimed (I am told), "Keep your hands off the girls or there will be a mummy around here!" True to tradition, any action with the slightest connotation of sex is incendiary. We cannot afford to risk any more incidents like this—we will have to give the non-violence rule more emphasis in our morning meetings.

Mildred Ward, the personable cashier at the college, has agreed to get one of the other ladies who work at the college to go with her to Rich's Laurel Room tomorrow. Their visit should let Rich's know that we don't consider our affair with them settled with the closing of their basement counter so long as they continue to operate a segregated restaurant on the third floor.

I had intended going tomorrow to Triads, a men's civic club which meets at the colored branch YMCA, to beg leadership for the sit-ins, but I am afraid that if I extend myself any further some of the Negroes may begin rightfully to feel, "This white minister is trying to take this project over from us." Jim didn't dispute this and agreed to get one of the Negro ministers to go instead. I may feel now like the man who was invited on the snipe hunt, but I must remember that I didn't start the movement, and if it's finished, it won't be I who finishes it.

Before he left, Waldo gave me half a watermelon. Today I offered what was left to Jim Reese and, remembering the cook's joke at Grant's, told him I hoped it wouldn't offend him to be offered watermelon. He laughed and told of an incident last summer at camp when melon was served without forks and the high schoolers from his church were embarrassed to eat it that way in front of the white kids. Jim joshed them, "Oh, be quiet and eat your watermelon!" Jim is a good influence on the Negro young people. I wish they all might attain his degree of self-acceptance. Waldo is not so free; when I started eating watermelon at his house without a fork just to tease him, he protested that he could never do that! I try to tease him out of his sensitivity. I do not know whether my method is right or whether I am only adding to his suffering.

Thursday, June 23

TODAY, for what I suspect is the first time in history, a nuclear physicist participated in a lunch counter sit-in! Dr. Robert Ellis, who is a visiting lecturer at the Science Institute being held at Knoxville College this summer, expressed a desire to experience a sit-in demonstration, so Dr. Harvey brought him down to Grant's today. Dr. Ellis is a Negro. He is engaged in Project Matterhorn at Princeton University, which is developing peaceful uses for thermonuclear energy. He and Harvey sat near one end of the counter and discussed—of all things—nuclear physics! The racial mores apply just as strictly to the Ph.D. as to the illiterate. This has created an insufferable situation in the South in which it is impossible to earn reward by merit. No matter how many degrees you earn, no matter how many books you write, even if you become a college president or a United Nations Secretary, you still cannot eat at the nicest restaurants, stay at the best hotels, see the new movies, own a business on Main Street, or buy a home in the fashionable part of town. The class system of medieval Europe never had the finality which race strictures have today in portions of the United States, for in feudal society the religious vocation offered a way of escape even to the peasant. Our segregated Church fulfills no such democratizing function.

Knoxville College finds it much easier to secure white professors than Negro professors at the Ph.D. level. Part of the reason is the reluctance of highly trained Negroes to live under the social restrictions that are placed upon them in the South. (If it were not for the persistence of racial prejudice in the hiring policies of Northern universities, the situation of our Negro colleges in the South would be even more difficult.) If he is one of those undemanding individuals who can be content with his work, his family, and a small circle of friends, he may live at peace in his little campus world. Unless he teaches at a state college, it will probably even be an integrated world. For the campus of the private Negro college in the South has much of the aspect of the overseas mission compound of a past generation—it is a little island of alien ideals amid a hostile culture. Its insignificance gains for it the freedom to exist. But when the teacher ventures outside this insulated area, he knows that he ceases being a professor and becomes just a Negro, and he must brace himself for humiliation at any contact.

The turnout for the preliminary meeting today gave me encouragement. Not only was Dr. Crutcher back, but so was Father Jones, who has been ill, and Carroll Felton. Jack Leflore, a handsome and aggressive young Negro businessman was there, an even more encouraging sign than the presence of the ministers. Dr. Crutcher laid before us the possibility of expanding our activities to include picketing. Bob West had talked with a man who is familiar with picketing as a technique in labor disputes and was able to explain to us that there are two ways to use the picketing technique—token picketing over a long period of time, or a mass picketing demonstration. The two differ in their objectives—the sustained picketing aiming to wear down the resistance of the organization being picketed, the mass picketing aiming primarily to dramatize the cause in order to win the sympathy of the public. We all felt the time had come to inject a new technique into our campaign; our problem was which type of picketing better suited our purposes. We decided that it would be easier to enlist many workers for one big day than to keep a few scheduled each day for a long period of time. Furthermore, we saw in the mass picketing idea a possibility of finally breaking the news barrier which has kept many people in Knoxville unaware that sit-ins are even going on. Unanimously and almost spontaneously we agreed that the target should be Rich's Department Store. Crutcher envisions a hundred picketers marching around Rich's all day long from 9 A.M. until 9 P.M. If we can carry this off, it should be a sensation! It must be soon, and it should be a big shopping day. Although I was skeptical of our ability to mount the operation so quickly, we decided on Monday. It is my understanding that both the store itself and the police will be informed in advance.

The group divided to go to Grant's and Cole's, but Father Jones was insistent that we should not continue to excuse Miller's, since it has become public information that they are not being open and aboveboard. They have escaped sit-ins up until now because of the fact that at each contact the management has reasserted the store's willingness to desegregate if the other stores do. But we have reached the point now where such reassurances are meaningless. Since the store is locally owned and has been in Knoxville much longer than Rich's, we have sentimentally hoped for better things from them. But apparently we were wrong; they have been less straightforward than Rich's. Father Jones himself wanted to go to Miller's and Felton volunteered to go with him.

Things were quiet at Grant's again today. I am coming to feel appreciation for their attitude toward us, which is almost hospitality when compared to that of any of the other stores which we have gone to with regularity. Yesterday one of the waitresses spoke to a white man who was eating beside a Negro woman and asked him to tell the woman that one of the white ruffians was planning to throw iced tea on one of our girls. The waitress explained that she would lose her job if she talked with one of the sit-inners. "But I want them treated fairly; they're fighting for their rights."

Mrs. Wiersema, who sat near me again today, said that yesterday two nicely dressed Negro women sat at Grant's counter. She assumed they were sit-inners, but upon conversing with them learned they were tourists from Ohio who did not know there was a sit-in going on. Invited to join it, they replied, "Thank you, but we want to eat."

The young man who was our leader today bought food next door and ate it while sitting at Grant's counter. Personally, I wouldn't do that; it seems impolite.

About 12:40 I left with the intention of joining Jones and Felton at Miller's. I found Miller's sign up as reported, "Please, Employees Only," but there was no one to stop me from entering.

The counter was full of customers. Many of them had on hats and obviously were not Miller's employees. I walked the length of the counter and saw no dark face. Upon leaving, I noticed lurking nearby the store detective, whom I had learned to identify at the Police-Community Institute.

Walking on down Gay Street to check what was happening at Cole's, I met Jim Reese with his camera in hand. He had been to take a picture of the hangman's noose at Cole's! He said he had tried to take a picture of the sign at Miller's but the store detective stopped him. "I'd sure hate to see you lose a good camera!" the detective threatened.

I heard this afternoon what happened when Jones and Felton went to Miller's. They were intercepted at the door by the detective, who for a while kept everyone from entering the counter. After a few minutes one of the top executives of the store came down and exchanged the sign for one reading, "For Employees, Their Families and Friends." Then whites were admitted and the Negroes kept out. This draws the line more clearly than it has yet been drawn by any other store; it tells the Negroes that Miller's store numbers only whites as its friends. My guess is that the Negroes of Knoxville will respond in an appropriate way.

The two ministers talked with the executive in his office. I understand that he repeated the promise that Miller's will desegregate when and if the other stores do. But Rich's would be first on any list of "the other stores" that Miller's would draw up, and with Rich's lunch counter closed permanently, of what value can this promise of Miller's be any longer? (Interestingly enough, Miller's did desegregate its eating facilities some four years ago. Negroes were served there for about six months, but when the disturbance over the integration of the schools at Clinton, only eighteen miles away, brought a flare-up of racial tension in the area, the management requested the Negroes in the interest of public tranquility not to come until the storm had blown over. They have never been invited back. Even so, the remembrance that Miller's did once voluntarily desegregate is one reason Miller's has been treated with more tenderness than Rich's during the sit-ins.)

I stopped by the cashier's office to find out how things went at Rich's Laurel Room today. Mildred Ward got Florence Olden, who works in the business office, to go with her during their lunch hour. They are both handsome women who carry themselves elegantly. Today they dressed in their stylish best. In short, they were in every way the kind of women the Laurel Room caters to, excepting their complexions, and even they are not dark. At the Laurel Room all customers wait to be seated by a hostess. Mildred and Florence were simply kept waiting, period. Mildred says they were scared, but gained courage when they saw that the store employees and the other customers were more embarrassed than they were. As soon as they arrived, they overheard one of the employees on the house phone saying, "This is an emergency. You promised us protection." (Protection!) Shortly, several burly detectives appeared. Meantime the hostess had begun to greet the whites who came with a cheery, "Oh, yes, we have your reservation!" We are sure that few of the people who eat at the Laurel Room bother to get reservations. After a time, Mildred and Florence left; they had not said anything to anyone.

Friday, June 24

TODAY was the day of our ministers' meeting. We called it at one of the big downtown "white" churches hoping to encourage white ministers to attend. While I have never known any white minister who would refuse to enter a Negro church—the pattern of paternalistic visits by white dignitaries upon special invitation being well-established in Southern tradition—still the separation of our lives is such that we rarely think of being included with the other group in any whole. White churches in the Deep South publicize their functions with the generalization, "Everybody welcome," or even, "Every citizen of Magnolia City is urged to attend," without remotely supposing that this would include Negroes, and even here in this more "liberal" city, many congregations would be thrown into consternation if a Negro responded. It is difficult to say whether racial separation or denominational separation is the more serious rupture in the Church Catholic, the more grievous departure from the holy fellowship in which "there is neither Jew nor Greek, there is neither bond nor free, there is neither male nor female," because all are "one in Christ Jesus." Few white ministers take the trouble to cultivate the acquaintance of Negro ministers. Interracial ministerial alliances such as we have in Knoxville are an important breakthrough. Still, we feared that if we set this meeting for one of the Negro churches, the white ministers would tend to discard the notice with the thought, "That is an interest of *theirs*." Probably it should be added that Negroes here in Knoxville, where some genuine opportunities do exist to mingle with the other group, generally take the same attitude unless the meeting has something specifically to do with race relations.

We had sent out over a hundred letters; six Negro ministers and nine white ministers attended. I was not disappointed, because some of the Negroes and most of the whites were men who had not shown much interest previously. This was not an official meeting of the Knoxville Ministerial Association. Most of the officers of that organization were absent, which may or may not indicate a lack of interest, since the notices arrived only a day before the time set for the meeting. Jim Reese presided and did a fine job of it. Charles Trentham, the courageous pastor of First Baptist Church, is out of the city, but we were fortunate to have present Joe Copeland, the other white minister who was active on the Mayor's Committee, to help fill in the group on the history of the negotiations up to the point where they broke down. Copeland is pastor of Second Presbyterian, the largest church of the United Presbyterian denomination in the city, and serves on the national

Social Education and Action Committee of that denomination. The congregation of Second Church during his nine-year pastorate has moved hesitantly but noticeably toward a more liberal attitude on race relations. (I recall that the first time our interracial Ministerial Association was allowed to hold a luncheon meeting there, only two and a half years ago, it was considered a triumph for the cause of race relationships; now with the integration of presbyteries in this area, mixed groups meet in the church almost every week.)

Bob West related the comment of the assistant manager of Cole's that "If this thing were right, there would be more ministers in it," whereupon the pastor of the Euclid Avenue Baptist Church volunteered, "If the ministers had been preaching the truth all along, their people now would *know* what is right!" I was pleased to hear such a forceful statement from a Southern Baptist man. I am told there are 66,000 Southern Baptists in Knox County. Among these are many from the lower economic and educational levels. If their ministers were to teach clearly the implications of the Bible with regard to race, our problem would be well on the way to solution. The great majority of Southern Baptist preachers feel their vocation is to preach the gospel of individual salvation from sin, but fail to identify our society-wide tyranny against a racial group as a part of that sin. Such "social questions" they believe to be outside their legitimate concern. However, several of the Southern Baptist seminaries are giving a sound theological grounding in the relationship of the gospel to social problems, and we can expect that, as a higher percentage of Baptist ministers secure seminary training, the social concern of that denomination will deepen markedly. This should eventually have a profound effect upon social attitudes in the South.

Jim Reese suggested that white ministers could help by encouraging their members to sit at the counters beside Negroes to eat lunch and to let managers know they would support a move to desegregate. He invited the ministers themselves to join the demonstrations. He got only one "taker"—a man who is leaving town in two weeks to take a pastorate in another part of the state agreed to go with him to the Laurel Room on Monday.

The group voted to ask the president of the Knoxville Ministerial Association to call an official KMA meeting for Tuesday morning. We agreed on two items to be taken up at that time: a proposal to send a letter to store managers to be signed by as many ministers as possible and a proposed chronology of the negotiations which could be accepted as "official" for the use of ministers.

Because we are ministers and ministers love to haggle with one another in meetings, it took two hours for us to accomplish this little bit of business. By this time the sit-ins were already in progress. I called Crutcher from the church to ask where I was most needed, and he suggested I could help most today by meeting with two ladies to shape up the legends for the signs we will use Monday.

As I was leaving the church, one of our sit-inners, a husky Negro youth, came running up, dripping perspiration. He was looking for Dr. Crutcher, but failing to find him, told me his problem. A sheriff's deputy had accosted him in front of Cole's and asked his name. The youth wasn't sure whether our rules allowed him to give his name or not. Rather than to risk betraying the organization, he asked the deputy's permission to go consult with Crutcher. He had run the seven blocks to the church to find him and would have run back had I not insisted on driving him. To me, this was a touching example of devotion to the cause. This is the same young man who walks two miles each day to catch an inter-city bus because the private bus line which runs to his community insists on segregated seating. This boy is unsophisticated, but he has the deep sense of personal dignity which so often marks those in every clime who live the simple life. This same spirit which has enabled Negroes to live with an oppressive social structure without losing their self-respect also makes them formidable fighters for justice.

I felt a little guilty to be eating my lunch at the normal hour, and wondered what was happening downtown. Mrs. Leflore and

Mrs. Edwards came to my home about mid-afternoon, and amid a torrential rainstorm we decided on the legends to be used and what materials we would need for the signs. Mrs. Leflore and Mrs. Edwards are two of the corps of women who have been giving loyal service to the movement as office help and in various other odd jobs. Most of them are school teachers whom the organization feels too vulnerable to risk in sit-ins.

Jim has spent much of yesterday and this afternoon distributing the handbills for the "Trade With Your Friends Movement" to the Negro pastors, who will in turn see that they get delivered door to door among the Negro families in an assigned section of the city. The leaflet lists the ten merchants who have failed to desegregate, despite months of negotiations, and then states: "The court, in a recent Alabama case, stated that 'every person has a right to trade with whomever he pleases and therefore the right not to trade with any particular person or business.' . . . Knoxville citizens can now determine who are their friends and who are not their friends." The message announces a mass meeting at Mt. Olive on Sunday and closes with this suggestive statement: "Many people have canceled charge accounts with merchants they do not consider friendly." It will be noticed that there is no exhortation on the leaflet other than to "trade with your friends"; thus it will hardly be possible to hang a charge on anyone that he urged a boycott.

McArthur came over tonight, and while the rain poured in torrents outside we worked for several hours at the kitchen table making signs for the picketing Monday. We made several copies of "No Eat, No Buy," "We Are All Brothers in Christ," and "We ~~Are~~ Were Rich's 2nd-Class Customers." I am glad to have this fellowship with Mac; although he lives just across the hall, we seldom get together except for a few words as we pass. During my first year at Knoxville College, it troubled me that the one or two close friendships I developed were with white faculty members.

Was it race prejudice? Then Jim came as pastor of the church and very quickly, because of our common interests and similar outlook on life, we became warm friends. I feel quite free now to let friendships develop where they will. As Mac and I work together, we have a sense of an even wider fellowship, realizing that in many different houses throughout the city tonight people are making signs for the same purpose. But what if it is raining like this on Monday?

Saturday, June 25

We had a meeting of the Executive Committee at Mt. Olive at 10:00 this morning. A young attorney from Nashville who was one of the seven-member Mayor's Committee there was present at Dr. Crutcher's invitation to share some wisdom from the Nashville experience. He attributes the success of the lunch counter movement in Nashville to the large economic loss suffered by the downtown stores when Negroes were conducting their "stay away from downtown" campaign and many whites were fearful to come downtown because of the violence that had been associated with the sit-in demonstrations. One interesting item the attorney told us is that when the merchants of Nashville finally decided to move, they requested the other side to appoint an *all-Negro* negotiating committee. "When whites are involved," the merchants said, "they always preach to us. We don't want to be preached to! This is a dollar and cents matter to us." This tends to confirm my conviction that talk alone will never move the merchants and that they really respect us more for dealing with them in economic categories, because these they understand. They may understand morality too "in its place," but not as a basis for business decisions.

We went on then to plan our picketing demonstration. We

figure it will take three hundred volunteers in order to keep one hundred there all day long, even though we have decided to terminate the picketing at 5:30. We are excited over the prospect of the picketing; our movement is gathering steam. More of the ministers are manifesting an interest now; I suspect some of them have come because they felt they had to in order to keep the loyalty of their people, but I am satisfied so long as they are here.

My sign-making has kept me up an hour past midnight. I pride myself in the cleverness of one pair: one sign to be carried by a white picketer reads "This Little Pig Had Roast Beef," its companion to be carried by a Negro reads, "This Little Pig Had None." Is this taking the whole affair too lightly? Yet we've got to remain able to laugh at ourselves—something which has always been one of the great assets of the Negro people.

Sunday, June 26

PREACHING at the Friends Church this morning, I took five minutes or more as I did last Sunday at Erin Presbyterian to tell about the lunch counter movement and try to get the congregation to see that here is an opportunity for Christians to bear a testimony. Both audiences received my remarks with almost complete impassivity; I do not know how to interpret this.

I tried to slip inconspicuously into a rear seat at the mass meeting, but it is hard for me to remain incognito in a sea of dark faces, and so I was called up to the platform. People continued crowding into the church until long after the hour set for the meeting. Even some of the city churches continue the old custom among Negroes of commencing when the people are gathered, and there is a permissive atmosphere about lateness at almost all group gatherings of

Negroes. As one who could never make it anywhere quite on the hour set, I appreciate this relaxation when I am a member of the audience, but it exasperates me when I am presiding at a meeting.

When all the seats were filled, chairs were placed in every available space, and then those still coming were directed to an overflow room in the basement. Crutcher says there were 1400 present; I question the figure, but there is no doubt that the crowded room contributed to the enthusiasm of the meeting.

Crutcher commenced the meeting on a rousing note by relating that he had received a call this afternoon from Dr. Hardy, one of our Negro physicians, urging him to come out to University Hospital immediately. When he arrived, he discovered that Jack Leflore, who had gone to the hospital to visit his mother, was conducting a one-man sit-in in the hospital's lunchroom! Leflore explained to the hospital manager, "The taxes I paid probably bought the bricks under the stool I'm sitting on, and I want to use my bricks!" University Hospital is the only one of the four general hospitals in Knoxville which admits Negroes at all, and not even the Negro physicians can eat in its lunchroom. This faces the Negro with the choice of humbling himself to ask for a handout in the kitchen, or else going hungry, for the hospital is located a mile outside the city in a field. Talking the kind of "turkey" that we preachers don't know how to talk, Leflore delivered the ultimatum—"I'll give you until Wednesday, and if you haven't opened up by then, I'll bring forty sit-inners out here with me and we'll stay until you do open!" Dr. Hardy added that if the manager shot one every day there would be a dozen more sit-inners to take his place the next day. (Crutcher confided to me that this was undoubtedly an exaggeration, but I wonder if it does not depict the deep feeling behind this movement for equality more accurately than the merchants in town have ever understood it.)

Father Jones continued the high spirit of the meeting in his hard-hitting main address. It was entirely read from a hand-written manuscript, but full of the power given it by a man of deep spiritual convictions, entirely dedicated to a cause. Father Jones is small; aroused, he conveys the image of a scrapping bulldog.

Recognition was given to representative sit-inners. Mrs. Davis told the audience that she rises a couple of hours earlier every morning in order to make up for the time she spends on sit-ins; she prepares lunch for her ailing father before she comes to the ten o'clock meeting. Her testimony was that for a cause as important as this we should let other things go. Lee Butler, the white University of Tennessee student who was roughed up on the street, got a rousing ovation. But it was little Annie Brown, one of our high school girls, who brought down the house. Annie loves—unfortunately, I think—to tantalize the assistant manager at Cole's. Apparently the pleasure is mutual, for she says he calls her "the beige one," and said in her hearing, "By next week they will all have dropped off except the beige one." Annie retorted so that he could hear, "Next week there will be forty more beige ones down here!" Annie pointed to a baby on the front row and asked the audience, "Do you want this little baby to have to sit-in when he grows up, just because you failed to do it when you could have?" She has a point.

When it came time for the offering, Crutcher explained that the organization feels responsibility toward those Negroes who have lost their jobs as a result of Rich's closing its counter. Several were heads of families. A Methodist minister came to the microphone and exhorted the audience, "Let's have fifty men give five dollars each! Let's start with the ministers!" No matter what anyone says, it really was past time that I should have left to make my evening preaching engagement!

It was with a colored congregation in a nearby town. After the service, the leading elder and his wife invited me to their home for ice cream. The Nashes own their spacious frame house and keep it up well. It is far nicer than any house I lived in during my boyhood in Iowa. Although he is retired, even some of the white townspeople call him respectfully, "Professor Nash." In the typical Southern town, the principal of the Negro school has the highest status in the Negro community, considerably higher than that of the minister, for the minister functions only with respect to the Negro community, while the school principal is the chief contact person between the white community and the Negro community. In a sense, he is the only Negro recognized as a person by the white community. I remember sitting with the white ministers of a certain town planning a city-wide religious census which was to include the Negro population. Being new in the town, I asked how we could contact the Negro ministers. "Oh, the thing to do would be to contact Jones, the principal of the colored school, and he will contact the ministers," volunteered one of the white ministers. I insisted on contacting the Negro ministers individually, much to the puzzlement of the white group.

Monday, June 27

THE big day! By 9:15 we were downtown; the station wagon bearing the signs was stationed in a parking lot near Rich's while each of us chose a sign. While our number was far short of a hundred, there were enough to put twenty-five picketers on each of the two fronts of Rich's. I led a group up the Locust Street side.

I feel very conspicuous; I have always thought picketers looked silly. I haven't even reached the end of the block, and here come the reporters! One who introduces himself as the Associated Press representative says accusingly, "This was billed as an interracial demonstration, but you are the only white person!" I assure him there will be numerous others, as there have been in the sit-ins. With relief I note Crutcher coming behind me and sick the reporters on him. I have no business making statements to the press.

Our signs are disorganized. A little Negro boy is carrying one reading, "Rich's White Customers Will Support Equal Treatment." I trade my "We Are All Brothers in Christ" for it. Oh, oh, there is Harry Wiersema, a Unitarian, carrying "We Are All Brothers in Christ" which someone has thrust into his hands. He looks slightly embarrassed. Should I offer to exchange with him? But far be it from me to keep anyone from making a Christian confession. Bob West, his pastor, comes to Wiersema's rescue by suggesting that I change with him, which I am glad to do. But the fellowship in Christ is real today, if not acknowledged.

After all the rain we have had over the weekend, this day is beautiful. The police, who have been alerted, hover near—a few on foot, one or two on cycles, several cruising around the block in cars. A few hecklers collect. I decide to count how many times I am called "nigger" or "nigger lover"; it reaches five times in one hour. Generally they say it low, so the cops can't hear, because the police have sternly charged that there is to be no heckling. Of course we couldn't get away with a demonstration like this at all if the city administration were hostile. (I understand the druggists asked Mayor Duncan last week to make arrests and he replied, "I'm not going to do your dirty work for you!" telling them they would have to swear out warrants if they wanted arrests. But to swear a warrant puts one in a position of liability for causing false arrest.)

The Negro janitor of a big "white" church across the street comes over and tells us to feel free to come into the church to use the rest rooms or get drinks. I guess he feels this can be his little bit—perhaps his sacrifice, for I wonder if the pastor knows, or what the Board of Stewards would say.

Traffic is increasing as the curious drive by to see what is going on. Some young fellows with a convertible have obtained huge Confederate and Tennessee flags and are riding round and round the store giving rebel yells and occasionally firing blank cartridges.

I think I had better rest for a few moments, leaning here against this low wall. A young white man introduces himself; he is a student from Union Theological Seminary in New York who is working with a Negro congregation in Morristown, Tennessee, this summer because of his interest in race relations. He is with a Negro youth. A hard-looking woman passes by and growls something in my ear which is too obscene to repeat. "What did she say?" the seminary student asks, and I tell a white lie.

Frank Haille, who operates a sign shop across Locust Street from Rich's, and who is said to be active in the White Citizens Council here, has arranged a large commercial-type sign, white letters on black, which he has propped up against a car sitting in front of his place. It reads: "Sit-In Demonstrations Are Un-American."

Reporters and photographers come back again and again. TV cameramen take movie film. Surely our first objective will be accomplished—the news barrier will be broken today! But the number of customers still going into the store does not give us any encouragement about the effectiveness of our demonstration as an economic protest.

By 11:00 A.M. my leg has given way. I hate to give up, but I must. But after some rest, I am back at 3:30 wearing a different pair of shoes; I hope they will keep me going until quitting time. The number of demonstrators has not fallen below twenty-five on each front all day. Apparently those who have come became so interested they didn't leave on schedule, while others who didn't sign up have seen what we were doing and joined us. In my absence, a Negro-owned service station has sent seven cases of soft drinks, while a truck from a white-owned dairy stopped momentarily, unloaded two crates of orange drink and moved on. No one seems to know who inspired the dairy.

The situation is quite different this afternoon! Large groups of hecklers and curious onlookers are gathered around each entrance. Traffic into the store has virtually ceased. The crowds around the entrances make it difficult to get in; probably also people who planned to shop today decided against it when they heard about the demonstration on the noon radio news. Police report the biggest traffic jam since Christmas as thousands of the curious circle the block in cars. Our Confederate battalion, however, is no longer in evidence; I am told the police stopped the convertible, found the boys were from a neighboring town, and suggested they go home.

Some young boys, poorly dressed, are displaying crudely lettered opposition signs. One says, "Is this a Communist Sponsered (sic) Organization?" Another large one says, "If you don't like the South, why don't you go North?" Another lad in dirty, tattered overalls carries a sign which is a take-off on one of ours, but makes our case even more effectively; it reads, "We Are Rich's 1st Class Customers."

One lad, obviously one of what we call the hill-people (though he may live in the city) has a sign scrawled on a piece of corrugated cardboard ripped from a box; it says "Half-Bread (sic) go North." I don't know why he has singled me out, but he has one end of the thing stuck against my back and is following me back and forth. This amuses the crowd, myself hardly less. After several rounds, I converse with him while we are at the far end. "You see," he says, "I don't have no truck with blacks." "Well," I tell him in a confidential tone, "the way I look at it, God made us all." He hasn't said anything more. Now he has given up.

I am carrying this afternoon my favorite sign, "We Are All Brothers in Christ." A young grown man passes behind me and growls in my ear, "You damn sonofabitch!" I think of the legend on the sign and get a thrill as I realize, "Christianity is still powerful! I know, because it still has enemies!"

My embarrassment of this morning is gone; now I am proud to be walking in this line. One fellow mocks each time I pass, "Here comes the Great White Father!" It does not bother me. McArthur and Harvey have walked nearly all day carrying their signs, "I'm a Ph.D., but I Can't Eat at Rich's!" I admire them for being such good sports. It must be an effective sign; Harvey says it agitates the hecklers more than any other. Others say our most effective signs are "We Are All Brothers in Christ" and "Khrushchev Could Eat Here—I Can't." Jim Reese was carrying the Khrushchev sign when one heckler said to him,

"Yeah, but Khrushchev ain't a nigger!" That's putting it pretty
plainly. Several times today I have been called a Communist,
but there are some at least who prefer Communists to Negroes. I shouldn't be surprised if the same people who charge,
"This is all Communist inspired" would rather eat lunch with
Khrushchev than with Ralph Bunche.

As I pass, another heckler mutters, "I wonder how much the
NAACP is paying him?" I can't really get mad at such a charge,
because it shows such ignorance of the actual situation that I must
feel sorry for the person who makes it. The NAACP has shown
little interest in the lunch counter movement. Here in Knoxville
the one Negro who has been most identified with the NAACP
hasn't attended even one of our meetings. I suppose it is easier on
the conscience to believe that some outside organization is pour-
ing in money and leadership to agitate the situation than to admit
that there are people in your own community being treated so
unfairly that they would do all this to gain their rights. Of course
sit-in demonstrations make the kind of situation that Communists
would love to get hold of, but anyone who knows the people who
are responsible for the lunch counter movement in Knoxville—
persons like W. T. Crutcher, who has been a beloved pastor in
this community for over twenty-five years—knows there are no
Communists under this woodpile. Once they become convinced
of this, people will have to cease looking for a scapegoat and look
at the cause on its own merits.

The policeman who in plain clothes was protecting the white
virginity of Rich's lunch counter the first day I went there is
dressed up like a cop today and is the only one I have observed
to speak curtly to the demonstrators. Another policeman warned
the crowd, "There will be no heckling, and if you don't believe
that, just try me!" One thirteen-year-old white boy has been arrested for throwing water on a Negro girl marching in the picket
line and for having a knife in his possession. Visitors from the
Henley Street side bring us up to date on what has been going
on over there: A white girl picket has been hit with an egg. One

heckler watched the pickets until he could stand it no longer, then strode out and grabbed a sign from a girl marcher, snapped the staff in two, and threw the sign on the pavement. The girl calmly picked up the sign and carried it on without breaking the line.

But some onlookers have been affected in the opposite way. An older white man who described himself as an old hand at labor picketing asked to be allowed to join the march, and took a sign. But when he kept talking back to the hecklers, Rev. Patterson had to call him to one side and explain that we don't do that in our kind of picketing.

It is 4:30. I see that Stuart Bacon has dropped by; he is talking with Crutcher, watching the signs go by. Dr. Bacon is a clinical psychologist who is a member of our interracial Knoxville Men's Fellowship. Now he is no longer beside Crutcher; I look for him and spot him in the picket line, carrying the sign, "We Are All Brothers in Christ." Yes, the brotherhood is real, for Dr. Bacon is a Roman Catholic.

It is nearly 5:30 and we are breaking up. One boy with a pedometer says he walked thirteen miles. I am just grateful I was able to make it to the end. Now I have a chance to talk with Dr. Bacon. "I had come by three times during the day, wondering what I should do," he confesses. "I have always preached brotherhood, and it seemed that now I ought to stand up for my convictions. But I was embarrassed. I know what was bothering me—I was afraid some of my patients would see me as they came out of the clinic. But you have to live with yourself too, so finally I joined in, and I feel much better about it." He tells me that his family spends a thousand dollars a year at Rich's on account, and he plans to write a letter of protest with the next payment.

I wonder, if we marched every day, how many others would eventually join us? I am reminded of the story of the forty Christian athletes in the Roman army who were sent naked out onto the frozen lake to die unless they should recant and do obeisance to the emperor's image. Long hours they marched, singing hymns in the icy cold, while soldier guards watched from the comfort of a bonfire on shore. Finally one of the Christians broke under the torture and ran to the fire, proclaiming his readiness to deny the faith. But by this time one of the guards had become so impressed with the courage of these Christians that he stripped off his own uniform and took the place of the defector on the ice, chanting with the others, "Forty wrestlers marching for Christ."

Our story won the front page of the afternoon paper. WATE-TV on its 11:00 p.m. news showed the heckler breaking the sign. We were delighted to read in the paper also that the Methodist ministers of the city have called for negotiations to be resumed—an action probably stimulated by our ministers meeting of last Friday. The thing is no longer under a bushel. The publicity plus the expectant enthusiasm produced among the Negro population by yesterday's mass meeting and today's demonstration mean that we have entered a new phase of the struggle.

Tuesday, June 28

CONTRARY to popular assumption, the Knoxville Ministerial Association embraces in its membership less than one-fifth of the four hundred clergymen in Knoxville and its environs, which is a major reason for the relative ineffectiveness of this group in furnishing community leadership. Our attendance of thirty-five this morning we considered good for a called meeting. I was encouraged by the fact that some were there whom we don't ordinarily see at KMA meetings. The meeting was stormy and confused. As usual, we were not arguing about objectives, but about procedures and words.

The principal accomplishment of the meeting was the adoption of a statement favoring lunch counter desegregation and asking the Mayor's Committee and the merchants to cooperate in the resumption of negotiations, which have been stalled now for five weeks. There was heated argument over a stipulation that "we agree to urge the members of our congregations to support merchants who desegregate their lunch counters and use their influence to see that the merchants suffer no economic hurt from this step." (It is difficult to understand why ministers bristle at any suggestion that someone is trying to tell them what to preach, when they use this so zealously guarded freedom of the pulpit so seldom for any courageous purpose. It is in effect declaring, "I will defend to the death my right to choose my own pious platitudes!") In the end, we only expressed the "hope" that Christian people will support the merchants who desegregate, a sentiment which itself seems certain to raise doubts in the minds of the merchants. I have qualms that we are on morally shaky grounds by asking the merchants to do more than we are willing to do ourselves—namely, to take a bold action for desegregation in their own bailiwick.

Most of the ministers present affixed their signatures to the statement, and it is understood that opportunity will be given to ministers not present to sign.

After the meeting, Bob West and I dropped by Todd & Armistead and joined the sit-in that was in progress there. This counter was reopened yesterday after being closed for ten days. In the interim the store has arranged a barricade of merchandise before the counter, but the entry was not manned when we arrived. I was glad to see among those sitting at the counter the wife of the president of Knoxville College. Dr. Colston himself has not participated in the sit-ins; both he and the other leaders feel that he can be of more service to the cause by remaining in a position where he can serve as a contact person between us, the Mayor, and the Chamber of Commerce officials, who in turn have contact with the merchants.

Having heard that there was a disturbance at one of the other stores, I walked down there in the rain only to discover that the "disturbance" was that the manager was disturbed because our group was there! He felt that because of the friendliness he has shown to our cause he should be exempted. Indeed it was a misunderstanding that the group was there, Crutcher having been involved in the ministers' meeting, but none of us is sorry. If a store can be excused simply by expressions of righteousness, there is no reason why every store should not gain exemption by the same tactic. Of course, this man's friendliness may be genuine; we can only play along until we find out.

I hear that Harry Wiersema, Jr., was struck by a white hoodlum in Cole's today! If so, this is our first open violence other than yesterday's egg throwing. I do not yet have the facts.

Harvey and B. A. Ward went to Rich's Laurel Room at lunch time today. They were refused outright without resort to the "reservations" gimmick. A lady customer emerging said to them, "I approve of what you're doing and wish you success." The guard at the door reddened. If the woman wants our success badly enough, she could cancel her account at Rich's, or at least communicate her sentiments to the management.

We hear that Rich's local management had planned to close the basement counter only temporarily, but a boss from the Atlanta office came up and said, "Rip it out completely!" We are aware that a large part of Rich's problem is the fact that its vital decisions are made in Atlanta, where the company has a larger store. No doubt the big bosses feel that if they integrate in Knoxville this will increase the pressure on them to integrate in Atlanta where the opposition is much greater. However, there are enough Negroes in Atlanta to wield the balance of economic power if they ever become united as the Negroes here are becoming.

We hear a rumor that some merchants are to meet tomorrow. (We exist on rumors.) Our contact man says that four stores are ready to move if they can get one locally-owned store to move with them. But our information is that Miller's is included in the four, so this does not improve our situation—Cole's and Todd & Armistead, the only other locally owned stores, seem rigid in their negative position.

Harvey feels that our group should be contacting the managers directly. A committee was given the assignment of doing that the early part of last week, but with Crutcher out of town the committee never got activated. What contact with managers has occurred has been spontaneous or accidental. Three Negro women went to see Mr. Handley, the president of Miller's, on their own authority last Friday. He told them once more that Miller's is ready to move with others, not alone.

A fairly accurate report of this morning's action by the Ministerial Association came out in this afternoon's *News-Sentinel*. This together with the Methodist ministers' statement of yesterday should have an impact.

Wednesday, June 29

TODAY our movement is in crisis and all of us know it. Open violence flared again, and one store has made a countermove we didn't expect.

Spurred by the rising excitement, between sixty and seventy came to sit-in today, enough to hit nearly all the stores whose counters remain open. Miller's was excluded because we hear they have at last completely closed theirs. I chose to go to Walgreen's because I hadn't yet experienced what it is like there. (I found out!) A tall brawny young Negro man named Logan was our leader. I asked him what his work was. He said, "I was working for a cab company until last week, but when I heard about the sit-ins I quit my job so I could help with them. I was only making fifteen or twenty dollars a week, and by working in the sit-ins maybe I can do some real good." What a spirit! Logan is not very well educated, but has a deep sense of justice and seems to know Christian love as more than a theory. He kept tight control of the group. One boy of twelve was with us; Logan called him "Junior" and kept reminding him sharply to sit back on his stool until I pointed out that when Junior sat back, his feet didn't touch the floor! The kids want to do their part, but we shouldn't involve them in some of the things that may happen.

Walgreen's is the only place we go that has booths; Logan and I occupy one together. A man in a white jacket who seems to be in charge of the counter manifests his hostility from the beginning. As he passes by our booth, he conspicuously spits on the floor. The next time he tosses a lighted cigaret on me; it rests in a fold of my coat. I would prefer to ignore it, but must pluck it off before it burns a hole in my good suit. I want to examine the coat to see if it is damaged, but I must not do anything here that will indicate anxiety. A young white fellow stops at our booth, inquires about Robert Booker, whom he says he knows. Now I see him bring coffee which he has ordered to one of our Negro boys and a coke to another. I wish he had not done that. The demonstrators do not touch the drinks. Logan suggests that the drinks may be drugged; I had not thought of that! The man in the white coat comes to pick up the drinks. He deliberately spills the coke over the demonstrator, and now the coffee, exclaiming with mock apology, "Oh, excuse me!"

A woman customer brushes close to our booth and mutters to me, "Take your niggers and get out of here!"

A group of white boys who appear to be high school age come up to our booth and begin to tantalize me. I do not recognize the fellow who heckled me before; these boys have a younger appearance, but their line is the same: "Come on with us, fellow; we're going to show you where you belong!" I am apprehensive, but somehow actual danger is never so fearful as dreaded danger.

As they continue their heckling, I look straight ahead at Logan.

Suddenly I feel myself drenched with what seems a terrific lot of liquid. My glasses are filmed over; I take them off and hold them in my clenched hands. My eyes smart—what was the stuff? The liquid has gone down all over my "preachin' suit." I notice crushed ice too, and realize it must have been a coke—a tall coke, not poured or spilled, but the contents thrown over me by one of these boys from a distance of two feet. Logan utters quiet words of encouragement; he is a great strength to me. I can sense as though I had eyes all over my head that everyone in the establishment is looking at me; I feel I have the sympathy of most of them. Nevertheless, it is a mortifying experience to be attacked in public by another person and not be able to do anything in your own defense.

I breathe a bit easier, for the boys have left us now, but I see one go into the kitchen and speak to some employee—the man in the white coat?—and I fear he is up to no good. Now they are back, heckling me again. I look straight forward, pretending to pay no attention. Suddenly I am jolted by a severe blow on the left side of my face. My first thought is of being hit by a batted tennis ball when I was six years old—it stings like that. It did not feel like the blow of a clenched fist; it must have been done with the open hand.

Logan reminds me I am not to strike back, but I hardly need that advice. I do not feel like striking back physically, but does one just sit here and let a young punk use him for a punching bag? Suddenly the blow comes again, again hard. Failing to get any response, one or two of the boys grab me and start pulling me from the booth. I slide my glasses to Logan as we have prearranged, and hold on.

At precisely this moment a young white man who has been eating in a booth near ours rises and takes the situation in hand. He is impressively large and young enough to be damaging. Sternly he says to the boys, "You fellows have gone far enough and now you'd better get out of here! Look, I'm neutral in this, but this fellow was just sitting here. You could be arrested for what you've done. You'd better get out of here before you get into real trouble!"

I wish I could see the boys' faces! They meekly leave and the man leaves too. I will never know his identity and therefore can never thank him, but I have a feeling he would not wish to be thanked by me. What he did, he did not do for me, but for his sense of decency and order. What a travesty of both it is that a *customer* should have to restore order! I cannot imagine why any hard-headed business man would allow his store to become a scene of riot.

Nevertheless, here is a clear example of the effectiveness of the non-violent approach. It has caused this "neutral" to declare himself for decency and order. A more crucial test will be what he now says about serving Negroes in Walgreen's, and this I will never know. About the effect of non-violence on the agitators themselves, I have some reservations. I believe now that if I had at any time risen from my seat and said "Boo!" to those boys, they would have left me alone. Declared non-resistance brings out the bully in those who are inclined to be bullies.

Logan asks me, "What did the man mean when he said 'impure?'" It takes me some time to realize Logan means the word "neutral." I explain to him what a "neutral" is and am even more impressed with the boy's educated heart. I suppose any one of the white gang could have defined "neutral," but their knowledge hasn't made them good citizens or given them a fair attitude toward their fellow-man.

Half an hour has passed. At exactly 1:00 P.M., the counter lights are turned off. The man who I assume to be the counter manager comes to our booth and says in a decent way, "We've closed now; wouldn't you like to leave?" Logan asks me for advice (since this is his first day as a leader), and I tell him, "I think we could leave as soon as all the others are gone," meaning the customers. This seems to satisfy the manager. Shortly after this, a man stops at our booth and says, "Hey, preacher." I turn, thinking he has a serious purpose. The man is of medium stocky build, black hair slicked back, and appears to be about thirty. He jeers, "Was your mother one?" Surprised, I treat it as a joke and turn forward again. The man proceeds to sit down in a booth along the rear wall with another man; a waitress comes, seems to be conversing with them. Suddenly the man rises from the booth, winds up like a baseball pitcher, and throws something with power down the row of booths at some target behind and to the right of me. I see a white object whiz by in the air.

A woman behind me screams, "Who threw that salt shaker? You've hit my baby! If I had hold of the dirty sonofabitch that hit my baby, I'd tear him in pieces!" The whole place is thrown into turmoil. A crowd collects, some coming in off the street. I can only think of one thing—supposing they charge that one of the Negroes did it! I get the impression the baby is badly injured.

A man who seems to be the manager of the entire store comes to our booth and advises, "You'd better go now." We are definitely ready, but the question now is, "Will we be allowed to go?" For by now the police have arrived and are talking to the woman. Logan goes over to ask the police if it is all right for us to leave. The police are not getting anywhere; nobody is admitting that he knows who threw the shaker. I keep an eye on the culprit who sits innocently in his booth. I am determined not to leave the store until I have told what I know; even if it were not for honesty's sake, it would be to protect our group. Perhaps the police will get around to questioning us. At last the manager comes to me and asks if I know who did the throwing. I tell him without pointing to where the man is sitting. "The waitress must have seen it, because she was standing right beside his booth," I add.

"The waitress says she didn't see anything." That figures; I thought she was flirting with them.

A siren wails, a man in a white uniform enters the store—apparently a police officer on ambulance duty. They talk with the woman some more. Logan finally gets through to the police and they give us permission to leave. The policemen now move back to the booth where the guilty party is sitting. The eight or nine Negroes encircle me to give me protection as we move through the crowd, but I tell them I will have to stay because I witnessed the offense; I ask for one Negro youth to stay with me. Just at this point the police officers escort the culprit and his companion from the store. They have apparently made an arrest. Greatly relieved that no one has accused us—for the opportunity must have made it a temptation—I give my name and address to the store manager and leave with our whole crew.

A crowd which includes a great many white youths is gathered on the sidewalk outside the store. Our danger is so real we can almost smell it, like dogs whiffing the wind. My only safety is in my Negro friends. How topsy-turvy my world has become, when I feel apprehensive among white strangers and perfectly safe only when Negroes are around! I have learned a lot since I came to the college three years ago; my attitude then was not unlike that of the department head at the University who avows that he always rolls up his car windows and locks his doors when he drives through a Negro neighborhood! The white South has always depended on the Negro population for its security and comfort, but in subtle ways that are easy to overlook. It would be good for every white person to have this experience I am having of knowing that my physical safety is completely in the hands of Negro friends.

A few steps from Walgreen's I run across a friend from Norris, Tennessee, who, not knowing our danger, expects me to stop and chat with him for a moment. I ask him to walk along with us, quietly explaining why I cannot stop. The Negro youths stay with me all the way to the parking garage and, despite my protests, wait outside until I drive off.

As I drive home, I am in a state of agitation. In my mind the pieces of evidence become exaggerated into a certainty that the baby is dead or dying. I suffer an agony of conscience: "If we had left immediately when we were first asked, none of this would have happened— Does this not make me a murderer? During those first calm days, it seemed impossible that it could ever come to this! How thin is the line between peace and violence, between life and death, between hope and desperation."

Because in my emotional excitement I do not wish to be alone, I stop at the Reese's and share my experiences with them. From there I call Crutcher, who gives as his opinion, "The papers ought to know about this!" Hardly any time elapses before reporters from both the *News-Sentinel* and United Press International call. I am almost afraid to ask about the baby, but one of the reporters mercifully tells me that he doesn't think there has been any serious injury. The salt shaker hit the mother and fell down against the baby. But the baby was only fourteen days old! The object was thrown with great force and obviously went far wide of its intended mark, whatever that may have been. Supposing it had hit just a few inches lower against the infant's head! The *News-Sentinel* reporter rings back, saying that his boss wants to know what kind of doctor I am—a medical doctor? "No, a doctor of philosophy—from Yale University." I sense his disappointment. I can appreciate that if he could tie in the American Medical Association with the sit-ins, it would make quite a sensational story! The word has spread quickly and friends are beginning to call to express their concern. I am basking in the glow of attention, to the point that I am almost hurt that the Associated Press has not yet called!

The tempo continued rapid. When I arrived for the Executive Committee meeting at four, some of the members had copies of the final edition which has in eight-column headlines across the front page, "Sit-Inners at Drugstore Enjoined." Judson K. Shults, owner of the Todd & Armistead Drug Company, has obtained an injunction from Chancery Court enjoining Crutcher, Jones, Patterson, *any* member of the Associated Council for Full Citizenship, or even any person sympathizing with them from attempting to obtain service at the Todd & Armistead lunch counter. The excitement of our group was at high pitch. We have never heard before of a store obtaining an injunction to prevent sit-ins. However we respond, we will be blazing a trail. "The time has come for some of us to go to jail, and I'm ready!" It was Jack Leflore who voiced this courageous sentiment. Others indicated their willingness to make the same sacrifice. We fear that if Todd & Armistead gets away with this, other stores will follow. But others expressed the opinion that the other stores cannot afford to do it, because it amounts to a plain invitation to all Negroes to stay out of the store forever. (Todd & Armistead is probably the only one of the ten firms whose business from Negroes is negligible.) They pointed out that anyone defying the injunction would make himself liable to the serious charge of contempt of court, and there would be little chance of getting off. It would place us against the due processes of law and order, to which we have so often had to appeal. It is the opinion of the Committee that we can legally *picket* the store, but no decision will be made until our volunteer corps of Negro attorneys is consulted later this evening.

Interestingly enough, Shults has named the fifth amendment to the U.S. Constitution as one of the grounds for the injunction. This raises the possibility that we may be able to appeal this all the way to the U.S. Supreme Court.

The Associated Press was on the wire, wanting a statement. Hurriedly we put our heads together and came up with one saying that the sit-ins will go on and that we are sure that our friends in every part of the city will be disappointed that Todd & Armistead has taken this negative approach to a community problem. The latter part of the statement is a veiled suggestion that white sympathizers join us in staying away from the store.

Another big question faced us this afternoon: Should we call another mass meeting for Sunday to start a "Stay Away from Downtown" movement? Up to now we have withdrawn trade only from the offending stores; what we are now considering is withdrawing trade completely from the downtown area. We decide that now is the time to strike, when excitement is high in the Negro community. After all, we have been given today a lot of free publicity! We will hold Sunday's meeting at First A. M. E. Zion Church, our first move away from Mt. Olive. This is part of our effort to make this a community-wide crusade.

Leflore reported that he went to University Hospital today—his deadline for action on desegregating its lunchroom—with a group of sit-inners he had recruited himself. The superintendent dickered with him for more time. Jack agreed to a week on condition the signs on the rest rooms, "Colored Men" and "Colored Women," be removed immediately. They were.

Mrs. Harshaw told us that while she was sitting at the Todd & Armistead counter today someone who apparently was not an employee sprayed a yellow substance on her. She went immediately to a doctor. So vividly did she conceive her fear that she could already feel the acid eating away her flesh. "Doctor, are you sure you don't see any blotches appearing on my skin? I'm certain that my arm is beginning to feel numb!" The doctor assured her that he saw nothing, advised her to go home and forget it. Most of the fears of the community connected with this transition to a different social pattern are just as self-generated.

The committee made the decision that only persons of high school age and above will be allowed to participate in sit-ins from now on.

The meeting over, I had a chance to read the salt shaker story, which also rated front page coverage. I was dismayed that the article highlighted a statement by the woman who was struck that the shaker came from the direction of a row of booths in which Negroes were sitting. My statement about what I had actually seen was reported only near the end of the article. That a man was taken into custody was not reported. The story leaves the impression that Negroes were responsible for the violence.

At 7:20 P.M. I picked up Anders and Inger Iversen, the Danish couple who are to be my guests for the next two days, at the

Greyhound station. They have come at an opportune time and to an opportune place to find out some things about American life that most foreign tourists miss.

After dinner I called one of the city editors of the *News-Sentinel* to protest the manner in which the salt shaker incident was presented. He was very easy to talk with, assured me of his personal interest in our cause, and explained that the pressure of having to meet a deadline was the principal reason for the story being as it was. From him I learned that the man was arrested, that he is a local man twenty-two years of age, and that he will answer in court to disorderly conduct charges next Wednesday. He confessed, but charged that one of the Negro boys had been throwing things in the store first. This I greatly doubt, because Logan and I, who were facing in opposite directions in the middle of the eating area, had the store well "covered" between us. Our group remained well disciplined throughout all the excitement.

Thursday, June 30

TODAY was the first day since the sit-ins began that I did not devote a large part of my day to the cause in some form. Today Jim and I decided we were due a respite, so the Reeses and I took our Danish friends to the mountains for an American-style picnic. I'm sure there are people who could take this fever excitement day in and day out and thrive on it, but I become too tense, get nervous indigestion, lose my appetite. My belt wraps around a lot farther than it did three weeks ago. I am unable to continue routine work; like a malignant infection, thoughts and plans for the crusade reach out to consume the normal tissue of my life until every cell is inflamed.

I seized the paper as soon as we got back to the apartment to find out what had happened today. There was a small article reporting that four Negro men picketed outside the Todd & Armistead store and that one elderly picket was knocked down. Apparently there were no arrests. Another item, ostensibly having nothing to do with the sit-ins, caught my attention: "The congregation of Euclid Avenue Baptist Church at a called business session last night voted 126 to 89 to 'vacate the pulpit.' The ... pastor is expected to leave within thirty days." He had been pastor of this 960-member white congregation located in a racially mixed neighborhood for only sixteen months. This is the minister who six days ago declared in our Ministerial Association meeting, "If the ministers had been preaching the truth all along, their people now would *know* what is right!" The paper gives no specific reason for the dismissal. Perhaps the congregation understood "the truth" differently from the way the preacher did. Perhaps he did not have enough time. Was he wrong about the reasonableness of congregations? Had he made the misjudgment of Socrates in assuming that to know the truth is to act upon it?

While we were preparing dinner, a long distance call came through from my mother in Iowa. A neighbor had read in the *Chicago American* that I was "attacked and beaten by a mob." (How determinative can be one's choice of words!) Mother called person to person, supposing that I would be in the hospital. She wants me not to participate in any more sit-ins, but of course I told her that as a grown man I will have to make my own decisions according to what I think is right.

From private sources I have learned that an instructor from the University was struck in the head at Kress's today so severely as to require medical attention. The victim is Dan Morgan, an economics instructor, whom I have not met and have not even heard of until today. The blow, which came from behind, struck just behind the ear in such a way that it seemed to impair the hearing. Morgan in the best non-violent tradition refused to turn around, so consequently never knew what his assailant looked like. It is encouraging to us to discover that there are persons who haven't even been a part of our group who care this much.

Today also another white minister participated in a sit-in. He is Dr. Glen Otis Martin, who until recently was Director of the Wesley Foundation at the University and now is a staff representative for the Methodist Board of Education. Our record remains clean, however, for not being able to attract any white minister of orthodox persuasion who has a congregation.

At Grant's today the gang of rowdies pulled two Negro boys off their stools onto the floor. The boys picked themselves up and calmly sat down again. McArthur is sure the toughs would have attacked him too had he not had in his hands a clipboard which could have served as a defensive weapon.

Friday, July 1

SINCE the Iversens were interested in the sit-ins, I took them this morning to the ten o'clock meeting. Bob West was not with us today, and will not be again, since he is leaving tomorrow to enroll in a summer course at his seminary. Our movement has survived by drawing into itself whoever was available at a given time. There were a number of Negro men with us this morning for the first time. They were businessmen and teachers, called out to help patrol the stores, now that the situation is becoming so tense, with violence flaring almost daily. A definite decision was made yesterday to let the public school teachers participate in the sit-ins. If University of Tennessee professors are risking their jobs, our group reasoned, should we not allow Negro teachers to do as much?

We have two concerns—the white gangs who are out to "get" the demonstrators, particularly the white demonstrators, and the Negro gangs who are out to "get" the white gangs. Strangely enough, in this struggle for human rights for Negroes, whites remain at the vortex of violence.

We have become increasingly troubled by Negro youths who, declaring that they will not be bound by a doctrine of non-violence, make unauthorized sorties into the downtown area when the sit-ins are in progress. A few of them are fellows who have earlier participated in legitimate sit-ins; the rest are kids who, with or without sit-ins, would find some trouble to get into. Yesterday word was passed along to our leaders that such a gang was forming to go to town. Rev. James, who returned yesterday, was asked to find them and reason with them and apparently convinced them temporarily that they would be doing us more harm than good.

At least two of the Negro men will be stationed at each store while a sit-in is in progress. The teachers will have charge of Cole's and Walgreen's, the businessmen will handle whatever is done at Todd & Armistead, and the ministers will look after the other stores. Their twin assignment is to be alert to call the police when any situation develops like the one in Walgreen's on Wednesday (for any movement on the part of the actual demonstrators there might have triggered further violence) and to prevent the wildcat Negro groups from causing trouble. I wonder if there has been another city in which sit-ins have been such a community-wide enterprise as here in Knoxville? When Dr. Crutcher told the youngsters who came yesterday of the Committee's decision that demonstrators had to be at least of high school age, their feelings were hurt. One little girl said as she was leaving, "I thought that's what we were fighting against—discrimination!"

I felt Grant's would be safest for the Iversens. They went in first so they would not be seen with me. They observed for about twenty minutes while sipping drinks, then told me good-by and left for the bus station. First a nuclear physicist from Princeton and now a couple from Denmark—these symbolize the international significance of what is going on here, a significance unrecognized by most of our own citizens.

Miss Boykin, an attractive Negro girl with light complexion and auburn hair, was our leader. When an exchange of personnel found me sitting next to her, I quietly moved one seat away, explaining to her that I saw no need of antagonizing our enemies unnecessarily. I recall that I came close to sitting down in a booth with a Negro woman at Walgreen's Wednesday before I remembered the mores; my sitting with a Negro man certainly proved antagonizing enough!

Miss Boykin's principal problem as leader was a group of four Negro boys who kept roving through the store. She told me they said they had come "to protect our sisters." Translated, that means, I think, "to have some excitement." The boys purport to be looking for the gangs of white boys. They should not be difficult to find. This causes me to wonder if they *really* want to find them. Miss Boykin says the Negro boys know some of the white boys because they played together when they were younger. There are neighborhoods in Knoxville where Negro and white kids play together as a matter of course. I have heard Dr. Crutcher tell of conversing once with a downtown businessman who expressed hostility toward any form of integration. Then as he was driving home, Crutcher saw the same man's two teen-age sons playing ball with a bunch of Negro and white boys who had chosen up sides at a neighborhood playground.

Once during our sitting we heard a police siren screaming down Gay Street. Momentarily, I grew pale inside. I can sympathize now with the way Anne Frank felt whenever she heard the ominous quacking of the Nazi police cars from her garret hiding place.

A young woman who works in another Gay Street store took a seat beside me and ordered a salad. After a bit she asked, "You're not eating?"

"I haven't been given a chance to eat," I explained. "You see, I have been to Grant's so many times with demonstrators that they treat me just as they do the others. Come to think of it, I have never been asked in Grant's if I wanted to order. Today I think

I really might have if I had had an opportunity." The girl clammed up.

At the ministers' meeting the other day some of the men were puzzled about how a white person could make an effective sit-inner. "Don't worry about that," I said—"within the first hour you'll have an honorary membership in the Negro race conferred upon you!" I was thinking of the epithet that would be used by hecklers, but it is just as true of the recognition that is accorded by employees.

I was curious to know whether a white identified as a demonstrator would be served if he asked to be, but though it sounds like an easy thing to do, I could not get up the nerve to ask. Later I suggested it to another white demonstrator. "Let's find out whether the policy is not to serve Negroes, or not to serve people with certain ideas," I proposed. As bad as racial discrimination is, the other kind is more to be feared. He was served.

Crutcher came by at this time to inform us that the city safety director has requested that we limit the number of Negro demonstrators in each store to six in order to avoid public agitation. Apparently he is borrowing a trick from Chattanooga, where this was done on a judge's order. This will change our operation significantly. I am not yet able to envision all its consequences. Miss Boykin immediately thinned out our little patch.

The evening paper carries on the front page a story that eleven Negro boys were arrested today and booked on charges of disorderly conduct and inciting to riot. The latter is a state charge. The boys are accused of roaming the downtown area in a gang, shoving people off the sidewalk, and refusing to disperse when ordered to do so by police. My first feeling was one of relief—"Maybe this will solve our problem!" But these are serious charges! It would seem there has been some partiality here, since white gangs have been roving the downtown area for weeks and the police have told us they could do nothing unless violence occurred. There have even been several acts of unpunished violence. The arrests may put the Associated Council in a difficult position. Even though the law director and the *News-Sentinel* carefully pointed out that these youths had nothing to do with the sit-ins, will we not have to come to their defense? Will these serious charges be used as a weapon over the heads of the entire Negro community?

Others besides the sit-inners have been active today distributing through the Negro residential areas thousands of leaflets announcing the "Stay Away from Downtown" movement. It is to begin July 5 and continue "until conditions improve for all." The leaflet exhorts, "Save Money! Stay Away from Downtown!"

The *News-Sentinel* finally broke its editorial silence on the sit-ins this afternoon. Of course the paper took a position against us —it is almost inevitable that a newspaper will side with the business community—but what discouraged me was the superficiality of the editor's thinking. It was based on an analogy between a place of business and a private home. "A store operator has a clear right to determine who his customers shall be, just as does a householder have the right to determine who shall enter his home." The falsity of the analogy is so glaring that I decided it must be challenged, so I spent the evening composing a letter to the editor and took it immediately down to the post office.

I have been reflecting about why most of the hostility is vented against the whites. The most obvious explanation is that, while the white segregationist can partially understand the Negro's trying to get something for himself, he looks upon us as turncoats and traitors to the race. But another theory strikes me as possible. It is suggested to me by the way the white gangs have shied away when even one or two Negro men were present. Could it be that in attacking the whites they see a "safe" way to express a deep hostility toward the Negroes? This would assume that there is a subconscious fear of race conflict instilled into both whites and Negroes by the culture of the South which prevents them from taking the fatal step that might bring the whole culture tumbling down on their heads. After hearing of Knoxville's race riot of 1919 when the National Guard sprayed the area of Vine and Central with machine gun bullets, I can understand how such a fear would exist. The fact that white and Negro mobs have battled one another in other cities may only show that tension had grown in those places to the point where the subconscious fear was trampled by stronger conscious emotions.

Ralph Ross thinks the first theory is correct. Ralph, who is one of my favorite pre-theologs, is working as a porter at the Trailways station this summer. Occasionally when I go downtown to mail a letter in the late evening I pick him up as he comes off work at eleven and am rewarded with a commentary on life from Ralph's unique point of view. A tall, lithe boy, Ralph carries himself with the dignity of a warrior and speaks with the fearlessness of a chieftain. In his face, the high cheek bones of the American Indian vie with the complexion of central Africa for the honor of having produced this exceptional individual. Jeremiah, Jesus, and Paul deserve as much credit. On a campus where students excuse one another rather too easily for lapses in morality, Ralph's name is synonymous with character. Furthermore, although he plays tackle on the varsity team ("I'm the religious athlete," was the candid way he introduced himself to me), Ralph is a practicing pacifist.

Knowing these things about Ralph enabled me to evaluate the story he told me. On Tuesday, Ralph joined the sit-in at Cole's. When the group was about ready to leave, Harry Wiersema, Jr., said he was going to call his father to come after him. As he moved toward the telephone, a white youth with a duck-tail who had been standing around intercepted him and without saying a word struck Harry hard on the jaw with his fist. Jolted, Harry doubled up and turned partially away. The assailant struck him again in the belly. Harry turned his back and his attacker hit him a third time, in the kidney region. By this time Harry had regained his composure and simply turned and faced the boy quietly with folded arms. I can picture Harry standing there—tall, well-built, blond, guileless—in every outward aspect the all-American boy. But here was the all-American boy in a role history has never cast him in before! The attacker was confused and frightened by this unexpected response. Ralph says the hoodlum stood there helplessly, as though questioning within himself, "What am I doing hitting this fellow?" The police were called, but Harry refused to prefer charges.

Ralph spoke as though he had seen Jesus himself: "I said to myself, 'This white boy doesn't have to do this for us. He could go into a drug store anytime and get anything he wanted at the counter.' We've talked a lot about Christian love in class. Now I know what it is; I've seen it."

Ralph didn't know Harry's name. He had never seen him before, and I doubt that their paths will ever cross again. But in their brief contact one transmitted a spark of divine understanding that may through the other reach countless lives. I am reminded of James Russell Lowell's words, "Once to every man and nation. . . ."

Harry's mother had worried that he might not have the self-discipline to refrain from striking back. She need worry no longer; Harry has won his wings.

Saturday, July 2

IT has been almost two weeks now since the Sears' manager closed his counter with the opinion, "This will all have blown over in two weeks time!" Perhaps now that he has discovered how much he misjudged us, he will be willing to work out with us some kind of gradual desegregation plan. After all, Sears' store is ten blocks from the central business district. If it would move in our direction now, it would profit considerably while the "Stay Away from

Downtown" movement is on. On the basis of this kind of thinking, Harvey attempted some negotiating there today. He discovered that our persistence has caused only one new thought at Sears'—that it will not be "safe" to reopen the counter on Tuesday.

Men have gone to Rich's Laurel Room at least twice this week and on one occasion talked to one of the executives. We have heard a rumor that Rich's Atlanta office has given leave for the decision about their basement counter to be made locally "depending on how many calls you get." This may be no more reliable than the other rumors the mill is turning out.

I spent some time today revising the sit-in rules, since we have decided to mimeograph them for distribution to all demonstrators. Our thinking has changed to such an extent that we now feel that a misstep by a demonstrator is much more to be feared than that our rules might fall into the hands of the enemy. Some new rules grow out of our continuing experiences. Several have to do with demeanor at the counter:

"Demostrators must face the counter at all times. Reading is permissible, but sit-inner should look up when waitress is near, as though to say, 'I am ready to order now.' Use care in selection of reading matter" (Harry Wiersema, Jr., says he noticed *Teen-Age Confessions* in the hands of a few demonstrators).

"Demonstrators must not eat or drink at the counter unless the food or drink is served them by employees of that establishment. If a sympathizer places food in front of you which he has ordered, thank him, explain your rule, ask him to remove it, but if he does not, gently push it to one side and to rear of counter." We hoped by this rule to avoid "accidental" spillings.

"Do not hide your face with your hands" (a temptation after you've been sitting in one place for two hours).

"If you chew gum, do it so people hardly notice it."

One very practical rule for hot weather reads, "Demonstrators should always be neatly dressed in clean clothing, and should be careful to avoid 'B.O.'"

While riding over with McArthur to the 6:00 P.M. meeting of the Executive Committee, I unrolled the evening paper and discovered a second editorial on the sit-in situation, which I read aloud as we traveled. It is surprisingly different in tone from the editorial of last night. Entitled "Why Not Start Over Again?" this piece concedes that the Negroes have a point, contends that it cannot be secured by "elbowing and squatting," and calls upon their white friends to "start all over again in an effort to resolve the situation." What influences may be responsible for this change in tone?

Rev. James was in the presiding chair again after his lengthy absence. It may be rather difficult for us to get used to looking to James as leader again after Crutcher has acted in that capacity for three vital weeks, but it must be even more difficult for the two of them to make the adjustment.

Crutcher answered anxious questions with an opinion that the matter of the boys' arrest is not serious. Although the charges are grave, the police have virtually assured that probation can be worked out. Rev. James and Father Jones bailed the boys out on their personal responsibility. James explained his position: "Strictly speaking, it was not the responsibility of our organization, but in a larger sense we have to share responsibility for everything that grows out of the sit-in movement on our side. If we had not bailed them out, our cause would have got some bad publicity in the Negro community because parents would have said, 'You got our youngsters into this, and now you won't help them out when they get into trouble.'" Fortunately the boys were not carrying weapons. (One of the demonstrators at Cole's Tuesday showed Ralph Ross a knife concealed in his sock. "If only one person jumps me, I won't use it, but if a gang attacks, I'll cut me at least one of them!" the boy promised. This is a new definition of non-violence!

I am still extremely apprehensive about what might be done to the cause by some "friend" like this.)

This meeting brought a sharp difference of opinion. It erupted first over this question: Should we agree to the safety director's request that we limit Negro sit-inners to six per store? Jack Leflore, the salesman, was strongly opposed to our making such a concession; he feels that we should go in force when we go, even if we are only able to make one store a day. Still at issue is the objective of a sit-in—is it to close off business? Leflore is in favor of filling every stool. Others are more moderate in their views. McArthur is concerned about protection; he thinks six would be at the mercy of the mob. Others feel this would make no difference, since the mob knows that we are committed to non-violence in any case. Someone points out that the violence has gathered around the white demonstrators, and the safety director has placed no limit on them. Harvey thinks we should bargain for more personnel at the larger counters, for some have as many as seventy-five seats; I share this view. Dr. Colston, president of the college, who is present at our Executive Committee meeting for the first time since the sit-ins commenced, surprisingly gives the opinion that when we demonstrate we should do so forcefully, but wonders if we may have arrived at a time for negotiation; it is logical, he thinks, that demonstration and negotiation should take place in alternation until an agreement is reached. Colston's suggestion is based on information we have not had until now—an official of the Chamber of Commerce has passed the word along to Colston that he is attempting to get the merchants together Tuesday.

The circuitous means of communicating with one another has lent a comic-opera aspect to the way this major community problem has been handled. It would seem sensible for one of the merchants to have called Crutcher or James and said, "Come on down and *let's talk!*" Instead the merchants hint to the Chamber of Commerce official that they might be willing; he contacts not Crutcher or James, but Colston—the one person in the Negro community who has greatest status (the school principal, as it were)—and he in turn makes the contact within the Negro community. The respect accorded to the one individual represents a sort of equality conferred upon the race in the person of its representative, who for this purpose embodies the race much as Adam does mankind!

(This traditional pattern has had its influence on the way negotiations have proceeded here, but it must be admitted that in our particular situation a more determinative factor has been the interest of the merchants not to get into a position where effective pressure could be brought to bear upon them. So long as no Negro is able to confront all of them at once, each can continue to throw the responsibility on another for not being willing to "go along." And now there is tactical reason for not appearing too eager.)

A daring strategy occurs to me: Supposing we were to call the *News-Sentinel* and announce that we are "responding to their editorial of tonight" by calling off demonstrations all next week in order to give the merchants a chance to work out a plan for desegregation? This appeals to me as a way of gaining the goodwill of the public, which is beginning to turn against us now that the demonstrations are drawing violence which has thrown the downtown area into a state of insecurity. It might bring moral pressure to bear upon the merchants. The suggestion is batted around for awhile, but declined because we fear that without the continual threat of demonstrations the merchants will simply procrastinate. It is better not to reveal our cards, better to keep our adversary apprehensive about our next move. Besides, Crutcher fears that any public announcement to this effect would undercut the mass meeting and make it difficult to get workers out next week. He is convinced the steam must not be allowed to escape from the boilers. In fact, Crutcher personally is against any moratorium on demonstrations until we know for a fact that the merchants are ready to "talk turkey." The fact that James has returned to the leadership of the organization is perhaps decisive at this point, because Crutcher stands against the group. One can understand that he has invested so much in the strategy of demonstration that it is difficult for him now to change stride. But we must remember that sit-ins are not an end in themselves; they are only one technique by which we work toward a larger goal.

Our decision is to extend the Fourth of July holiday by not demonstrating on Tuesday, the fifth, or on Wednesday; this will be "leaked" to the merchants. Then if no decisive action has come from the merchants, a committee will go to the safety director Wednesday afternoon, tell him that we are going to demonstrate en masse on Thursday, and in the light of the fact that we have completely suspended demonstrations for a five-day period, ask his cooperation. This seems to kill two birds: the question of a moratorium on sit-ins and the question of the number of demonstrators. It will have the additional advantage of puncturing the expanding tension downtown to let off some of the pressure.

Although the meeting has gone on too long, I feel impelled to bring up one other concern which I am perhaps in a better position to feel than some of the others: our critical need to interpret our cause to the white community. The editorials show the utter lack of understanding of our position by intelligent whites. There is a general misapprehension that sit-inners forcefully take over another person's property. I tell everyone I can privately that we have never refused to leave when a manager firmly requested it. Most people are astonished to learn that very seldom has a manager asked us to leave. We cannot say this in public, for then the managers might begin to force the issue. But we can explain that a sit-in simply consists of going to a counter for the purpose of getting food service and waiting there for the waitress to take one's order. And we can explain why we think we have a right to expect such service. The group decides to meet this challenge with a large-size newspaper ad and appoints to draft it a committee consisting of Pete Bradby (the Knoxville College public relations director), myself, and Robert Weeks, a white physicist at Oak Ridge who lives in Knoxville.

Personal concerns seem to get pushed later and later into the evening. At 11:30 tonight I took my clothes to a new laundromat over near the University which I had thought might be the solution to my laundry problem. I didn't even get out of the car, for in big letters on the window was the notice: "For White Patrons Only." I tried another out beyond the college, feeling it was so surrounded by Negro residents that it could hardly subsist without their patronage, but there too was the offensive sign. Were the signs up before the sit-ins, or are they evidence of a growing apprehension that Negroes may not continue to respect the invisible walls of custom? I came back to our colored business district where there is a laundromat which I don't much like because the washing cycle is too short, and there I sat in the open doorway while the Saturday night life of black Mechanicsville paraded before me. I felt a bit strange, perhaps, but at least I knew that both my friends and I were welcome there. I do not make a fetish of boycotting discriminatory businesses. I attend perhaps two movies a year, generally when some white friend is visiting, and go to one of the restaurants when there is occasion. If I simply refused these privileges, I am not sure my position would be understood by my Negro friends, who are struggling to attain the same privileges. But I just do not receive much joy from going places where my friends are not welcome. And when those places become so vulgar as to post their prejudices on signs, I will not patronize them at all.

Sunday, July 3

AT our campus church this morning, "Stay Away from Downtown" leaflets were passed out with the Communion bulletins, a strange juxtaposition but one that illustrates better than words could explain that for the Negro American to live and to pray is to fight for equality. Many people who had read or heard of my being struck on Wednesday had words of encouragement. Mrs. Rakestraw, a gracious elderly friend, grabbed me with a burst of emotion and gave me a kiss on the cheek. "I always did love you, and now I love you more than ever!" she said. I felt humble and deeply grateful. Harvey had a comment that was less encouraging: "Well, have you got your speech prepared?" He had heard I was to be one of the speakers at the mass meeting in the afternoon. Although it was the first I had heard of it, I did not doubt that it was true. The casualness of our organizational planning to some degree simply reflects the lower degree of intensity in Negro culture as compared to Anglo-Saxon culture.

(I use the term "Negro culture" with considerable reservation, recognizing that the culture of Negro Americans is by and large simply the culture of America, learned from and shared with white Americans. But there are some prevailing differences of temperament and of values which make life among Negroes continually interesting to one who comes from outside. It is with these differences that Negroes as a group enrich the cultural pattern of our nation. At the very points where the prevailing culture of America is dullest and weakest the contribution of Negroes is most striking: they help to compensate for our prevailing Anglo-Saxon depreciation of emotion and beauty; our reticence they make up for by their genuine appreciation of personality; our puritanism they correct with their frank enjoyment of life; and yet they compensate for our materialism with their almost innate feel for the spiritual. Like any generalization, this will not necessarily hold true for individuals, but as a generalization it contains truth.)

Having been duly forewarned, I tried to collect some thoughts as I dashed through an afternoon full of errands. We arrived ten minutes late for the mass meeting to find seats scarce in the 1100-seat auditorium that belonged to a white congregation as recently as four years ago. It is now the First A. M. E. Zion Church, ruled over by Rev. J. A. Babington-Johnson, a giant of a black man from the African Gold Coast whose clipped speech no less than his hyphenated name betrays his British background. I tried to jot down some notes as the others spoke. First, W. T. Crutcher. Today his slow, quiet manner was gone, and he was the fiery Baptist preacher, preaching for conviction, only today it was not individual souls he was trying to save, but a whole society: "We're for states rights, and against states wrongs!" was his theme, and each time he mentioned it, he got a rousing "Amen," or "You tell 'em, Reverend!" "We want our rights, and we want them NOW!" he roared. Much as I respect Crutcher, I couldn't help worrying a little about the effect of his speech on the less stable members of the audience. And yet there is a lot of inertia to overcome among his own people. Crutcher has often been criticized for being too easy a mark for the whites; today was his opportunity to get rid of that burden.

After Crutcher came Harry Wiersema, Jr. In introducing Harry, Rev. James related a remark that Harry had made to him this week: "I don't care so much about dying for my country—that's land; but for this cause I am ready to die, if my dying would cause people to see what is right and change things so everyone would be free." Maybe James had touched it up a bit, but nevertheless it touched me; I'm beginning myself to think of Harry as a saint with a slide rule. Harry spoke simply, without affectation, of his participation in the sit-ins. "When I go home after a demonstration, I feel *good* inside, better than I've ever felt before."

Then Father Jones, the Episcopal priest, made a few remarks intended as a tribute to Crutcher. "When I came to Knoxville several years ago, I looked to find who the leaders of the Negro community were. It did not take me long to discover that the one who stood out above the pack was W. T. Crutcher. Many people criticized Dr. Crutcher—they said he was too much of a pushover for the white city slickers, that he believed everything they told him. There were times when I felt this might be true. But now I know these charges were not true. In this struggle for equal rights W. T. Crutcher has proved himself a real fighter, a man who has the interests of all of us at heart. Here is a man who will *not* let the city slickers put anything over on him!"

In his almost childlike frankness Father Jones had perhaps expressed more than he had intended to say about the personal jealousies and suspicions which tend to vitiate the potential strength of Negro urban communities.

Then my turn came. I told of seeing flags around Rich's as I came through town on that holiday weekend. I would be more impressed with their patriotism, I said, if they practiced the *creed* of the Declaration of Independence, "All men are created equal." The department stores have closed their counters. This means one of two things—either, "We would rather close than serve Negroes," or "Let the others take the risk; we'll come along and make the profits." In either case, the motive is not very noble. In view of the attitude of these stores, I went on, I expect to see no faces of darker hue in those stores or anywhere on downtown streets for some time to come. I urged the people not to act from a spirit of retaliation: "Repay no man evil for evil, but repay evil with good." But it is not morally right for us to support injustice with our dollars! I went on to explain in terms much like those I had used with Byrl Logan why I, a white, sit-in: because I cannot let my Negro friends think that this is a racial fight. "If we whites can siphon off some of the hostility coming from the community, I am glad, for this helps to keep it from *becoming* a racial fight." Finally I asked the crowd to help us in our efforts to interpret our cause to whites. I was thinking about those who work for whites, or with them. "When they ask you what you think about the sit-ins, don't tell them what you think they want to hear! Tell them the truth! After all, this is not 1860, it's 1960! This is not

Mississippi, it's Knoxville, Tennessee!" Pete Bradby said I got as excited as Crutcher and was waving my arms like a rabble-rouser.

Again Crutcher spoke, this time to back up the "Stay Away from Downtown" movement. He told of standing on a street corner in downtown Nashville, observing the progress of their "Stay Away" campaign when a hotel bellboy came up, looked him over, and said ominously, "Mister, you're not from here, are you?" Crutcher implied that any Knoxville Negro who is seen downtown will be embarrassed and may find his friends behaving coolly toward him. He held up the leaflet and asked, "What does this handbill say?" The audience obliged with, "Stay Away from Downtown!" although on the whole it was an audience too sophisticated to bring the roof down.

After the passion of the various addresses, James, as chairman, came back to the mike and said in his droll way, "We're making a lot of noise, but that doesn't mean we're angry at anybody. If you have no love in your heart, stay at home. Why, even Jack Leflore's got it now, a little bit!" The ribbing that goes on between preacher and layman furnishes us a relief from our tension.

After the meeting I worked with Bradby until after 11:00 P.M. getting information from his notes on the negotiations which will go into the chronology we hope will be made public in time to help our cause.

Monday, July 4

A YEAR ago today my nephew Bill and I took a cable car up one of the German Alps and later celebrated Independence Day by begging our way into a cowboy movie at the U.S. Army Rest and Recreation Center in beautiful Garmisch. This Fourth of July has been much less spectacular. I sat all day at my typewriter working on the chronology. But in all honesty, I believe this summer has been as interesting as last summer's tour of Europe, and I believe I am growing just as much from its experiences.

Since the news media barely mentioned the fact that the Mayor's Committee existed and that negotiations were in progress from March 1 almost through the month of May, there are many, perhaps the vast majority of Knoxville citizens, who suppose that Negroes and a group of white radicals leaped into these demonstrations without any attempt to work out the problem with milder methods. We feel that, if somehow we can get this chronology before the public, the contrast between the long-suffering of the Negro group and the procrastination of the merchants will win us many supporters.

People will see, for instance, that Knoxville College students planned a sit-in as far back as February 17, but were persuaded by President Colston to negotiate instead. That on March 7, while students in many other Southern communities were staging full-fledged sit-ins, our students contented themselves with a pitiful "file-through," in which all they did was walk past the counters looking hungry. (But even this caused some citizens to register shock at the students' "bad faith.") That Negro leaders agreed as early as March 21 to a plan of controlled seating by a hostess at each counter.

The chronology will reveal that on March 23 agreement seemed so near that President Colston actually announced to the student body that they would be able to eat at the counters the following week and that students were preparing to go throughout the Negro community with a program of education to make the desegregation work smoothly when they learned that the step had been rejected by the home offices of some of the chain stores. It will show that the Mayor's Committee secured endorsement for a desegregation plan by the boards of five of the most important organizations in Knoxville—the Chamber of Commerce, the Downtown Knoxville Improvement Association, the Association of Women's Clubs, the Central Labor Council, and the Ministerial

Association—but that, despite the most diligent effort of the Mayor's Committee, two locally owned downtown drugstores adamantly refused to cooperate with the others in opening their counters to everyone, even though their participation would undoubtedly have broken the log-jam. It will show that the students pressed adult Negro leaders on April 6 to join them in a withdrawal of trade from merchants who discriminate but that the students were again persuaded to keep working through the Mayor's Committee.

The chronology will attempt to acquaint local people with one of the most astonishing developments which has occurred in any Southern community in connection with the lunch counter movement—that on May 6, at the suggestion of Mayor Duncan and at city expense, the mayor, two Chamber of Commerce officials and two Knoxville College students flew to New York to confer with executives of the four dime store chains to influence them to allow their local outlets to desegregate even without the participation of the local drug stores. And furthermore, that these executives refused to see the Knoxville College students! (They explained that, if they admitted students from one school, delegations would be coming from every campus. Personally, I should think they would be quite safe to agree to see any students who came with their mayor at city expense! It would seem to me they should have embraced this delegation with open arms: in the midst of all the trouble they were having throughout the South, here was one Southern community which had come to say, "We are ready to desegregate; we can't take you off the hook in Atlanta and Greensboro, but we *can* solve your problem for you in Knoxville.")

About noon the phone rang, and when I answered it, the other party hung up without a word. Others whose names have been in the paper have been getting nuisance calls. I decided to take the fun out of it for this fellow immediately. When he rang again—which I knew he would as soon as I put down the receiver—I simply let the phone ring—thirty or more times before it stopped. This picador type of annoyance continued for about an hour. Apparently someone found it more fun than shooting firecrackers.

The chronology will reveal one point that looks bad for our side—namely that the students stubbornly persisted in conducting sit-ins on May 13 even though the Mayor had passed word to them that the merchants were planning to meet that afternoon and that he believed "things were nearly worked out." (The students said they didn't believe the merchants anymore and thought this was a ruse to keep them from sitting-in. Subsequent events proved the students in the wrong, but also indicated that the mayor's optimism was not justified at that time.)

The chronology will try to clarify that confused period beginning May 18 which led to a breakdown of negotiations and the demise of the Mayor's Committee. The merchants asked for a ten-day "cooling off period"; members of the Mayor's Committee understood that the merchants were promising at the end of that time to put into effect a plan of gradual desegregation. When no such step was forthcoming at the end of the ten-day period, both students and adult Negro leaders felt they had been betrayed. Meantime, the merchants had replied that they were misunderstood—they had promised only to *consider* desegregating. But by this time the Mayor's Committee had disbanded, thinking a solution had been reached, and the merchants' further statement never reached those who had the greatest stake in the outcome. It would have made little difference anyway, since the result in any case was negative. The chronology finally will show that all of these involved dealings had succeeded in taking up the entire spring semester so that the Knoxville College students were removed from the picture and that adult leaders waited an additional ten days and then tested the practice at the counters before commencing any demonstrations.

Surely when all this is known, I thought as I added the finishing touches to the document, no one can say our side has acted hastily or without regard for the peace of the community. Officials of the Knoxville Area Human Relations Council have agreed to have this chronology multigraphed and distributed widely.

Tuesday, July 5

AT the ten o'clock meeting the chairman turned part of the hour over to me for instruction in sit-in procedures. I hardly remember how it was that this job fell to me; I certainly have had no training in it myself. But starting with the idea and spirit of non-violence, which we have imbibed from hearing about the movement elsewhere, we can pretty well figure out from our own experience here what is necessary to make that spirit effective. This morning we set up the piano and organ benches as stools in front of a counter made of pulpit chairs, and right there in the sanctuary of the church we conducted a mock demonstration. Four boys volunteered to be called "nigger," to be pushed, struck, and pulled from their seats. It was easy to do in fun. I told them there were only four types of abuse I knew of that could happen to them: insults, having something thrown at or poured on them, blows, or being pulled from the stool. Any one of these things can be endured by a person who makes up his mind to it in advance.

Not until this moment did Crutcher reveal to the group that there would be no sit-in today. Instead, he explained, for today we will use a different technique. We will invest everything we have in the "Stay Away from Downtown" movement. So the workers were organized into groups to go into the colored residential areas in all parts of the city to tell people about the "Stay Away" campaign. They were provided with mimeographed sheets reading, "To stay away from Downtown is your protest against segregation . . . against injustice." The group scattered to hand these out at bus stops and deliver them door to door. I did not feel a white would be very effective in saying, "*We're* not going to town," so I went home to spend the afternoon writing a draft for the big newspaper ad. As we prepared this, Bradby and I had in our minds the example of the "Appeal for Human Rights" published by the Atlanta students. We borrowed their title outright and listed the grievances which apply to our own situation in Knoxville.

About 5:30 Dr. Colston, my "boss," called and congratulated me glowingly for the letter to the editor which he said was printed in tonight's paper. He asked if I knew anything about a wildcat sit-in today. The report had reached him that some Negro kids sat in on their own initiative and had eggs thrown at them. I agonize over this type of thing; can't they realize that they endanger the whole project? No, of course, they are just kids and should not be expected to be able to reason the matter through like adults. On the other hand, it is difficult to prevent their going. Some people seem to think that the Negro leaders, the "contact" persons, should be able to crack a whip and get every Negro to obey. These people have an exaggerated idea of the unity of the Negro community, probably because in their own subconscious minds they apply one stereotype to every Negro. These are the people who say, "Negroes are musical"—"Negroes are born athletes"— "Negroes are less intelligent than whites"—"Negroes are good-natured"—"Negroes have body odor." The only cure for this kind of delusion is to get to know a number of Negroes well. The first one you make friends with you may find to be like my friend Jim, who sings lustily, but makes a few tones do for every pitch. After that, the preconceptions begin to topple pretty rapidly. I have no quarrel with a generalization made on the basis of sufficient data, so long as it is made clear that it is a generalization and not an inclusive description.

The phone was keeping me busy. Each time I thought, "This will be the heckler again" (exactly the way he wanted me to react), but first it was Bradby, then Ward, calling to thank me for the letter to the editor. They are thrilled to see *their* side presented in rebuttal to the editorials of last week. It was the editor's comparison of the place of business to a private dwelling that I was challenging. This was a part of the answer I gave in the letter: "If you are going to compare it to a dwelling, then compare it to the man who invites—indeed, entices—guests into every room of his home except the dining room, but deems them unworthy to share his fellowship there. Add to this that the householder profits financially from their presence in his home, and then perhaps the analogy of a home would fit." I challenged the assumption that the merchant has an unlimited right to do as he pleases with his business. Supposing, I suggested, that the *News-Sentinel* should refuse to allow people who live in a certain section of the city to obtain copies of its paper. Or supposing the telephone company would refuse to grant service to Republicans. The community would not tolerate either situation; if moral pressure did not suffice, no doubt the discrimination would soon be held illegal. I am convinced that all racial discrimination by private businesses will ultimately be held to be illegal, either by means of new statutes, or by the courts through the extension of the principle of non-discrimination inherent in our Constitution. Ultimately our communities will determine that the freedom to be a whole personality is more to be valued than the freedom to discriminate. Here lies uncovered the moral flaw in every defense of discriminatory practices which is based on freedom or states' rights.

Two notes of encouragement that came today made the insults recede into insignificance. A lovely lady in our church wrote that she prays for me by name every day during the sit-ins. Then from Chicago came a note from Kenneth Howard, a handsome black 1959 graduate of whom I am especially fond. Kenneth said he had seen the name "Knoxville" in large headlines in the *Chicago Daily News* as he rode the bus to work and was sick at heart when he read about the attack on me. Kenneth is over-serious; I will have to write and cheer him up.

In any war there are the little incidents which the group seizes upon and fondles for morale-building purposes. Especially good for this purpose are instances of defection within enemy ranks. This morning at our meeting one of the women demonstrators gave us such a morale builder. She reported that a Negro friend of hers from Cleveland, Tennessee, who knew nothing of the struggle going on here, came to Knoxville to shop on the day of our picketing of Rich's. She had picked out a dress at Rich's when the white clerk got her to one side and asked, "Honey, do you really have to have this dress? Don't you see what your people are doing outside?" Embarrassed, the customer left the dress. Crutcher says that plans are being made to contact all the towns within a seventy-five-mile radius of Knoxville to inform Negroes of our "Stay Away" movement. This will cause the business community deep concern, so contrary is it to every effort of theirs.

Carroll Felton says one businessman who has no lunch counter called him this morning to ask if the innocent are to suffer with the guilty. Felton replied, "Yes, because you all meet together, and you are the ones who can apply effective pressure to the merchants who do have counters." While we were meeting this morning, the manager who has maintained contact with us reported to Crutcher that there was a lot of money lost in downtown Knoxville last week. That would be because of the "Trade with Your Friends" movement and the general unrest; today is the first business day that would be affected by the wholesale "Stay Away from Downtown" program.

Wednesday, July 6

As I write this, in early afternoon, the day is ominous; everything hangs in the balance. On one hand are the indications that the merchants may be beginning to stir. But on the other hand, we have heard that the police chief has put out orders that whenever more than two Negroes are seen together on the downtown streets, officers should stop them and, if not satisfied that their business is legitimate, arrest them. This sounds like decision time. If it is true, then the time has come to get arrested. I have been examining my own conscience: Am *I* ready to get arrested? Obviously it would work less hardship upon me than it would upon most of the others working in the movement, since I have no family and no work responsibilities during the summer. But am I willing to go all through life with a "record"? On the other hand, how could I get arrested, since the order is against Negroes? If I go with a group of Negroes, will the police arrest me with the others? If they should let me off because I am white, it would infuriate me!

But this is getting ahead of the story. I had the idea today of presenting the training session in the form of a sit-in in which everything is done wrong. The first step was to stop at the College Drug here near the campus and pick up a copy of *Jive* magazine with a near-naked woman on the cover. "Anything for the sit-ins won't cost a dime!" protested the owner. Strange what it takes to aid the sit-ins!

We have always closed our morning meetings with prayer. As a rule, those who pray ask for divine guidance and protection as we go forth into a situation which may bring violence and injury; for God's blessing upon the merchants, that they may be led to see their moral obligation to treat all men as children of God and brothers in Christ; and sometimes even for those in the gangs which collect to heckle us. But the past few mornings we have also begun our meetings with a brief devotional service conducted by one of the ministers. I am glad for this because it helps us to keep the religious motivation which is always in danger of being exchanged for the primitive desire simply to *get* something for ourselves, or—worse yet—the desire to retaliate.

A reporter and cameraman from WATE-TV showed up at the meeting. I assumed they were going to photograph our training session. I was alarmed, knowing it just would not give the right impression over TV if a white were seen leading the training session. A lot of people would be convinced that I had been sent down here from New York by some sinister organization "to stir up our Nigras." Hastily I got Felton to assent to handle the training session (for he has actually had far more experience than I). But what the cameraman wanted was some film of the group leaving the church, being handed "Stay Away from Downtown" leaflets to distribute. Although the shots will give a true picture of what we were doing today, the actual scene was posed. But surely no one will charge that WATE-TV *staged* a sit-in, as the Tennessee governor charged against CBS during the sit-ins in Nashville!

Rev. James asked me to read to the demonstrators the copy we have prepared for the newspaper ad, which lists the sixteen areas of community life in which Negroes are not allowed to participate on an equal basis with whites. It was embarrassing to have to remind Negro youth of the discrimination that is practiced against them. My embarrassment grew partly from shame for my share of the moral responsibility for this as a member of the white race. But aside from this, as an educator I think it is a much more wholesome approach to Negro young people to help them prepare for the rights they are going to have than to remind them of the ones they don't have. Their tendency to inferiority feelings is already great enough. The ad was prepared for whites to read.

To encourage the group, I told them about the University wife who had called me that morning to tell me that three prominent white women were going to make another approach to Miller's management. They will promise to use their influence to see that Miller's doesn't lose business if the firm desegregates its counter and perhaps delicately suggest that Miller's would get the business we normally would be taking to Rich's. The woman also told me that some of the male professors are conducting a telephone campaign to tell other University personnel about the trade withdrawal.

Since the TV men had left by this time, I proceeded with the sit-in training. Lorenzo and Mrs. Harshaw displayed considerable histrionic talent as "bad" sit-inners. Lorenzo chewed gum voraciously, leaning on his hands at the "counter." Mrs. Harshaw drooled a cigarette, talked with standees, spoke sarcastically to the waitress. Both of them got up from time to time to change places. Meanwhile playing a sympathizer, I put drinks in front of them, and Mrs. Davis as waitress went through the pantomime of throwing the contents on the demonstrators. Then we let the audience point out all the things that were wrong about this demonstration. It was just another way of reminding them of some of the things we don't do.

With the training session over, none of our leaders was in evidence to take charge of the meeting. Investigating, I found them in the church parlor with long faces. They had just received from a source they considered reliable the report about the police chief's new order against Negroes being downtown in groups. There seemed to be no explanation for this unexpected blow other than that the city administration had finally turned against us under pressure from the business community. It was at this moment that this present sense of crisis gripped us.

I taxied several workers to their zone in the east part of Knoxville, where they would distribute leaflets. One was the young man who ran seven blocks the other day to ask if he should give his name to an officer. His brother was buried yesterday, but the young man was right back with us today and brought another brother who had received time off from his job because of the family tragedy and decided to invest this one day in his people's struggle for freedom rather than in mourning for the dead. That kind of spirit can't be defeated!

Just a few minutes ago Harvey told me on the campus that Crutcher has called off the committee's visit with the city safety director this afternoon. We cannot understand this in view of the new police order.

In view of the above facts—which I jotted down this afternoon—we assembled for the six o'clock meeting of the Executive Committee in the spirit of convicted men presenting themselves for sentencing. But we were to be surprised. As to the police order, Crutcher had inquired directly of the safety director who told him that the order applies to white and Negro alike, and that it is not aimed at legitimate sit-in groups, but at the roving gangs of teen-agers whose presence downtown threatens the outbreak of rioting. This gave to the whole picture a different hue.

Dr. Crutcher then told us in confidence that he had that morning had a long conference with the editor of the paper. Crutcher had asked for it because of the unfavorable editorials that appeared last week. The editor's attitude during the first part of the conversation had been unfriendly to us. He had heard that demonstrators had been imported from New York together with a large amount of money to finance the movement, and that the group leaders were being paid $100 apiece! Apparently he half believed these fantastic stories.

"Are you really putting on a boycott?" he asked.

"No," replied Crutcher, "we're just staying away from town."

"You will put merchants out of business!"

Crutcher explained in his quiet way that we don't want to put anyone out of business, that we are just going to stay away from town until we get justice, and then we'll increase the business of the downtown merchants.

The editor expressed amazement after Crutcher had detailed for him the long history of negotiations which occurred before we finally decided to start demonstrations. He confessed that he had not kept well informed on events having to do with the counters. There was much irony in this, since the policy of the news media not to publicize the negotiations has resulted in not only the public but also the news people themselves being uninformed!

At the conclusion of the conversation, this fair man said, "I'm a Christian and I believe in the Golden Rule. I want you to know that I will work actively from now on to help bring about a just solution to this problem." This, coming from the man responsible for last week's editorials, almost renews my confidence in the power of morality and religion, which has been considerably shaken of late.

But these reports concerning the police order and Crutcher's interview with the editor were only appetizers to the main item of news which was now uncovered. Twice during the day the circuits have opened to connect us with the remote world of the merchants. Crutcher's contact person called during the day to tell him that a man from the head office of one of the variety chains is in town to help the stores work out the desegregation of their counters. They have gone far enough in their thinking to speak about a signed contract of some kind with our group. We do not know yet what stores may be involved in this venture.

Then at 4:45 this afternoon Mayor Duncan's office called both Crutcher and Colston asking them to meet tomorrow at 11:00 A.M. at the Chamber of Commerce office. We assume that the meeting has to do with the lunch counters. At last something seems to be breaking for us. We can only keep our fingers crossed, or pray, according to our inclinations. James, Crutcher, and Colston were named as our official negotiating committee; Dr. Colston will request that Rev. James be included in tomorrow's meeting.

But these hopeful developments left us with another critical problem: should we continue *not* sitting in so long as there are hopeful signs of activity from within the other group? Or should we as a matter of course resume our regular schedule of sit-ins now that the declared holiday is over? Father Jones felt strongly that we should resume demonstrations. His principal argument was that if we do not, we will lose the enthusiasm and loyalty of our people. He reminded us that this could be a "ruse" of the opposition intended precisely to secure the cessation of demonstrations in the hope that our enthusiasm will die out. He is convinced the merchants have deceived us before. One or two other committee members supported Jones, but most of us agreed with Crutcher and James that for fruitful discussions to occur, we too must show a certain reasonableness and concern for the well-being of the entire community. We must not repeat the mistake of the students who demonstrated on the very afternoon they had been told the merchants were to meet.

We had come to feel rather expert on the subject of conducting demonstrations, but now we are moving into territory that is relatively strange to us. Crutcher, feeling the need of counsel, contacted by phone today a fellow Baptist minister in Nashville who was one of the leaders in the movement there. This simply highlights the fact that we have had very little personal contact with those who have been working in the lunch counter movement elsewhere. What contact we have had has been informal and at our initiative.

A small article on the second page of this afternoon's paper admits that Negroes are "boycotting" downtown stores. It includes a statement by Dr. Crutcher that the Associated Council is ready to negotiate at any time.

Thursday, July 7

INSTRUCTIONS in the technique of sitting in begin to seem more and more pointless as negotiations get under way. Of course, all our hopes may be dashed as they have been more than once before, and then there will be nothing to do but resume our demonstrations. If this occurs, they will undoubtedly be carried on with more intensity and result in greater violence. At any rate, we did not have any instruction session this morning, although we did have our meeting, and after praying for the success of the conferences, the workers went out as they have every morning this week to distribute literature and tell people that we are not going to town. Two workers went to Alcoa, fifteen miles away, where there is a heavy concentration of Negroes who work in the huge Alcoa plant, while other workers accepted assignment to other nearby towns.

It is not easy to interpret just what "Stay Away from Downtown" means. The demonstrators told of one woman who called the police chief after she received a "Stay Away from Downtown" leaflet and asked if it was true that it would be against the law for her to come to town! Not many miss the intent so completely as that, but they do ask questions that are difficult to answer:

"How do I pay my bills?"

"Send in a check."

"But I don't have a checking account."

"Then buy a money order at the branch post office." (For one woman who called, James drove to the post office, paid for the money order, and delivered it to her!)

"But I must go to the doctor."

"There are a lot of doctors whose offices aren't downtown." (This is considered an exception, however, if it is absolutely essential.)

"Is it all right to buy at the shopping centers?"

"Some of the stores which discriminate have branches in the shopping centers. Why would we treat these areas more favorably?"

"But what place does that leave to shop in?"

"Economize by restricting your shopping to necessary foodstuffs until we win this battle for equality, or else drive to Maryville or Oak Ridge."

Then of course there is the response that the workers resent the most: "But I don't care about eating at the lunch counters anyway. Why don't they work on something that would help *me*?"

We just must face it—Negroes, being human beings, react with all the human responses. However, those who are responding with wholehearted cooperation far outnumber the cynics.

The advertising manager of the *News-Sentinel* informed Bradby this afternoon that the editorial department has turned thumbs down on one statement in our ad which read, "We cannot support a business structure which discriminates against us. We think our friends will feel the same way." We rather anticipated this, however, and were ready with a substitute ending.

The present climactic stage of events necessitates a meeting of the Executive Committee almost every evening. But we do not resent the time spent when the meetings bring us the fresh scent of victory, as did the one today!

Dr. Colston first reported on the meeting which our negotiators had today with the Mayor and the president and manager of the Chamber of Commerce. The decision has been reached that the Chamber, with the Mayor's support, will officially request the merchants to desegregate. Two possible schemes for handling the "adjustment period" were presented for our group's opinion. One would be to limit the number of Negroes eating at a counter to two at any one time, but allow them to eat at any hour of the day. The other would be to allow a larger number, perhaps an unlimited number, but only at certain slack hours. The group readily agreed that the first plan is better because the restriction to certain hours, which was the Nashville plan, represents a situation less like that which will actually exist when desegregation is completed and would be more difficult to administer.

The Chamber officials were to meet with the merchants at 2:45 P.M., presenting to them the results of the morning meeting. (Even at this advanced stage of decision, the merchants are still keeping their distance from the petitioners.) At 4:45 P.M. the Chamber secretary called Crutcher to report "real progress for the first time in many weeks." It would seem that the break has finally occurred! It comes in this form: some stores have at last agreed to desegregate without all the stores. Tomorrow our three representatives are to meet with the Mayor, the president of the Chamber, and another prominent citizen who at this stage remains unnamed, even to our leaders, to work out the details of a plan. There is a certain aura of secrecy over all the proceedings because of the merchants' dread of publicity.

The Executive Committee moved into a discussion of how the desegregation of some counters would affect our economic withdrawal. It seemed evident that the "Stay Away from Downtown" movement would have to be abandoned in order that we might cooperate with those merchants who cooperate with us. It would mean reverting to the "Trade with Your Friends" movement. Nashville's experience is encouraging to us; there also some of the downtown stores did not participate in the initial move, but before much time had passed, most of the hold-outs had volunteered to join. Two factors that were important there we expect to be operative here as well: the influence of the merchants who do desegregate, and the demonstration that integrated counters do work. We hope that no further sit-ins will be needed. As things have been, we have had nothing to lose from sit-ins, but after some stores desegregate, we would be risking a great deal.

The group of white women planning to confer with Miller's has felt there was no hurry. In the light of what is happening now, the Committee asked the women's representative who was present to impress upon them the urgency of going tomorrow if possible. We do not yet know what stores are breaking over, but we are quite sure that none of the department stores is included. We still have some hope that Miller's, which does not have to answer to a headquarters in some other city, may take courage and come with us.

Harry Wiersema, Jr., reported that he and Lee Butler distributed 2500 handbills to cars in the University parking lots today. The bill, which was their own idea, did not ask persons to stay away from town completely, but only suggested not trading with those who discriminate at their lunch counters. Practically all the comments they received were favorable.

One solid success we have as of today. Negroes who go to the lunch room at the University Hospital from now on will be served. The management asks only that there never be more than twelve at one time.

Crutcher's spirit is the key to our mood. Relaxed for the first time in a month, he said, as one already savoring a delicacy, "I hope to rest tomorrow." Yet, acting as a counterweight is the sense that something precious is slipping away from us—the enthusiasm and comradeship generated by our crusade. I feel almost a disappointment that the battle seems nearly over.

Tonight on the way to the meeting I saw two white boys and two Negro boys, all about twelve years old, bumming along the street together, oblivious that there is any problem. God grant that by the time they are grown there may be none.

Friday, July 8

OUR leaders are feeling the difficulty of keeping up the enthusiasm of our corps of workers when we are not demonstrating. Some even made this their major consideration in advocating that sit-ins be continued during this period of exploratory conversations. But this would have been to admit that we are caught in a web of our own construction, that we are prisoners of our own followers.

James disclosed at the morning meeting that at last our negotiating committee is to meet today with the merchants themselves. This will make only the second time in the long process of negotiation and demonstration since March 1 that a committee of our people has sat down to meet with a group of the merchants who have lunch counters.

Now that the downtown area is self-proscribed during business hours, I find myself looking forward to picking up Ralph Ross at the bus station as often as I can, partly for the thrill of the nocturnal drive down Gay Street. As unattractive as the inner area of Knoxville is, I prefer it to all other cities in which I have lived with an unreasonable love like that which a mother showers

on her ugly duckling. In the daytime, not even love can conceal
the city's blemishes, but at night she gratefully tucks her ugly
features back into the shadows while Gay Street, her principal
thoroughfare, bursts forth in an electric brilliance that gives the
city an excitingly different personality. I feel possessive toward
this city, even including Rich's, Miller's, and the Todd & Armistead
Drug Store. It is my city; I want to be proud of it.

"A lot of Negroes think there is no such thing as a white Christian." Ralph can always be counted on for frankness; tonight was
no exception. He went on to tell me that he had made it the aim
of his sermon last Sunday to prove that there *is* such a thing as a
white Christian. His chief evidence was the scene he witnessed at
Cole's last week when Harry willingly accepted suffering for no
other cause than to help remove the burden of discrimination
from his fellow-man. Ralph's report meant a great deal more to
me than a topic of conversation—it meant that whatever happens
with the counters, our efforts have not been in vain. Testimony
has been borne to the message of reconciliation. The Church as a
whole has not yet learned that the call to bear this testimony is
a call to suffering. Twentieth-century Christianity speaks of rap-
port, of acceptance, of understanding, of forgiveness and of love,
even of guilt, but little of judgment and therefore little of vicarious suffering. For if one presupposes no judgment on sin, then
vicarious suffering is beside the point, since in the Christian understanding vicarious suffering is an acceptance unto one's self of
the judgment due another. Perhaps it is belaboring the obvious to
add that, among all the Knoxville ministers concerned with "rap-
port with the congregation," there should be some who instead
would demonstrate to their congregations the way of redemptive
suffering for the judgment God is working on society.

We stopped at Cas Walker's, which never closes, to pick up a
few groceries. Ralph dumped his items in my cart, which meant
no little trouble in separating them when we got to the cash register. "That cashier sure did look at us funny," Ralph observed as
we left the store. "I'll bet she was saying, 'What was that white

man doing with that nigger?'" I too had been conscious of the stares. We agreed it was good that people in business have learned to treat all customers courteously even when they are thinking things like that. When desegregation comes downtown, there will be no trouble from the employees, because they have their code of professional courtesy. As one of the merchants expressed it to James, "You will be our customers," implying that would take care of the matter. The employees were generally courteous to us during the sit-ins when they took any notice of us at all, and certainly as courteous to the Negroes as to the white demonstrators. While we deplore the fact that the Christian merchant does not let his moral judgments intrude into this "business" decision, we can only be grateful that the non-Christian merchant does not allow his to intrude much more. "Business is business" is a truism which is both a curse and a blessing to us.

Saturday, July 9

At four o'clock we were again at Mt. Olive Church to get the report of yesterday's meeting of our negotiators with the merchants. Now at last came the definite news for which we had been waiting such a long time: five Gay Street stores have agreed to desegregate—Woolworth's, Kress's, McClellan's, Grant's and Walgreen's. These merchants have organized, selecting as chairman the manager who has all along been the one most desirous of desegregating. This man we now recognize to have been sincere in his protestations of friendliness. The manager of the J. C. Penney Store, who is president of the Retail Merchants Association, is also lending his aid to work out a solution. These and others who have become concerned because of the "Stay Away from Downtown" movement have promised that they will continue to work on the holdouts and express the feeling that these will come along after a while.

A careful plan has been formulated. The Mayor and Chamber of Commerce will call together a "Good Will Committee" of about fifteen of the most prominent white citizens in Knoxville, most of them persons who have not been involved at all up to this time. This committee will request the merchants to open their counters to all. The merchants, meeting the same day, will reply in the affirmative. The text of the committee's request and the merchants' answer will be published in the afternoon paper the same day. It is understood that the names of the Good Will Committee will not be released locally, but will be sent to the home offices of the stores to demonstrate that the initiative for desegregation came from local people and is backed by the most influential citizens. All these plans are for the present being jealously guarded from the press because, if it were known that the merchants had had any hand in calling the Good Will Committee together, the influence of the Committee both on the local populace and on the stores' home offices would be undercut. (As a matter of fact, the statement that will be released to the press after the two meetings has already been worded.) Such is the theory, but in actuality a group of unnamed persons can hardly have much influence with the local citizenry. I believe the local people are ready and have been ready all along to accept desegregation as the reasoned decision of the store managers themselves.

Joe Copeland, pastor of Second Presbyterian Church, worked most of the day yesterday contacting persons for the Good Will Committee; apparently he is taking a major responsibility for this phase of the operation. There is a spirit of haste in carrying through the plans which is in curious contrast to the lassitude and deliberate procrastination which has marked the dealings since the middle of February. The other side is almost apologetic that the Good Will Committee can hardly be assembled before Tuesday. This does not mean, however, that the counters will be opened Tuesday. The merchants say they will need several additional days to orient their employees to the change; some personnel may have to be transferred to other departments.

Downtown merchants who do not have lunch counters are being requested to ask their employees to continue supporting the stores that desegregate their counters. These merchants will point out to their employees that all businesses are suffering from the Negroes' economic withdrawal and that the security of everyone who gets his living from downtown business depends on making the counter desegregation work. The merchants' chairman was jubilant when he called Crutcher this afternoon because every one of the merchants he had contacted about this had readily agreed to cooperate. Thus a great many people who thought they were being personally threatened by the request of Negroes to eat at the same lunch counters with them will perhaps be rather surprised to find themselves allies of the Negroes' cause.

To the anxious questioning by our negotiators, the merchants replied that they do *not* intend to wait for the approval of their home offices before putting desegregation into effect, or even necessarily for the word of the local decision to reach them. This proved to be the snag once before, before the sit-ins ever began; we do not want that kind of disappointment again. The merchants' chairman states flatly, "There is no doubt this time—we're going to do it!" But none of us dares join him in that optimism. We will wait for our celebration this time until Negroes are actually eating in the variety stores and the drug store. We can appreciate the caution of the secretary of the Chamber of Commerce when he says, "This is the *nearest* to it of anything that's happened yet!"

But suppose, after getting an agreement with these five stores, we go right on demonstrating at Miller's and Cole's, the crowds of agitators increasing and the violence flaring on Gay Street? In dread of something like this, the merchants who are party to the agreement have requested, although they did not demand, that for at least thirty days after desegregation starts there be no demonstrations on Gay Street. Their motive was not kindliness to the non-cooperating stores, but the knowledge that any such state of affairs would hurt their own business and make it difficult for desegregation to be successful. The fact that they would make such a request is strong evidence that they feel the demonstrations thus far *have* been effective in keeping people from buying. Of course we will abide by their request. Actually it leaves us free to deal with Rich's and Sears' as we see fit, since they are some distance from the main street.

Sunday, July 10

VIOLATING my usual Sunday morning routine, I grabbed the Sunday paper as soon as I arose this morning and tore through it looking for our ad. The second time through I found it, and was disappointed that it seemed so inconspicuous. Yet we planned it for those who read their paper carefully, hoping these would be the thinking people. I tried to picture the impact it would have on the comfortably fixed white businessman browsing through the paper while the children are at Sunday school, on the stalwart church-going couple relaxing on Sunday afternoon who fancy they are already treating their fellow-man according to the Golden Rule. People like these can live very comfortably in a Southern town, hardly aware that a large portion of the residents of the same community are denied the privileges that make life so comfortable for themselves. If they think about it at all, they have rationalizations ready at hand, such as, "The Negroes are happy with things as they are." And so we have tried to shock some of these people into a recognition of the real state of affairs. The ad asks in a straightforward way, "Why are Knoxville Negroes not satisfied?" Speaking in the first person, it proceeds to answer the question:

". . . we cannot send our young people to summer junior and senior high schools. We cannot attend the University of Tennessee as undergraduate students. . . .

"We cannot get jobs as city bus drivers, even on routes which carry predominantly Negro passengers. . . .

"We cannot get service at East Tennessee Baptist Hospital, at Presbyterian Hospital, or at St. Mary's Catholic Hospital. . . .

"We cannot stay at the leading hotels. . . . We cannot live in the better residential areas. . . .

"We cannot point to a single Negro representative on the City Council, the Board of Education, the Knoxville Housing Authority, the Library Board, the Knoxville Utilities Board, or the Board of Directors of the City Auditorium. . . .

"We cannot play golf or bowl in Knoxville. . . . We cannot see a first-run movie. . . .

"We cannot patronize many businesses, such as laundromats, which exhibit signs reading: 'For White Patrons Only.' . . .

"We cannot eat at most of the restaurants in Knoxville. We cannot get food service in downtown Knoxville. We cannot eat in variety, drug, and department stores which gladly take our money in all other departments."

"Is it any wonder that Negroes of Knoxville are dissatisfied?" the ad queries. It then gives a brief explanation of the sit-ins and concludes with this statement: "We and the white friends who have accompanied us have suffered physical violence without retaliation because we believe in the way of Christian love. 'Repay no one evil for evil . . . but overcome evil with good.' "

We can only hope that some comfortable minds will be made uncomfortable.

The deacon who welcomed me this morning to the pulpit of the Rogers Memorial Baptist Church, a colored congregation, assured us of his own interest in the desegregation movement by repeating a dialect incident that may actually have happened in a Florida town as he said: A prominent Negro, consulted by the city officials about some prospective improvement in the colored section of town, replied in words calculated to impress the white leaders with his degree of literacy, "Gen'men, you can be suhtain that anythin' that's detrimental to mah race, Isaiah Jones'll be fur it!" (It's much more fun to laugh at oneself than to be laughed at.)

Speaking on "The Cost of Discipleship," I mentioned as a timely illustration the local Negro minister who is reported to have said when asked to participate in the sit-ins, "I was sent here to preach the gospel and protect the property of the Methodist Church. I cannot afford to have my church or my parsonage bombed." Both races have their status-savers. As a positive example, I pointed to the white minister, a native of Mississippi, who had told me with a sob in his voice, "My brother is the ringleader of the segregation forces in our entire denomination. Our family has split in two over this question of race." It did not seem to me that he had placed himself in a very advanced position, but I try to be understanding of those who have taken even small strides at such tremendous sacrifice. Had I been preaching to a white congregation, I would have used a white as the negative example and a Negro as the positive example.

For the first time the mass meeting was at James's church, Mt. Zion Baptist. The crowd was only a little more than half that of last Sunday, partly because of rain, but probably the fact that we are no longer in danger has sapped some of the enthusiasm. In contrast to the beginning phase of the movement, today only a handful of whites were present. The day after the picketing of Rich's our conservative morning paper went to pains to list the names of certain picketers who are TVA employees. The next day these persons were requested by their superiors "for the sake of good public relations" not to participate in any further demonstrations. In some cases this affected other members of their families as well. Shortly thereafter the commercial sign shop across from Rich's changed its sidewalk sign to read, "TVA Supplies Power and Sit-Inners." This kind of pressure has had some effect on white participation; another probable factor is the increasing violence during the last week or two of demonstrations, and another the absence of the Unitarian minister from the city. Yet after the organized effort began on June 9, there never was a sit-in in a single store without white participation, so far as I can recall now.

Father Jones reads the scripture, "Here beginneth the fourth verse...." Immediately my mind wanders to marvel at the many different strands of church-ism which are united in this movement. A Baptist would never say, "Here beginneth." "We are one body in Christ"—"differing gifts"—"be kindly affectioned one toward another, in honor preferring one another"; he prays that our leaders not sell their birthright for a mess of pottage "as has so often been the case in the past." I recollect his remarks about Dr. Crutcher at last Sunday's meeting. With the negotiations going on now, the implied caution is clear.

James: "The 'Stay Away' movement was so effective that after it began on Tuesday, July 5, before Thursday night the merchants were making moves to desegregate." Was it that simple? Hadn't the Chamber already been urging the merchants to meet after the sit-ins became so threatening? I remember there was enough promise by July 2, the day after the handbills were passed calling for the "Stay Away" movement, that we agreed to withhold sit-ins. In such a complex situation, it is impossible to tell the relative weight of the various pressures.

The splashing of water from a drainpipe, the whirring overhead of breathless fans, hardly moving the damp air.

James introducing Colston: "I stood in this same spot four months ago and said that Dr. Colston was one of America's greatest educators and that he had made the wisest possible decision in persuading the students not to demonstrate. Dr. Colston thought a victory could be won through negotiation. He had a right to believe that—wasn't East Tennessee different? Don't we do things in Knoxville that are not possible in any other city of the South?" (He is apologizing for Dr. Colston, for all of us.) "But now we have found out that somebody has been kidding somebody!"

Colston expresses the conviction that we are now about to have the kind of success that will *keep* us believing that Knoxville is "special." He reveals few if any facts from the negotiations, but promises that we will be getting specifics from the leaders in a few days. He encourages the group to cooperate with whatever plan is worked out. He urges the group to remain mobilized to achieve other victories.

One of the Negro attorneys follows Colston to tell us that the Todd & Armistead injunction will be contested in court and that it has the makings of a unique case. "All the Negro attorneys are banded together to fight this case—it is our case as well as yours!" he promises.

Crutcher, after last Sunday's oratorical flourish, is his usual relaxed self today. Crutcher is one of those persons who has an amusing story for every occasion; he begins with one today: A colored man who was traveling found it necessary to stop in a small Southern town overnight. Not finding any lodging places for colored folks, he was getting desperate when finally the local mortician told him he might sleep on his embalming table. When the mortician arrived the next morning at his place of business, he asked his assistant, "Sam, did you cremate the three bodies that were laid out in the embalming room?" "Yes, sir, I cremated them, but there were four bodies, not three." "Sam! One of those bodies was a colored man I let sleep in here last night!" the mortician gasped. "You know, boss," said Sam, wide-eyed, "he kept telling me he wasn't dead!"

The point of course is that the Stay Away from Downtown movement is not dead. "Any Negro who goes downtown to buy is a traitor to the cause!" Crutcher exclaimed. The strong language is understandable in view of what he himself has undergone for the cause. He says that some of the Negroes who work downtown he has had to restrain from "going home with some of you" when they saw Negroes shopping downtown. One asked, "Reverend, I know you're a preacher and can't approve of violence, but if I don't say anything to *you* about it, is it all right for me to take care of that fellow?" Crutcher replied no, that this was a non-violent movement. "And those who are still going to town should be glad that it is," he adds in telling us about it.

Most of Knoxville's Negroes will cooperate, if not out of conviction, then out of group loyalty or desire not to be criticized. But there are a few mavericks. Crutcher reports hearing of one who said, "Those damn Crutcher and James Negroes don't have anything to do with me!"

The scent of success has aroused action on many fronts. There is increasing evidence that what we are experiencing in Knoxville is the belated awaking of a sleeping giant—the Negro populace. A meeting has been held during the week for the purpose of organizing the city under block leaders to get out the vote and to communicate news of the crusade. "The largest number of Negro businessmen ever seen together in Knoxville," Crutcher comments. The giant is stretching his limbs.

"I don't care how many years Colston has been president of Knoxville College, or Harvey and McArthur have had Ph.D.'s; when they go to town, they can't be served any more than the rest of us! So until we get this thing won, there won't be any big I's and little you's." I wonder if Crutcher is acknowledging that several on today's program have acted the part of "the big I." Some have seemed more intent on impressing the audience with their wisdom or leadership qualities than with doing the job they were asked to do. I can't help thinking of what Jim Reese's wife Neola once told me: "Movements for social progress among the Negro people practically always get messed up by too many individuals wanting to be 'the big cheese.' There seems to be a craving to be considered the leader. It's something you wouldn't understand unless you'd had long experience in the Negro community. It's our greatest handicap."

Next to the singing, the offerings are the most fascinating thing to experience in those of the Negro churches that still follow the old pattern. I use the plural, "offerings," advisedly. One soon learns not to surrender all the money he brought with him the first time the plate comes around. It is not uncommon to have three different offerings during the Sunday morning service, all attended with much congregational participation, and often with the intake counted and announced on the spot. (Yet in spite of all this emphasis on money, the Negro churches as a group are notoriously poor in stewardship. Unfortunately typical is a church of over three hundred members in the presbytery to which I belonged in Texas which after thirty years was still receiving mission funds. A dedicated stewardship of income based on proportional giving remains the single greatest need of the Negro churches.)

The ways of cajoling people to give are legion. This afternoon Crutcher suggests we take the offering the "old-timey" way. He calls for a volunteer to be "Miss Mt. Zion," someone from his own congregation to be "Miss Mt. Olive," finds someone in the audience from Felton's congregation to be "Miss Logan Temple," and so on until he has a "princess" from each of a dozen and a half congregations. He has them stand facing the audience, holding offering baskets while the congregation files by a section at a time, each person putting his offering in the basket of the church he favors. "A freedom dollar!" Crutcher cries as the plates begin to fill. "That's little enough to pay for freedom!" Two kinds of pressure are employed here—the pressure of publicity and the pressure of competition. Although fully a third of the audience slips out the door when the rest rise to bring their offerings, enough respond to raise over $500, matching the giving of last Sunday.

We leave with the promise that next week there will be the VICTORY meeting.

Monday, July 11

THE ten o'clock workers' meetings will be continued this week, but I no longer feel that my contribution to them can be enough to justify abandoning my study. Yet I got no study done this morning. Instead Jim Reese and I chased around on separate circuits getting the signatures of ministers on the letter which the Knoxville Ministerial Association adopted for transmittal to the merchants. We hope also to get it to the press this week together with as many signatures as possible. This could play an important role in marshaling community support for the change.

More "fan mail" resulting from the press service dispatches on the Walgreen's incident came in this morning. The first letter I opened was from a stranger in Chicago who said, "I am writing to commend you for your stand on this matter." The next, from Knoxville, was signed simply "C. N. Smith." I think I will quote a portion of it, using the same spelling produced by Mr. Smith's typewriter:

No doubt the attitude you take toward the association of the white and Negro races, you stronly favor miscegnation. I would suggest since Africa wants black rule, that all Negroes in this coutry migrate to this continent and establish themselves. This is the rightful place for them. . . . The Belgian Congo could now use many of the American Negros who think they are brainy. . . .

It is true we have many Negro-lovers in America like yourself, Earl Warren, Frankfrutter, Leehman, Elnor, Javitts, Cellers, and some others. Of course well know the supreme court edict on desegregation is causing all the troubles. . . . Tehn we had some left-winger in America who led poor Ike into sending troops into Little Rick, the most disgraceful act any person ever did again his own people. . . . What a man. . . .

We all know Knoxville College is operate thru the Presbyterins, Ike is a presbyterian, and also so is Theo. Smith and Carson Blake, both of whom advocated that Ike intergrate Central High at Little Rock if it took tanks and guns. . . . Such men as these two is why many prominent people have stated that there was more than 30,000 reds in our churches in America.

This country some day will be swallowed up by a Red China or some other red country. . . . There is not one person in Knox County who could make an automatic dispensing soft drink machine which takes twenty-five cents gives you your drink and correct change back. . . . You cannot have brains by mixing the blood of the white person and the Negro. . . . Today this country would have long been take by Russia had we not imported brains from Germany. Had it not been for Von Bruin and his colleagues of German scientists we never would have had the ballistic missels etc. Today it is too complicated for the

American scientists to comprehend. We are becoming weaker thru mixed bloods daily.

... Why did God give the birds of the air an instinct to choose their mates from their own species? ... Now we have become so ignorant many people like yourself think you can breed the Negro and White race and get brains, when you know better, but NAACP money and politics is doing a stinking job.

No doubt your conscience tell you better than you are acting but Colson perhaps has stated to you and other whites associated with Knoxville College, you job hinges on what you do for the NAACP....

I would like to have given this one the soft answer that turneth away wrath, but Mr. Smith gave me no address.

There was a third letter which affected me more deeply. It was from my friend Ernest, a young officer in the church of which I was pastor back in Texas. He had seen a clipping from a Denver newspaper which named me as "a white antisegregation demonstrator," and which said I was "attacked and beaten" in a Knoxville drug store. Ernest made these observations: "It would seem you have changed your profession, no longer being either a minister of the Gospel or a teacher of philosophy but a 'demonstrator.' How fortunate we are that your zeal didn't mature until after you left here." (Even so, my zeal had me in continual tension with my congregation in that East Texas town.)

Ernest continued: "I can respect your ... opinions, differ though I may; however, I cannot see how your right to hold these views also gives you license to enter a private business establishment and encroach upon the proprietor's right to run his business as he chooses.... Neither can I justify your apparent abandonment of the pulpit where you could preach the Word and arouse a Christian social conscience within your listeners, in favor of agitating on street corners in defiance of court orders. I lament the loss suffered by our denomination...."

Ernest's letter hurt me, but his sentiments were no surprise to me. I well remember the night not long after I had announced my resignation when Ernest came into my study greatly concerned about something. Half apologetically, he began, "There is a rumor going around the town—I feel certain it isn't true, but I think you ought to know about it so we can set it straight by revealing the facts. Because if the rumor is allowed to go on, it will hurt you and hurt the church. . . ." The rumor of course was that the college where I was going to teach was a Negro college. Ernest's feeling was like that of one of the few other persons in the congregation who felt close enough to me to tell me what she really thought—"You've given us a slap in the face, to leave us to work with niggers!"

But Ernest and I liked one another enough that we could quarrel even about this and remain on friendly terms. There had been another occasion when because of our friendship Ernest was able to save me from pushing the congregation too far. I can understand him a little. His racial views would have been molded in childhood by the monolithic sentiments of that plantation-belt town. As an adult, he wants from life only the opportunity to enjoy the quiet happy life of his hometown with his family and friends—and the Southern town can afford a lovely life for its upper-class whites. Vaguely he is aware that the price of this happiness is the acceptance of the community's racial mores. But Ernest has to contend also with a conscience informed by a deeper-than-ordinary understanding of the Christian faith and four years of university education. He struggles valiantly to keep the conscience repressed.

Ernest closed his letter with some family news, as though to say he wanted to continue our friendly quarrel on the same basis as always.

Jim and I worked again all evening on the ministers' letter, he telephoning and I typing names, faintly aware that the Democratic Convention keynoter was striving in vain to be heard from the kitchen radio.

Tuesday, July 12

SOME early morning calls brought the total of signatures on the ministers' letter to seventy-five. Jim rushed it over to Joe Copeland at Second Presbyterian Church, who was to take it to the meeting of the Mayor's "Good Will Committee" this morning.

At 12:30 P.M. the crucial announcement came on the radio news! The "Good Will Committee" of white leaders has requested the merchants to desegregate their counters and the merchants have agreed! The plan is being carried out according to promise. The afternoon paper carried the statement agreed upon by this committee and the merchants:

The Knoxville Good Will Committee, appointed by the mayor and the Chamber of Commerce, met with merchants of the community. This committee recommended that the lunch counters be open to all people. The merchants agreed to comply with this recommendation and with the committee are working out a plan to put it into effect.

The committee appreciates the patience and co-operation of the people and the merchants of the community and is confident that every one will continue to exercise the same restraint and good judgment in the matter as they have previously demonstrated in matters involving community relations.

I was able to read this statement to Union Presbytery, meeting this afternoon, before most of the commissioners had read it in the papers. I suggested that this is a time when we can show our Christian convictions on brotherhood by quietly urging members of our congregations to patronize these stores, sitting beside Negroes at the lunch counter. I told the ministers they might be asked to arrange for groups from their churches to be in the stores on one of the days during the initial period. Will the ministers and churches of Knoxville respond to this challenge?

We are assured by Dr. Copeland, who participated in this morning's meetings, that the ministers' letter with the seventy-five signatures was received with surprised gratitude by the merchants who are planning to desegregate. They felt it would impress their home offices. However, I am considerably agitated over a misunderstanding that has developed as to whether the signatures on the letter are to be released to the press. I will be extremely disappointed if the Ministerial Association loses this opportunity to take a courageous stand before the whole community.

Wednesday, July 13

STAYING away from the workers' meetings for the past two mornings has given me an unhappy feeling of no longer being a vital part of things. I just couldn't stay away this morning and miss experiencing the reactions of the group to the reality of success after such a hard struggle.

Upon arrival I learned that James and Colston at that very moment were meeting with the merchants to work out details of putting desegregation into operation. While we sat waiting for our meeting to begin, one of the high school boys said to me, "Dr. Proudfoot, there's something I've been wanting to ask you, and maybe now would be a good time. Why are you participating in this? You know, you could go down there anytime and be served. Some of us fellows have been discussing it this morning. . . ." There was in his voice a sort of disbelief that any white could care.

I was silent for a moment, thinking. "Well," I finally said, "imagine things were reversed—you could go and whites were being discriminated against. How would *you* feel?"

He thought he would not feel good about it, "because I don't like to see *anyone* discriminated against." I told him that maybe that was his answer. But I was not satisfied that this was any real answer. Why *am* I participating in this movement? I continued trying to formulate an answer in my own mind.

When therefore I was asked to lead the opening devotional (a thing which it was assumed any minister should be able to do without preparation), I knew exactly what I wanted to do: I wanted to give my answer to that question. First I read the passage from Ephesians 2, "For he is our peace, who has made us both one, and has broken down the dividing wall of hostility." Then I repeated the young man's question and said, "Both the democratic ideals of our country and my Christian faith teach me to believe in brotherhood. But I am participating in this movement primarily because of my Christian beliefs. The Bible makes clear how Christians are to regard those of other races and groups. In the first place, we were all created by one God as a single human family. Secondly, Christ came to redeem us all, regardless of race or country. Thirdly, there are no distinctions in the Church, for it is Christ's Body; it has diverse members, but all are made harmonious with one another by virtue of the unity they have with Him. And finally, Jesus made very clear that many will come from the East and West and sit down at table in the Kingdom, but the children of privilege may be cast into outer darkness. He taught us that the commandment, 'Thou shalt love thy neighbor as thyself' is 'like unto' the first commandment, 'Thou shalt love the Lord thy God,' and Jesus himself gave us the supreme example of humble, selfless love."

I added, "The Christian basis is the best basis for what we're doing, for then we can never do it for purely selfish reasons. We're doing this as much for Rich's and for Walgreen's as for ourselves." (Do we always remember that?) "If we participate in the crusade for equal rights out of Christian motives, we will never fall into the temptation some Africans are now falling into of substituting black supremacy for white supremacy. The goal we seek is not the supremacy of any group over another, but brotherhood in Christ."

This is the completest statement I've made of my reasons for participating in the movement. Ironically, it comes now when my participation is almost over, but I feel good for having had the chance to make it.

During all of this there had been two free-lance reporters, one with camera, from Bristol, Virginia, in the auditorium. When James and Colston returned from the official meeting with the intention of disclosing the terms to the workers, they were frustrated to find these reporters present, for they had signed an agreement absolutely not to release to the press any details of the agreement just made. Rather embarrassedly, we had to ask the reporters to remain in another room while first James and then Colston spoke to our group.

The negotiators had agreed on the following terms: The four variety stores and Walgreen's will begin serving Negroes next Monday, July 18. Included in the deal also will be Woolworth's two stores in suburban shopping centers. There will be a transition period of ten days during which no more than two Negroes will request service at a counter at the same time. Our organization has accepted responsibility to "police" the counters to see that no more than two try to eat at one time. There will be no restriction on the time of day Negroes can be served. At the end of ten days, the merchants and our negotiators will meet to decide whether the restrictions can be taken off.

Several questions immediately occur: What if a Negro tries to get served before Monday? What if a Negro not a part of our organization doesn't wish to abide by our rules? These questions were raised also by our representatives, who were told by the merchants that a Negro requesting service before the agreed date would be told of the agreement and courteously refused. In the case of a Negro who insisted on service when two others were already eating, if our overseers were not present or could not handle him, he would be served, but the merchant would expect to register a complaint with us asking us to do a better job of policing. It is also understood on our side that we will continue to stay away from town until we actually *eat!*

Dr. Colston counseled the group: "You can live without eating at Woolworth's. The thing is you want to know that you *can* eat there when you want to. So *do it naturally*. Don't go downtown in a big group just to eat at Woolworth's. But when you are downtown anyway and are hungry, go in with whomever you are with and get something to eat."

Colston commented that the store managers now feel there is some *righteousness* in what they are doing and want to show the uncommitted stores that it will work. Can it be that they are relieved to be free at last to act as *persons* on the basis of conviction, rather than as computing machines on the basis of profit?

The Bristol reporters followed me to my home for an interview, and Harry Wiersema, Jr., joined us there. It was Harry, the Unitarian, who turned the conversation toward the role of religion in all this. He said that when a white girl asked him during the picketing, "Why are you down here with these niggers?" he explained it was because of his religion. (A frank testimony that non-Unitarians might well emulate.) The girl, a Southern Baptist, answered, "That's not what my preacher teaches." Harry's simple reply was, "I'm sorry your minister and mine don't agree," which taken in a general sense is a rather profound comment on the status of segregation. For, as I told the reporters, if all the ministers would speak and act on the basis even of what they believe, the problem would be far along toward solution. Christian conviction put to work by individuals is having a considerable effect on race relations, although it is an effect impossible ever to measure. But the Church as an institution and the ministry as a group have been distressingly cautious, as often as not putting God's blessing either overtly or by implication on whatever social patterns already exist. Here for instance is a prominent minister who moves that a resolution before the denominational assembly be sent to a committee "for further study," explaining that it may be construed as putting pressure on the churches, "and if there is anything we don't need in our present situation, it is pressure." There was once a mighty prophet who called out, "Let justice roll down like waters, and righteousness like an ever-flowing stream!" (Amos 5:24.) Perhaps to fit our modern situation, this sentiment should be revised to read: "Let the principle of eventual justice be acknowledged by appointing a committee to study the matter, but let us not stir up the people of Bethel at this time by a hasty action which they would interpret as an attempt to bring pressure upon them."

Harry and I agree that we are both in danger of coming to despise whites who don't agree with us. A Northern liberal visiting here recently told me he suddenly became aware while he was walking down Gay Street that he was feeling, "You damned whites! I hate you because you don't like Negroes!" We all recognize when we are rational about it that if God is not prejudiced against Negroes, he isn't prejudiced against our fellow whites either. Is the problem really racial, then? Or is it the same old difficulty of human beings understanding and forgiving one another? Is not "human relations" after all the *right* term, and not just a euphemism for "race relations," as I have always secretly supposed?

Meanwhile Negro Christians are giving us one of the outstanding examples in all history of Jesus' teaching, "Love your enemies and pray for them who persecute you." Harry expressed amazement that the Negroes do not seem to hate whites. One person he asked about this explained, "We've been taught in our churches not to." Is it as simple as that? Don't whites study the same Bibles? Perhaps the difference is that we whites have not suffered enough really to understand a gospel of suffering love.

The reporters asked if my stand on race had not hurt my effectiveness as a leader of my East Texas congregation. "No," I replied, "I don't think it did, except that in this one area of race relations the congregation developed such a hyper-sensitivity that it was impossible for me to accomplish any short-range objective. If I had kept quiet, I probably could have slipped some things over on them which they did not understand as steps in the direction of full brotherhood. But if they had acted only because they were assured the step would fit in with the pattern of segregation, I would only have been supporting their prejudices. On the other hand, I am encouraged to think that the direct testimony I gave in speech and action may live in their thoughts long after the value of some small compromise may have vanished." We pay a high price for "making a little bit of progress" when we give up the prophetic role of the pulpit, which is effective only in a testimony for absolute, not relative, righteousness.

We were at Reese's tonight watching the convention balloting on TV when Reese related this anecdote: At a burial this morning, Rev. James whispered to Reese, "Well, the promised land is in sight! We are about to taste of the milk and honey." Reese chuckled, using the Negro dialect which he can switch on and off at will, "If the milk 'n honey's gonna be this hard to git in the promis' lan', you jes' make mine chicken!"

Thursday, July 14

AFTER further queries, I finally had to admit this morning that apparently the members of the Ministerial Association, when they adopted the letter to the merchants, did not intend their names to be published. I accept this as a fact, but with considerable disappointment that we ministers did not identify ourselves *individually* with the group's publicly reported position. In a way, we have asked the merchants to lay themselves on the line when we are not willing to do the same ourselves.

I am impressed by the fact that virtually all the ministers whom I contacted to get their signatures for the letter agreed, even after I told them the names would be published. This encourages me in my perverse conviction that people in general and ministers in particular are more courageous alone than in a group. If we ever want to get a ministers' manifesto like that of the Atlanta ministers, I can see now that we should not work through the Ministerial Association, because there we are reduced to the strength of the lowest common denominator.

The Knoxville Area Human Relations Council has given me permission today to take the chronology of the negotiations which I worked out on the Fourth of July, expand it to include the sit-ins themselves, and publish it as a newsletter of the Council.

When I saw Jim Reese this afternoon, he and Neola had just returned from registering as voters. They did not mind standing in line for two hours, they said, because in the ten years they ministered in the "Black Belt" of Alabama, they could not even find a white person in the town who would tell them the location of the registration place. This in spite of the fact that both are college graduates, and Jim has in addition two graduate degrees.

But Jim was more concerned just at this time about a call he had just received from the president of the Knoxville Ministerial Association, who was indignant upon hearing that his name was included among the 75 signatures on the letter to the merchants. He had not intended to sign it, he asserted, and furthermore was against the action on principle! Jim as secretary had attached the president's name when the document was typed, supposing (naively, as it turned out) that the president would certainly wish to support the action of the group and that in the confusion after the meeting he had forgotten to sign it. The president insists that Jim must sign a letter which the president himself will write to the Chamber of Commerce and Mayor disclaiming his signature. The fact that an executive of one of the stores which has not agreed to desegregate is a prominent layman in the church this man pastors is probably a significant factor in his attitude. It is unfortunate that the Ministerial Association should be under such tepid leadership at this critical time.

Friday, July 15

IN the eighth chapter of Romans we are assured that, when we do not know what to pray for, the Spirit searches out our need and interprets it to the Father. This must be what has happened, for today I have received an encouragement I would not have dared pray for. It came in the form of a letter from an older member of that same Texas church—a man who partly because of his deep personal piety has difficulty comprehending the social impact of the gospel. By no means a bigot, his weight as acknowledged leader of the congregation nevertheless pulled in the opposite direction to mine when it came to integration. Now he wrote that as he studied his Sunday school lesson about Isaiah, his thoughts were drawn again and again to me:

I still think as I did, but there is a depressing sense of guilt in that we were not as understanding as we should have been. . . . Not a great many of us are yet ready to stand up and be numbered alongside of you in your campaign. But we are ready to argue with you unheatedly, . . . and maybe admit within the profoundest secret inner sanctums of our hearts that possibly you have a point. . . . The drops of water that you must drip on our granite convictions have to wear down stone that was evolved through 200 years of formation. But maybe soon Christ will open our blinded eyes and we will be able to see an integrated church and society. . . .

In this note is a response that must be measured alongside Ernest's. It comes from a man who has been moulded by similar conflicting influences, but has had longer to wrestle with them in the inner man. I wrote back to this kind friend that his letter had enabled me to re-evaluate my entire ministry in that community. It gave a confirmation more explicit than any I had ever hoped to receive to the words that I noted here two days ago, expressed almost as much in hope as in conviction to the reporters from Bristol.

Another note came from Miss Julia, my Baptist lady friend in the same Texas community:

Dear Reverend Proudfoot,
Visitors last night told me of recent indignity at the hands of mob characters mistreating you. I was shocked and incensed at such conduct. It was all so unnecessary! The approach to the situation must be slow and gradual. I am not capable of an opinion about desegregation. I am so *Southwestern*. . . . I will be 92 my next birthday.
Love and best wishes, your friend
Julia D. Owen

Dear Miss Julia! If everyone in the town were as unbigoted as she, it would have been a happier place for me.

It has been a thing of wonder to me to discover again and again that it is not always the old who are prejudiced nor the young who are liberal. The implications of this for the general situation are not encouraging; it gives the lie to the widespread attitude, "Time will take care of this problem if we don't stir it too much."

Sunday, July 17

PREACHING this morning to a white congregation, I mentioned the demonstrations in an illustrative way. As the congregation filed out, one little lady stopped to say, "I was so glad to hear you speak of integration this morning. We never hear it from this pulpit, you know, and I think it *ought* to be mentioned!" That set me to wondering: granted that many ministers are going to let their policies toward integration be influenced by the attitudes within their congregations, why is it so many choose to be guided by the "anti's" rather than the "pro's?" Apparently it goes back to the fiber of the minister himself.

Our "victory" mass meeting at Logan Temple A. M. E. Zion Church this afternoon was well attended, but the spark is gone.

It is not success which generates enthusiasm, but danger or moral indignation. Those now are past.

"Let justice roll down like waters and righteousness like an ever-flowing stream," read Jim Reese from the prophet Amos, then prayed that the kingdoms of this world might become the Kingdoms of our Lord and Saviour Jesus Christ. Every person present felt he knew what justice demanded, what it would mean for the Kingdom to come among *us*.

At last the people heard the terms of the agreement, stated by President Colston. He named the stores, told of the ten-day easing-in period with its limitation of two Negroes at a time at the counter. But even this will allow thirty-two Negroes to be served at one counter during an eight-hour day provided each stays one-half hour, he had calculated. After all, this will be thirty-two more than have eaten there before! He urged the group to "do it naturally," not going to the counters just because they are open.

Rev. James picked up the phrase, "do it naturally," and in his comic fashion protested, "Yes, but I'm concerned that some of us do it naturally *tomorrow!*" The fact that he would be concerned lest Negroes fail to take advantage of the new opportunity, and thus give back the ground they had gained with so much struggle, would have been a revelation to many whites who fear that Negroes will "take over" desegregated institutions.

James had asked one merchant what would happen if a Negro who didn't know about the restrictions sat down at a counter when two were already there. "We would serve him," the merchant replied. "After all, you are our customers, and we treat our customers courteously!"

"Did you hear that?" James mimicked. "Now I'm a customer! I can tell you that's a good feeling! I've been that man's customer all along, but now I'm a customer in an unaccustomed way!"

James's banter was delighting his audience. "You weren't even hungry in the first place! You wanted respect! I'm so full up with pride, I don't know when I'll be hungry again. I don't need a hamburger!"

There had been some apprehension that since the public announcement of the anticipated change was made several days ago, some Negroes would anticipate the D-Day. The managers reported to Crutcher that only one little Negro boy came to one of the counters, and he was served without comment. Little does the lad know that he is a historical "first!" The youngsters aren't as timid as their elders. Southern whites pronounced the death sentence upon segregation long ago when they set up public education for Negroes based on the assumption that a Negro can learn anything a white can learn. Some men, good and bad, must have realized that then. The Afrikaners know that segregation and education cannot survive together, so they do not educate. Providing this kind of public education is the finest thing Southern whites have to their credit in their treatment of the Negro.

Aside from eating at the counters, the other significant thing that will happen tomorrow is that we will take our trade back to town after withholding it for two weeks. "But it is crucial that we return to town in the right way!" Crutcher emphasized. He read from some scurrilous handbills that had come into his hands, to show that we still have enemies. One which he said bore the imprint "U.S. Klans, Inc., Knights of the Ku-Klux-Klan," featured a drawing of a repulsive looking Negro woman holding a spotlessly white infant in her arms. It queried, "Should we have them (Negroes) in our home, pay them hard earned money for them to fight us with?" A counter-boycott against Negroes in both employment and sales will show them "how well off they were before the existence of their 'COMMUNISTIC, AGITATING, STRIFE INCITING' NAACP!"

The other, more libelous, was entitled "COMMUNISTIC MINISTERIAL ASSOCIATION" and obviously was inspired by news reports of the resolution on lunch counters adopted by the Ministerial Association:

This infamous hypocritical Communist organization of sixty-two (62) White Trash and African Idiots are trying to tell the citizens of Knoxville to go against the laws of God and mix with Negroes.

Charles ———, pastor of the ——— Baptist Church [1] ... stood in a basement room at the Central Methodist Church and called an agitating trouble making Negro by the name of Crutcher, Brother, and remarked I am with you. This is practically the same system used in Russia to destroy the Churches by making them a source of trouble so they would have an excuse to close them.... Every Christian denomination in the City of Knoxville has been infiltrated with Communists. ... If your Preacher is this type who advocates your becoming a mongrel by mixing your White blood with Negro sickle cell anemia—he is a rotten Communist and is unfit to stand in the pulpit. Will you run him off or let him run you off? Remember the Church is yours and does not belong to him....

This message, press printed, was unsigned.

"Now you see from these handbills that not everyone in Knoxville is our friend yet. We go back to town but we go back to shop with *friends!*" Crutcher emphasized. This means we will trade with everyone except those who continue to discriminate at their lunch counters.

"You know, there was a man who asked a carpenter to make him a baseboard with fourteen cat holes for his kitchen. 'But wouldn't one cat hole be enough? Why on earth would you want fourteen?' the carpenter asked. 'Because I have fourteen cats, and when I say *scat*, I mean *scat!*'" The moral of course was: "What we say, we mean!" "I don't understand," Crutcher charged heatedly, "how anyone with an ounce of respect for his race, or for that matter, for the human race, can walk in and spend a *dime* in one of those stores that closed rather than serve you!"

He spoke of the need to move on to further goals. He mentioned the hospitals, stores which employ no Negroes though they do much of their business with Negroes. "You will get nothing unless you fight for it! We have learned from this struggle that nobody is going to give you anything!" (This is sad, but true. Whites know what is right and may even feel sympathy, but such is the weight of tradition and fear of community pressure that they will seldom move until Negroes apply counter-pressure.)

1. The names were spelled out in the original.

One of the school principals spoke on the block organization which is aimed primarily at getting all Knoxville Negroes registered to vote and conveying information that will help them use the vote to gain civil rights. Among the first objectives is to get Negroes on city and county governing boards, into clerical positions in the court house and city hall, and into white collar jobs with the Knoxville Utilities Board.

The minister of Tabernacle Baptist Church emphasized, "Voting must be the key to all we're trying to do. . . . Negroes have got to divorce themselves from the practice of being a 'certain-white-man-voter.' We've got to get away from the idea that we have to be paid a dollar to get our vote, or have to be driven to the polls in a Cadillac. No one will ever respect any Negro who takes a dollar for his vote—that official owes you nothing more. You were worth one dollar and he gave it to you!"

I agreed to serve as one of the "hosts" at Grant's from 10:00 A.M. until noon tomorow.

Monday, July 18

THIS is written just before I leave for Nashville. I feel I deserve a little vacation.

I was extremely nervous about playing "host" this morning—almost more nervous than I was about sitting-in. I took over from a Negro boy of high school age. He said that he and a woman had eaten individually since the counter opened at nine. I couldn't get in touch with the manager to report; he stayed in his office most of the morning, apparently taking the new step rather nonchalantly. Feeling extremely self-conscious, I stood around fiddling with artificial flowers and records, read greeting cards and finally bought one so the clerks wouldn't get too suspicious. At 10:10 a dirty looking Negro boy entered the store; I was relieved when he did not go to the counter. In fact, I realized with some chagrin that I was hoping *no* Negro would seek to eat while I was there! It seems that the more violence and tension I have experienced, the more I have come to fear it.

I noticed many Negroes on the sidewalks in sharp contrast to the pattern of the past two weeks. Several more came into Grant's to shop. At 10:25 the youngster who had been supervisor before me returned with a girl chum and treated her to a milk shake. At 10:40 Carroll Felton and another Negro minister sat down at the middle of the counter. I was a bit resentful that they had chosen to sit in the most conspicuous position, when nearly the whole counter was empty. It seemed ostentatious. Two nicely dressed white girls looked, turned and left. I heard as they passed me, "Well, they're serving them. Apparently they don't care whether *we* eat here or not." Other whites took seats at some distance from the Negroes.

At 10:55 Rev. Patterson sent word for me to come to McClellan's, providing a replacement for me at Grant's. I went fearing the worst, but he only wished me to sit beside two Negro girls who were eating there, just to make them feel good. He had also observed that few whites were taking seats next to Negroes. A white woman on the other side of the girls was sitting in a sort of side-saddle position, facing toward her companion and with her back turned rudely upon the girls. As I sat there sipping tea which I didn't want and chatting, I noticed a hefty dowager come up, put her nose in the air and walk out.

At 11:15 I went back to Grant's and stood talking for a few moments with Carroll Felton. The dowager came in there, looked, saw two Negro boys at the counter, and as she passed us on her way out, said testily for us alone to hear, "I can't find a place to eat!" I wanted to tell her there were several empty stools there, or that she could go to Cole's, but I was able to hold myself in check.

As Carroll and I continued our chat, the same high school boy came back into the store with a different girl and headed for the counter. Carroll accosted him, discovered he had eaten at three other counters during the morning besides his two previous forays into Grant's. We convinced him that he had eaten enough for one morning. It apparently meant a great deal to him to be able to display his bravery to the girls.

By noon, Grant's counter was nearly full. There were two vacant stools on one side of the Negro boys, and two white women had seated themselves on the other side of them. We assumed these women to be "friends" who had been alerted through the organization.

Later this afternoon I talked with Joan Livingston, who has taken the big task of enlisting the support of white churches and other organizations. She has had a fairly good response. Each organization that agrees is assigned to a particular store on a particular day. Since the Negro customers may come at any time while the counter is open for business, we can hardly have white persons there for every occasion, as was done in Nashville, but the hope is that at least enough of these special persons will come in during the day to offset those whites who stay away from the counters, and that some of them will be able to demonstrate their friendship by sitting beside Negroes. This latter objective is of special interest to the managers. The manager who is leading the group complained today that not enough white friends had showed up, which caused empty seats on either side of the Negro customers and, he felt, a consequent loss of business.

Incidentally, none of our assisting organizations has yet come to feel as possessive toward a counter as did the woman in Nashville who, when a white Baptist pastor wandered in to see how things were going, accosted him with the indignant query, "What are *you* doing here? This is the Unitarian counter!"

My experience in the store today causes me to think that the managers had a point in saying that they would not desegregate unless some other stores would join them. A single store which integrated might lose a number of hungry bigots. But I am confident that, once people like those who departed today find out that most of the stores are doing the same thing, they will accept it with a shrug of the shoulders. For one thing, there are not enough unsegregated counters left downtown to absorb a large shift of business.

Wednesday, July 20

IT is rather shame-faced I feel in confronting my Nashville friends, since when I was last here in late March I was so sure that Knoxville was handling its lunch counter problem better than Nashville! The only flaw in that judgment was that Nashville's disturbances brought quick results while our affair dragged on until now. It is still debatable whether their clamorous approach or our quiet one will prove to have been the better, but whatever the decision, one must confess that each city did as it did because of the personality of the town and no theoretical judgments would have dictated a different approach.

In the afternoon I was seated in the grill of the Vanderbilt Union with several friends when a large man brushed against my chair as he made his way out. I started suddenly with the momentary fear that I was going to be attacked. As I analyzed my own emotions, I realized that I do not feel secure in going into any place that suggests a lunch counter. I remembered then that I had subconsciously looked all around for possible antagonists as I entered the grill.

On the way home I stopped at a nice restaurant in Sparta, Tennessee. The place has Negro waiters. This means it aspires to be a "classy" establishment. Some people who would protest if they saw a Negro waitress serving behind a lunch counter will go out of their way to patronize a restaurant just because it has the "class" that having Negro waiters betokens. It will take someone wiser than I to figure out these emotional reactions, but of course they do correspond somewhat to the different roles the Negro traditionally had in relation to the plantation family on the one hand and the poor whites on the other.

Thursday, July 21

THERE have been no incidents reported during my absence; this I heard with considerable relief. Galen Martin and I toured the Gay Street stores during the noon hour and found only one Negro eating. She wore a white uniform, an obvious indication that she works in some downtown establishment. She is the kind of person who will benefit most from the change of policy. Even to me it seemed odd that this first week, with all the excitement that preceded, there should be only one Negro eating during the rush hour. Yet this is what we had tried to convince the managers would be the response of Negroes after the newness wore off.

There was a good business in all the stores and at all the counters. At McCellan's we saw one of our white women supporters, who said that the manager there reports everything is going well and that he can tell no difference in his business. She had identified three white persons who had come down to eat because they had been asked to by our supporters.

While we snacked at Grant's, two Negro boys joined the counter. They caused no stir.

The cashier who was working the lunch counter at Kress's yesterday was much disaffected by the new policy, complaining to almost every white customer about the Negroes, Galen says. When he paid his bill, he said, "Ma'am, do you mind if I tell you something my father, who is eighty-two, often says? He says

there are some things the more you stir them, the more they stink."
"Well, it's a free country!" she pouted. (But freer for some than
for others.) Today there was a different cashier at the counter.

Friday, July 22

I CALLED Pete Bradby to go to lunch with me today. He suggested
Walgreen's. I understood he was gently pushing me, sensing my
reluctance to go back where my traumatic experience occurred.
Mrs. Griffin, who had participated in the sit-ins, was supervisor.
There were no Negroes eating. The only place free was a booth
in the far corner. This involved our winding through the entire
eating section, a colored and white man together. Despite my
uneasiness, we managed it with no hurt more damaging than a few
curious stares. I grabbed the seat which put my back to the wall;
there no one could get behind me, while I could see the entire
room. I looked for the employee who threw the lighted cigarette
on me, but could not recognize him. Fired? On vacation? Transferred to another department? The food was excellent. The waitress was most courteous to Pete—"More coffee, sir?" Here again
was evidence that once the businessman says, "You're my customer," the human relations problem is settled.

Pete kept me interested, if not entertained, during lunch by a
tale of his past. He prefaced it with the remark that Carroll Felton
had said he deliberately adopted non-violence eleven years ago
after almost killing another man in a fight. "With me it was just
the opposite," Pete said—"I adopted it as my only practical defense
after someone almost killed me!" He had been hailed into court
some years ago in Norfolk, Virginia, his home town, on a minor
traffic violation. A police officer directed him to sit in a particular
section of the courtroom designated as the "colored" section. Pete
sat somewhere else. The police dragged him into an anteroom,

handcuffed him with his hands behind his back, and began to beat him up. When one of the officers put his thumb in Pete's mouth, Pete, unable to defend himself any other way, bit it. He was charged with assaulting an officer and eventually paid a fine of $250. Pete calls this "the justice of the Southern white man."

As we left the store, Mrs. Griffin told us surreptitiously that three white toughs, one of whom was brandishing a knife, had just left there for Kress's. She asked us to tell the supervisor at Kress's. At Kress's we could find no one we could identify as either supervisor or toughs. Two elderly Negroes were eating there, whites on either side of them. Harry, Jr., Lee Butler, and a girl were eating. They told us they had first gone to Cole's, having misunderstood which places were cooperating in the desegregation move. As they sat at the counter there, they noticed a new sign, "We reserve the right to refuse service to anyone." As they started out, a waitress asked if she could serve them. "No," one of them replied, "we don't like your sign."

The evening paper carries an eighth-page ad by the owner of a cafeteria in Oak Ridge which is being picketed for holding up the desegregation of eating places in this near-by nuclear workshop. The owner states: ". . . I must continue to operate my restaurant the only way I know how to operate a restaurant . . . against the background of our Southern traditions." In this case the Southern traditions exclude one of the city's councilmen. It is an amazing fact that considering Nashville, Knoxville, and Oak Ridge only, the dispatch with which desegregation of eating places has occurred has been directly proportional to the percentage of Negro population. If there is anything at all to this little rule of thumb, it has tremendous implications for the speed of integration in the Deep South once the initial break is made in the wall. Significant factors in the three cities mentioned are the degree of self-identity and the strength of leadership within the Negro group, plus the fact that where there are fewer Negroes there is often less for them to complain of.

Sunday, July 24

As I entered Tabernacle Baptist Church for the mass meeting, Rev. James called me back to the office and asked slyly, "Which of these three topics would you prefer to talk about this afternoon . . . ?" Since I had all of five minutes to prepare, I chose the philosophical topic—a "reappraisal" of what we have accomplished. Actually, having kept this journal of everything that has happened, I couldn't have avoided doing some thinking about what it all means. During the few moments I had, I scribbled a few notes on the back of a handbill I had received at the door which announced a meeting tomorrow night of all those interested in creating new jobs and new businesses for Negroes, a project being pushed by a group of the women, I understand.

Although this meeting was scarcely advertised, the auditorium of this large newish church was full. On this extremely hot afternoon, everyone was fanning vigorously with fans that advertised a Negro-owned funeral home on their reverse sides. (Not the mortuary operated by the physician; there *is* one such monopoly in Knoxville.)

In his welcoming speech the host pastor, Rev. Baker, told of a white soldier and colored soldier who were buddies in the army. The white soldier was always getting wounded and his Negro friend would have to visit him in the hospital. Finally the latter gave his friend some advice: "Friend, why don't you do like I do— I run zig-zag when the firing starts." His white buddy replied, "I run zig-zag too." "Yes," said the colored boy, "but I watched you and you were zigging when you ought to have been zagging, and zagging when you ought to have been zigging."

I can imagine this story had a different application when it was first told, but the pastor made this point with it: "Now is the time to zig when we are *supposed* to zig!"

Rev. James, who was presiding, cried gaily, "How many of you feel better than you did at the first mass meeting?" Everyone raised his hand enthusiastically.

Dr. Crutcher began his report by announcing that a discount store and a suburban drug store have joined the downtown stores in desegregating their counters and that two drugstore chains without downtown outlets have made commitments to desegregate as soon as some details can be worked out. He emphasized that we are moving ahead at the same time on other fronts. An investigating committee has discovered shockingly unequal conditions at the local state mental hospital. "And we are not going to stop before we have a student in the undergraduate department of the University of Tennessee!" (The graduate and law schools have been desegregated since 1952; Negro high school students are on the campus this summer in federally-financed science institutes, but the undergraduate college remains segregated—largely, I think, because no Negro has ever gone to court to seek admission.)

Then Crutcher turned with vehemence to the subject of the trade withdrawal from the five stores that have refused to open to us. "The Negro can no longer be pushed aside and deferred until tomorrow. He is ready *now* for full first-class citizenship! There are some who are dragging their feet, but the majority of the Negroes of Knoxville are marching. And I can tell you that those who're dragging their feet are going to find it mighty uncomfortable to drag their feet when they're with a crowd of marching people!"

A woman had told him this morning that, as she was leaving Miller's store on Thursday, she was followed by a group of youngsters who took her package away from her. (Approving applause.) "I told her, and I want to warn all of you, that we are not responsible for anything that happens from now on." Anyone who slips into one of these stores by a back entrance "is less than a traitor!" he declared. Miller's store has three fronts, he explained. "They've got an alley too!" someone shouted from the audience. "Yes," quipped Crutcher, "and some of the folks that go in there are alley folks!" He warned that every time a Negro goes into one of the "off-limits" stores the organization gets notified by one means or another. Furthermore, a group of young people has said they are going to stand in front of the two downtown department stores and take snapshots of any Negroes who go in. "At the mass meeting next Sunday we will have some pictures to show you!"

One particularly shocking incident burdened Crutcher. A truck from Miller's was seen unloading furniture at the home of a prominent Negro businessman. "He has stabbed us in the back!" Crutcher cried, and added, "I'd rather do without something now, even though I needed it badly, so that my grandchildren could have it in dignity tomorrow!"

James followed Crutcher to urge the people to keep with care the agreement with the merchants so that at the end of the ten days we will stand a good chance of getting the restrictions removed. He disclosed the reports he has had from the merchants, which show that the terms have not been kept in every instance:

On July 21, at 4:10 P.M., two colored boys entered Kress's, split up, and one sat between two white women, even though fourteen seats were available. The other boy sat by himself looking embarrassed. James's comment was: "If this movement doesn't mean more to us than sitting between two women, we ought to stop it right now!"

On July 22, at 12:45 P.M., a large colored man and woman took seats at one of the counters. The man, who apparently had been drinking, was loud and boisterous. Customers seated near him left. James's comment: "Be foolish somewhere else. This is too serious a thing to play with!"

On July 23, at 3:30 P.M., two Negroes were seated at Woolworth's when two others came in and sat down before the hostess could intercept them. To save the situation, our "hostess" told the manager, "Those are dark white people." (At this, James's audience howled with laughter.) James continued: "The manager suspected, but you know it is not always possible to tell one of us with complete accuracy. Now those insistent people made the hostess tell a lie—but the Lord will forgive you for a *good* lie once in a while. But now let me give you a little advice: If your color is light and you think you can get by without being counted on the quota, do it in such a way that you won't get *us* into trouble. Leave that little dark one at home, because otherwise it's a mark against us. Don't carry *me* with you, in other words. If my wife wants to go somewhere where there are restrictions, she doesn't carry me along. The Bible tells us: 'Be as wise as serpents and as harmless as doves.' "

The manager of Walgreen's complained one day that Negroes were singling out his store to eat in. He had confided this concern to his district manager, who after looking in all the other stores and finding no Negroes eating, believed the complaint justified. He went to James. "I'm an unhappy man," he said. "Well, let's talk about your unhappiness then. Because it makes me unhappy when you are unhappy." (I never know when James is adding window-dressing to a story, but don't really wish to be disenchanted.) James's answer to the man's problem was that Walgreen's serves the best food. A disarmingly simple answer, and one I could well believe true after sampling their fare there Friday. The manager had been circulating through the stores again while James was there conversing and returned to report, "I withdraw my complaint. I found Negroes eating in all the other stores." James added to his present audience: "I'm not telling you not to go in there, but now that you've heard the problem, I'm sure you'll know how to adjust yourself to it. If you're going to get hungry downtown, manage to get hungry in front of some other store this week."

Then James made some comments about the approaching state primary election which illustrated how potentially powerful on the political level this new sense of unity among the Negroes may become. "Tip Taylor is spending a lot of money. Some of you may be tempted, but certainly Estes is the man we want to vote for— he is for full citizenship for all citizens." (Choruses of "Amen.") "Now in regard to this race for sheriff, you all remember, because it was reported in the papers, that E. B. Bowles said in a meeting at the First Presbyterian Church that he would use his office to prevent school integration. E. B. is still in the fruit business, but you forget about all those free bananas he's passed out. We're not going to vote for E. B., are we? In fact he doesn't employ any Negroes. We ought to stop eating those old rotten bananas altogether!"

To a white minister, these seem extremely pointed political comments for a minister to make, but I have the impression that they are no more direct than many of the Negro pastors are in the habit of being about politics. Politicians know that, if they can win the minister's affection, they will have many votes besides his own. This puts the minister in a fearfully responsible position. Some of the Negro ministers here are active Republicans and some active Democrats, so their influences tend to cancel one another in most races, but whenever a clear-cut civil rights issue is felt, as in the two contests James had just mentioned, party affiliation is likely to fall increasingly by the wayside.

Finally James introduced me with a flowery tribute to the part I had played in the demonstrations. I felt it the part of modesty, in my turn, to mention the exaggerated character of the press reports of the Walgreen incident. I remarked that friends in Texas had written expressing the hope that I was "getting better," to which I replied by quoting Mark Twain—"The reports of my death are greatly exaggerated." Since my talk this afternoon represented a summation and estimate of the whole movement, I think I should record it in some detail from my notes. (No doubt some of the rough spots will have to be smoothed a little to get it down here in written prose.)

"The daily news from the Congo reminds us that all over the world there is a great movement of those who have been oppressed to gain freedom, of those who have been 'have nots' to become 'haves,' of those who have had things done for them to do things for themselves, of those outside the pale of full citizenship to get full citizenship. By an accident of history, this is largely an upward movement of the colored peoples of the world. To evaluate properly our movement here in Knoxville, we must see it as a part of that larger movement.

"Yet we are not working *against* America; rather we are working *as Americans* to secure that which the American ideal has always claimed—and to serve a *better* America. What has happened here this summer has been truly amazing. *For the first time* in Knoxville the Negroes have become a united, inspired force, moving together toward the accomplishment of goals they ought to have attained years ago. I often think that, because of the experiences we are having in this movement, a disproportionately large contribution is going to be made by the Negroes of Knoxville to the community of the future, because we have learned the value of civic rights by first being deprived of them and then having to struggle for them.

"As I view the effort of these past few months, I find five things unique and important about the movement here in Knoxville as contrasted to the lunch counter movement in other cities. The first is that it has been an effort of the *whole* Negro community—not just students. The students started it and got the rest of us interested; but again by an accident of history—the fact that things came to a head just as school let out—we adults were forced to pitch in and carry on, and this may have been a very fortunate thing. It enlisted the whole community in a united way. On our sit-ins we had youngsters as young as two and adults over seventy.

"A second unique thing is the degree to which this movement has not been limited to Negroes, but has been carried out in cooperation with significant numbers of friends in the white community. I think we can get even more cooperation from the white community if we can strengthen our lines of communication. We've been depending mostly on the ministers, but I'm not sure they're the best channel of communication. Often lay people will do things their pastors won't ask them to do.

"A third important thing is that the city administration has been with us. I don't know of any other city where the Mayor has worked so hard to get the lunch counters desegregated, even to the point of taking a committee all the way to New York to plead with the store executives to let us desegregate our counters in Knoxville. This augurs well for the future. We ought to be able to attain many more goals with the friendly city administration we have.

"A fourth significant thing is the extent to which this movement in Knoxville has enlisted those who had been leaders of the Negro community all along. An article in *Harper's* magazine several months ago pointed out that in very few places have the "old leaders" continued to be leaders once the struggle for equal rights moved out of the courtroom and took up newer, more vigorous techniques. Rather, new and younger leaders have come forward to take the leadership of this new phase of the movement. For some reason, the ones who had been the leaders couldn't seem to adapt themselves to the new objectives or the new methods, or manifested an interest too late. But I'm glad to say that here they did rally to the cause—not 100 per cent I'm sorry to say, and some rather slowly—but nearly unanimously, the ministers, the businessmen, the teachers, and all the other existing leaders of the Negro community gave themselves to the cause. Now certainly we want new leaders as well. It would be very bad if we ever became so rigidly structured that there was not opportunity for others who want to become leaders to find places of leadership. We must see that they have that opportunity.

"A fifth thing is that there has been no one personality here around whom everything has centered, who has pulled it along by the force of his personality. There has been no Martin Luther King, not even a Jim Lawson—but just everybody working together on a project from which everybody stands to benefit equally.

"In spite of the cynical comments we have allowed ourselves from time to time about the so-called 'good race relations in Knoxville,' I do believe that our movement has been not so much to secure good race relations as to realize the potential of those that have long existed. I know people have always said, 'We have good race relations in Knoxville,' and used this as an excuse for not doing any of the things which good race relations would seem to make mandatory. But I still think that there is a great deal of good will, that attitudes are not fundamentally hostile. If they were, we wouldn't have got public acceptance so easily of this lunch counter move. Now I'm going to say something frankly—when I preach to a predominantly white congregation, I criticize their sins, but when I preach to a colored audience, I tell them about their sins; I think that is only realistic preaching! (Sounds of 'Amen,' 'Go ahead!' come from behind me on the platform.) I think this failure to make more progress has a lot of it been your fault, because you haven't told the white man what good race relations demand of him. You haven't pointed out these things to him often enough or loudly enough. A lot of it he doesn't know or never thinks about; he lives a comfortable life, he doesn't get bothered about these things unless you bother him. We've got to speak up, to show him what our needs are, to show him some spine, some courage, and that we are determined to go forward!

"Now we've had some success with these stores, but what we've done is only a very small proportion of what remains to be done. The true value of what we've started will not be evident until we see how well the group stays together and goes on to greater achievements. Do you remember the ad in the paper two weeks ago today? I hope you cut that out and saved it. The Republicans are meeting in Chicago right now hammering out a platform; the Democrats gave us one a couple of weeks ago. Everybody it seems is getting a platform! Well, that ad is our platform! It listed at least sixteen areas of community life where we have inequalities. Our job will not be done until all sixteen of those are made right.

"Just think—we've done all this in the summertime! In the summertime generally all that people want to do is sit on the front porch and fan themselves. But if we've done this much in the summertime, think what we can do in the winter!

"Now it will not all be as dramatic as sit-ins. Some will be very dull, even negotiations—as much as that word has fallen into disrepute. It will take patience. On the part of our leadership it will require sharp thinking to pick the next objectives and outline the strategy to achieve them. For the movement as a whole, it will take clear organization, firm direction, and most of all—*full participation*."

The meeting moved into a hymn singularly appropriate for the occasion that could well have been the theme hymn for our entire movement. Significantly it was written as a passionate challenge to the eradication of slavery by an ardent believer in justice and brotherhood, James Russell Lowell. The audience, most of them nurtured on gospel hymns and spirituals, had difficulty with the complicated tune, but the power of the message nevertheless came through:

Once to every man and nation, Comes the moment to decide,
In the strife of truth with falsehood, For the good or evil side;
Some great cause, God's new Messiah, Offering each the bloom or
    blight,
And the choice goes by for ever 'Twixt that darkness and that light.

Then to side with truth is noble, When we share her wretched crust,
Ere her cause bring fame and profit, And 'tis prosperous to be just;
Then it is the brave man chooses While the coward stands aside,
Till the multitude make virtue Of the faith they had denied.

The community will accept and be secretly glad for the results of this "radical" effort of ours. In a decade or two decades, the faith that is now denied will have become virtue to all except the most raucous elements in our Southland. But then when 'tis prosperous to be just, will justice have come too late? Will the Ghanas, and the Guineas, and the Indias by that time have decided that democracy is unable to produce justice? Will the Negro Americans have become disillusioned and embittered? Will the cause of Christ have become hypocrisy in the eyes of a mankind too just to be religious?

Indeed, I believe America and in particular its Christian citizens have come to the moment to decide.

Demonstrators outside the Tennessee Theater. The sign on the marquee, "Never did so few cook up so much excitement," refers to the movie, but it applied more aptly to the protesters. Reprinted by permission of The Knoxville News-Sentinel Co.

Picketers demonstrating outside Rich's. The sign at the left appeals to the basic principles of the United States. Reprinted by permission of The Knoxville News-Sentinel Co.

Picketers demonstrating at the Locust Street entrance of Rich's. Reprinted by permission of The Knoxville News-Sentinel Co.

Picketers outside Rich's. Note the cold war theme: "Khrushchev can eat at Rich's. We Can't." Reprinted by permission of The Knoxville News-Sentinel Co.

Sitting in at the lunch counter of a variety store. Note the attitude of white passersby. Reprinted by permission of The Knoxville News-Sentinel Co.

Students sitting in at Grant's lunch counter. Reprinted by permission of The Knoxville News-Sentinel Co.

Afterword to the First Edition

AT the end of the ten-day "adjustment period" neither side contacted the other. The Associated Council simply quit sending supervisors, while the stores on their part continued serving everyone who came. Several outlying stores quietly advised Negro leaders that their people would be served. The manager who had served as the group chairman in the negotiations remarked a few weeks afterward, "I don't know why we didn't do this long before we did." This seems to typify the attitude of the merchants. The attitude of the Negroes was well expressed by a prominent Negro who is on the executive level with TVA: "I drop into Walgreen's every now and then to eat my lunch and they treat me as though I were a king; if I'd gone in there before July 18, I would have had the whole store in a turmoil. I don't understand what the difference is. Discrimination is just silly!" Were it not for the continued resistance of several leading stores, we would all feel now that the sit-in strife was just some bad dream from which gratefully we have been aroused.

But unhappily the campaign for the lunch counters is not yet over in Knoxville. More than a year after the beginning of desegregation, the counter of one of the three department stores (Sears') remains closed. Cole's, the city's most widespread drugstore chain, has made no move toward integration. Negroes continue to be excluded by injunction from the Todd & Armistead counter while the case remains tied up in the courts. The withdrawal of trade from these establishments by Negroes continues, though not perfectly observed. Numerous other establishments throughout the city, mostly drugstores with soda fountains, remain undeclared and untested. The main cafeterias at the Greyhound and Trailways bus stations have been opened to those Negroes who are "in on the know," but most of those who are traveling continue to go obediently into the "colored" luncheonettes kept open in both places.

Miller's, the home-owned department store, continued to have trouble making up its mind. The counter there had been closed during the demonstrations in June. In September the executives of Miller's called upon the president of Knoxville College in his office, told him they planned to reopen their counter, and asked him to persuade the Negro community to accept separate facilities. Those of us who had participated in the demonstrations were appalled that these intelligent men had learned so little about the spirit motivating the Negroes. The counter was opened for whites only. Various conferences with deputations from the Associated Council and other groups ensued with no apparent result. Unexpectedly then on November 17 the vice-president of Miller's called Dr. Crutcher to say that Miller's was tired of the whole affair and wanted to get it over with. He promised that Miller's counter would be open to Negroes beginning the first business day in January. That promise was kept, and of course Negro trade returned to the store when the counter was opened.

The management of Rich's disclosed in October that permission had been secured from the Atlanta headquarters to reopen the basement counter as a stand-up snack bar, with no customer discrimination. This, they said, was as far as Atlanta would yield. For a time this confronted the leaders of the Associated Council with the perplexing problem of whether to encourage the people to go back to Rich's to trade on the basis of only "vertical integration." As it turned out, this question did not have to be decided, because the store's Atlanta office withdrew its permission when the demonstrations broke out against Rich's in Atlanta.

Some rather half-hearted stand-in demonstrations were carried out in connection with Rich's Laurel Room in November by students from Knoxville College and the University of Tennessee. These were the only group demonstrations against lunch counter segregation carried on in the city during the school year after the major effort terminated. Adult members of the Associated Council have been hesitant to jeopardize their gains, while student interest has declined, partly as the result of having yielded leadership to the townspeople.

Suddenly in January, just three days after Miller's store had begun desegregated service, Knoxville was startled by the report that Miller's was in the process of purchasing Rich's Knoxville store outright. The multi-million dollar purchase was consummated January 29 with the announcement that Miller's would continue to operate both establishments. There was no indication that the sale had anything to do with the lunch counter demonstrations which had broken out in Atlanta, placing Rich's in the embarrassing position of having to go against the community in Knoxville in order to stay with it in Atlanta. But at least we knew now why Miller's had at last developed the courage to act independently, for the purchase negotiations must already have been underway in November. At last the city's largest retail store was in a position to join the rest of the business community in the elimination of discrimination. The basement lunch counter was promptly reinstalled, and both it and the Laurel Room were opened to *all* the store's customers.

This, then, is our part of the lunch counter story—a victory not complete, but nevertheless astounding in its extent and the rapidity with which it was accomplished, compared with the snail's pace at which progress has been made in other areas of equal rights, especially school desegregation.

What accounts for this extraordinary swiftness with which the change was achieved? The answer lies partly in the nature of the problem, partly in the technique employed, and partly in the spirit of those who tackled the problem. ("The condition of the patient, the type of operation, and the attitude of the surgeon," I like to call these three factors.)

Obviously the lunch counters are a vastly different type of operation from the public schools. The lunch counter is, first of all, a voluntary operation on the part of both merchant and customer. I do not have to patronize the lunch counter; I do have to send my children to the public school. (At least there is no practical alternative for most citizens.) Furthermore, the merchant who does integrate his counter does it as a result of his own decision. It is hard for the opponent of integration to question the merchant's right to extend service when the opponent has previously taken his stand on the merchant's right to serve whom he chooses.

In the second place, an integrated lunch counter does not pose the threat that a Negro may "marry my daughter." The public schools are centers of social life. In the South, and especially in small communities, they are often operated as though they were private clubs. ("We just invited every one of Junior's little classmates to his birthday party"—"All of us senior class mothers will work together on the spaghetti supper"—"Why not have the entire cast drop by the house for refreshments after the play?") But at the lunch counter I speak only to those I came in with.

For both these reasons, the general public feels much less involved in the lunch counters than in the schools. But even more important to the success of the effort is this fact: no one can deny that the Negro has a clear point of justice on his side when the entrepreneur invites him into his place of business, makes money from him in all other departments, but treats him as unwelcome at one department.

Let us turn to those elements in the "operation" itself which helped make it a success. First of all, the technique was one that enlisted the economic interest of the discriminator. In our part of the country the lunch counter proprietor is not likely to be so prejudiced that he does not covet the additional business he could get from Negroes if he served them. At first he could not be persuaded that he could have this business without losing the business of whites. It was in the negative form, therefore, that the economic motive proved decisive. The stores lost so much business from the economic "boycott" by Negroes, from the sit-in demonstrations during meal hours, and from the general disturbance of the downtown area that they decided they risked greater losses by not desegregating than by desegregating. This is *the one decisive reason* for the speedy success of the movement.

The demonstration technique makes use of one powerful factor that has thus far worked *against* school desegregation. This is the fear of community unrest. The moral implications of this I will discuss later; here I am concerned only with the fact. Southern communities, which have shown a high toleration for violence so long as it remained private and unadmitted, have a horror of open friction. Here society pictures itself as monolithic rather than cosmopolitan. Preying upon this passion for peace, a handful of die-hard segregationists in community after community throughout the South created the fear and sometimes the reality of violence whenever school desegregation seemed imminent. Said one school board member in Knoxville when pressed by a church group favoring integration, "After all, we school board members are no more anxious than any other parents to have stones thrown at our children, or our wives receiving threatening telephone calls." This fear of community friction delayed the start of school integration six years in Knoxville, whereas most informed observers agree that it could have been effected without disturbance in May, 1954. Thus a minority in the South has inflicted its will on communities by the threat of civil disturbance, carried out by techniques of public agitation and private pressure. The minority favoring integration, sometimes actually larger than the minority aggressively opposed, has been kept virtually impotent because it has insisted upon "dignified" methods.

Now in the lunch counter movement it was different. The technique employed, the sit-in demonstration, was, in and of itself, such as to place the fear of community disturbance on the side of civil rights.

The city administration, striving zealously to sell industry on coming to Knoxville, was willing to go a long way to keep from having to apologize to Northern industrialists for racial disturbances in the city. Downtown business leaders saw the economic withdrawal and the disturbances which were keeping shoppers away as working directly against their efforts to revitalize the lagging central business district. As demonstrations grew to the size where they could no longer be kept quiet by the tacit consent of city administration, business leaders, and news media (for up to the time of the picketing at Rich's, more news about the Knoxville demonstrations was being carried in other cities than by our local press, radio, and TV), something simply had to be done. The issue was forced with decisiveness and in a way that made it clear that the petitioning group was a force indigenous to Knoxville—a real community interest that would have to be taken into consideration in the future if Knoxville were to thrive.

To put all this in few words, integration in general has gone slowly because Negroes have not really made a fuss about it. In the lunch counter movement, they learned how much can be accomplished by making a fuss.

A third element in the technique which made for success was the factor of surprise. The technique was new. It had won its victory before the opposition had opportunity to group its forces and devise effective counterweapons. In many areas where the lunch counters were not desegregated in the first year, success may become increasingly difficult.

When everything has been said that may be said about the nature of the lunch counters and the sit-in technique, a large part of the success of the lunch counter crusade must be credited to the persons who carried it out—that is, primarily the Negroes themselves. There were revealed in connection with this movement assets among our Negro people which had hardly been suspected before. There were the enthusiasm and initiative of the students who launched the movement. They, it seems, had taken seriously what they had been taught in school, that "all men are created equal," that America is "the land of the free." "If you see something that needs to be done, form a committee and do it," has always been the American spirit; this is exactly what these Negro students did.

There was the leadership ability which made itself available. In some cases the leadership too has come entirely from within the student group; in Knoxville it came from three additional groups—ministers, college teachers, and housewives. In the face of this wealth of leadership, whites must ask themselves, "Are we going to have to discard Rastus and Hambone as caricatures of the Southern Negro?"

There was the courage these Negroes displayed. Even at times when they have had reason to believe that every community power was arrayed against them, individuals have had the courage to face violence, arrest, and imprisonment. They have met the greatest test of courage—the ability to endure humiliation.

Finally, there has been the religious spirit which has enabled Negroes to feel that they marched to battle in the strength of the Lord, even as they prayed for their enemies.

It has been crucially significant to the success of the movement that the response of the Negro community has been essentially a united one. The enthusiasm for the movement ran through Negro communities like an electric charge, arousing them from the attitude of resigned, sometimes bitter, acceptance of segregation which had been characteristic of the past; it even replaced jealous rivalries between Negro leaders and groups with a united march toward a common community goal. In contrast to the tedious court maneuvers that have characterized the school battle, the lunch counter movement has had drama and excitement. The technique of the sit-in has a certain flamboyance about it—the appeal of Jerry the mouse teasing Tom the cat. It is true that the unity of the Negro community in Knoxville came very slowly. This I believe has been true of the movement in general. Coupled with the historic reluctance of both races in the South to force the issue and the feeling on the part of the Negro that the white man will somehow manage to keep the key to all the doors has been in this case a hesitance to become public demonstrators, for that form of expression had been as foreign to the thinking of American Negroes as to that of most American whites. But when the demonstrators began to be subjected to threats and physical indignity, Negroes felt it a personal affront and began to call and to come asking, "What can we do to help?"

In evoking this united response, the lunch counter crusade had one further advantage over the school desegregation movement —it did not run counter to any vested interest in the Negro community itself. While Negroes in principle want a society in which all racial stigma is removed, there are nevertheless many who are unenthusiastic about desegregation of schools in practice. There is, for one thing, the well-founded fear of Negro teachers that they would lose their jobs if the local schools desegregated. (It would be difficult to overestimate the threat this poses to the Negro community, since in the Southern states teaching is almost the only vocation in which Negroes are on a parity with whites with respect to both employment opportunities and pay scale.) Furthermore, there are many who are reluctant to give up the neighborhood school as a center of Negro community life. They are not sure to what extent they would be able to build a new community feeling together with whites. Thus there have been substantial forces in the Negro community that have not been impatient with the slow progress of school desegregation. The lunch counter movement encountered no such drag; it brooked no vested interest.

Thus, the nature of lunch counters, the nature of the new techniques employed, the character of the Negro people, and the nature of their response to this cause all must be considered in accounting for the rapid successes of the movement compared to the slow progress of school integration.

What have been the results of the lunch counter movement? A look at the Knoxville situation discloses some clues.

(1) The most obvious result of the movement in our city is that Negroes are now able to eat in at least sixteen lunch places where they were not eating before. Throughout the South, counters have been "mixed" in perhaps one hundred cities. The effect of this on the way of life of the average Negro has been small, but on his morale the effect has been tremendous.

(2) An effect that may ultimately be more far-reaching is the awaking of a slumbering giant—the Negro population. For the first time many of our Southern communities have become aware that their Negro residents constitute an economic and political force to be reckoned with. The Negroes have been as surprised to learn this as anyone else. The Negro community has yawned, stretched its limbs, and felt a surge of youthful vigor which has sent through it a tingle of excitement at the prospect of new victories.

The organizations formed to wage the lunch counter battle may be turned to other objectives. Our Associated Council began to work on voter registration even before the counter crusade met with success. The enthusiasm engendered by the mass movement spilled over to cause a Negro student at last to apply to the undergraduate school of the University of Tennessee, and in November the Board of Trustees of that institution announced that race would no longer be a factor in admissions. Meanwhile the new *esprit de corps* had been an important factor in persuading the parents of twenty-nine Negro children to enroll them in the first grade at previously white schools when the Knoxville school system in September was finally forced by a long court struggle to begin desegregation on the grade a year plan. (The number may seem small, but is many times the percentage response achieved in Nashville three years earlier, B.L.C.—"before lunch counters.") The Associated Council in ensuing months began to turn its attention to segregated hospitals.

The potential effectiveness of an aroused Negro populace has been demonstrated; the question that remains is whether the will and the unity can be retained when the cause offers no such dramatic excitement as the sit-ins created. Will the giant settle back for another nap? Hardly had the victory been won in Knoxville before meetings of the Executive Committee of the Associated Council began to break out in bickering between individuals jealous of leadership roles, while the Council and the local NAACP chapter were playing Alphonse and Gaston to one another without the customary smiles. Observers at the area-wide organization meeting of the Student Non-Violence Movement in Atlanta in October, 1960, noted that even at that early date the students spent much of their time wrangling over parliamentary procedure.[1] This is the institutional rut which threatens every new movement once the original enthusiasm begins to wane.

(3) The lunch counter crisis brought about in Knoxville and scores of other Southern cities an unprecedented contact between whites and Negroes on the level of community leadership. For a long time community relations groups in Knoxville had been urging the mayor, the city council, or the county commission to create a Human Rights Commission, but with no success; now overnight something like it came into existence. Though unfortunately most of these biracial committees created in Southern cities to grapple with the lunch counter crisis were set up on an *ad hoc* basis, nevertheless the protracted negotiations gave white and Negro leaders opportunity to gain a new respect for one another and a better understanding of one another's burdens. If, for example, white leaders learned that there is more than one Negro in the community worth knowing, or that Negroes do not always think as a unit on every community problem, then prog-

1. I am indebted for this observation to Paul Rilling, Director of Field Activities of the Southern Regional Council, Atlanta. My outline in this section also owes something to a talk Mr. Rilling made to the Knoxville Area Human Relations Council on October 18, 1960.

ress was achieved. Interestingly enough, when Negro and white leaders in this Middle South community got together, they registered very little disagreement on principle. The difficulty was not caused by and large by personal prejudices, but by fear of that other group "out there," that is, the uncultured whites.

(4) It would seem hardly possible since the lunch counter demonstrations for Southern whites to continue believing the favorite rationalization, "Our Negroes are satisfied with our arrangement here in the South," and its corollary, "The trouble is all being caused by outside agitators!" When scores of local Negroes of all ages filed day after day into eating places, braving taunts and blows and possible arrest to register their protest against "things as they are," the person would be hard-headed indeed who did not get the point. With those whites who really cared—and there were many—this revelation will make a difference. Those on the other hand who are determined to resist any change now know that they must entrench for a bitter struggle.

(5) The lunch counter crusade threw the spotlight dramatically on group discrimination and demonstrated that something can be done about it by ordinary people. This has stimulated interest among white groups in working for the removal of discrimination. The increased activity has been especially noticeable among students. Never have Knoxville College students found themselves so popular among white students as during the year following the sit-ins. The Presbyterian students at the University asked a group of our students to join them in a weekly study group on race relations. The Methodist students at the University invited some Knoxville College students to Sunday evening supper and enlisted one for a part in a play they were presenting. Weekend student exchanges between Knoxville College and nearby Maryville College became a monthly occurrence, and Maryville students set up two committees to work on different aspects of desegregation. The Catholic, Episcopal, Presbyterian, Methodist, and Baptist student groups at the University of Tennessee joined to petition the Board of Trustees to integrate the undergraduate

departments of the University. While it is impossible to trace a history from these efforts back to the sit-ins, we have a strong feeling that, had it not been for the sit-ins, most of these things would not have happened. The current student generation, which has been pictured in all surveys as indifferent, may be finding for itself a cause.

(6) Concurrently, the success of lunch counter desegregation has helped to bring about a community atmosphere more favorable to such race relations activity. Take Knoxville, for example. With lunch counter desegregation, the beginning of school desegregation, and the dropping of the race barrier at the University, Knoxville in the space of one summer turned from a community segregated in principle to a community desegregated in principle. Among the leading stores the principle is now fairly well agreed upon: either you have an integrated lunch counter or you do not operate a lunch counter. It has therefore now become "safe" to advocate integration. School teachers, for example, need feel no reluctance in mentioning it in the classroom. Why, in fact, haven't we *always* been for integration?

(7) Not everyone approves of sit-ins, but at least we have discovered that there are other, more direct ways than court action for achieving fair treatment. Although the spotlight was on the demonstrations, it is nevertheless true that the lunch counter effort brought about more face to face *negotiation* of civil rights grievances than had ever been carried out before in the South. In only a few localities did reasoning alone prove enough; nevertheless, reasoning together may get more results in the future, now that communities have the lesson of the lunch counters to look to.

While it would be a mistake for integrationists to seize upon the sit-in as the answer to all problems, the peaceful demonstration carried out in a spirit of good will offers itself as an effective means of appealing to the public conscience. If the success of the lunch counter movement was partly due to the novelty of the technique, this constitutes the challenge to Negroes and their friends to engage in creative thinking for the purpose of devising new techniques and new ways to use the demonstration. The possibilities are exciting.

In the lunch counter movement Southern Negroes discovered their own economic power as an instrument for securing their social rights. In the sit-ins and their accompanying "economic withdrawals" they learned one effective way to use this power, but in that case the discrimination was by businesses that depended on Negro trade in other departments. Can Negroes find ways of using their economic power to bring about desegregation of restaurants, movies, hotels, and hospitals? The general withdrawal of trade from white-owned businesses during a protest period suggests itself as a possibility.

(8) On the national scale the sit-ins caused a stepping up in political efforts to establish civil rights. The sit-ins were sufficiently significant that both political parties felt compelled to say something good about them in the party platforms of 1960. John Kennedy's phone call to Mrs. Martin Luther King, Jr., while her husband was in jail on charges growing out of his participation in an Atlanta sit-in, is the best indication of the issue's importance. No less a personage than the then-president of the United States is reported to have remarked that this phone call (plus another made by Robert Kennedy) won John Kennedy the election.

(9) The lunch counter movement brought forth new, young Negro leaders for the cause of civil rights. Many of these are still in college; if they retain their enthusiasm, the full force of the new leadership will come in a few years when these persons have assumed the positions of power and influence in the Negro communities.

It is to be hoped that the leadership ability of these youths will not be restricted to the Negro community, however. For those who have eyes to see, the sit-in movement has revealed the tremendous resources we have in our Negro people as potential leaders of our whole society. This comes at a time when three of the four "trouble spots" for the United States identified by President Eisenhower in his farewell message to Congress involved the aspirations of the darker-skinned peoples. The nineteen million dark-skinned citizens of the United States could be our greatest asset in our relations with these areas.

Public captivation by the sit-in has obscured the fact that in many cities—perhaps we could say most cities—the sit-in technique was unsuccessful. Typically the lunch counter struggle went through three phases before a bargain was finally struck. Negotiation was the first phase. This failed in almost every instance, whereupon Negroes turned to the public protest—the sit-in—hoping to afflict the conscience of the community sufficiently to prompt action. But the sit-in, in and of itself, also usually brought no results. It was finally the economic boycott or threat of it which was effective in the key cities. This means that—much as we may prefer the contrary—the issue was not settled on the basis of morality, but on the basis of economics.

As we demonstrators began to realize that the store managers respected economic power more than moral power, we became increasingly cynical. We tended to think less of our Christian witness and more in terms of winning the game by whatever means should prove effective. "He doesn't understand our language; therefore, we will just have to speak in a language he does understand!" came to be our common rationalization. So the sit-in, which began as a moral protest and demonstration that integration would *not* hurt business, many of us came to think of as an instrument precisely for hurting business. The sit-in became for many of us an arm of the economic withdrawal; we were even quite aware and not displeased that customers were staying away from town because of the unrest provoked by our quiet and peaceable activities. "Six demonstrators will not be enough to make any dent in business at all!" some of us complained when we were requested to restrict our numbers. One of our group consistently urged, "When we go into a place, we ought to take enough people to occupy the counter completely!"

The question was, "Should we adapt ourselves to the value categories of our opponent in order to deal with him effectively, or would this be to desert our own moral position?" Involved was not only the objective of the sit-in but also whether the economic boycott itself could be morally justified. Perhaps the answer depended ultimately on our answer to another question: "Just what *is* that moral value we are trying to achieve? Is it to rid society of a social evil or to convict society of its sin?"

Those who look at the *fact* as the main thing tend to feel that in accomplishing desegregation, by whatever means, the moral imperative has been followed and the testimony borne. But there are some who are extremely concerned about the right and wrong of segregation who would feel that little has been gained unless we get society to recognize that right and wrong. These persons tend to feel that not only the goal but the method itself at every step of the way should be of such stuff as justice and love are made. They would feel that a genuine moral advance can be made only as men make moral decisions and that a moral decision must be an unforced decision—that it is different in this respect from a "good" decision.

It is true that the economic withdrawal is less objectionable from two standpoints than the use of the sit-in as an economic weapon. The withdrawal seeks only to withhold support, while the sit-in as an economic weapon aims to inflict injury; the boycott is a withholding of one's own support, while the sit-in used economically seeks to prevent others from trading. Yet the economic withdrawal—non-violent, to be sure—is certainly not non-forceful. Furthermore, the economic withdrawal in the form that has proved effective—the withdrawal from the entire business area— is subject to a criticism that the sit-in is not, namely, that it intentionally hurts the "innocent" as well as the "guilty." The same question may therefore be raised about both types of economic weapons. Put in a religious frame of reference, is it "Christian" to hurt another individual for any purpose? Framed in a more general way, in those areas in which the law allows individual choice, have I a right to force another person to do what is right even though he does not wish to do what is right or may not agree with me as to what is right? It is difficult for supporters of integration to see the validity of the question; we can perhaps see it more objectively by turning the tables:

The white landowners and merchants in Fayette and Heywood counties in Tennessee used "non-violent" economic pressure to get rid of the Negro sharecroppers who had upset the traditional arrangement between the races by registering to vote. And if the Negro customer in Knoxville protests, "Yes, but surely I have no duty to continue to buy from a merchant who discriminates against me!" the white wholesaler in Heywood County can say, "Surely I have no duty to sell to a Negro merchant who is pursuing a course which would make this an undesirable community for me and my family to live in!" (He fears that relatively uneducated Negroes would control local affairs to the disadvantage of the white population.)

The two arguments are identical. There is not even any certainty that the individual Negro's motives are more noble. The majority in both groups are seeking some benefit for their own group more than they are concerning themselves about the general welfare. A distinction can be made in the two situations only by resort to some standard of values which would enable us to judge the end being served in either case as distinguished from the personal motive that causes individuals to seek that end. The Christian ethic, since it is claimed by both groups, affords such a standard, and its testimony at this point is clear. The faith which declares that "in Christ there is neither Jew nor Greek" certifies the goal of the Knoxville Negroes (equal treatment in a society which makes no race distinctions), but rejects the goal of the Heywood County whites (the continuation of white supremacy). The same is true if we use our "American ideals" as the standard. The Negro is saying, "I want this right *too!*" while his white opponent is saying, "I want this right *exclusively!*" In the light of the creed, "All men are created equal," it is easy to see which goal is approved. So the Negro is in a different position morally than the Heywood County white in resorting to forceful, non-violent means to attain his social objective. But how different?

What we have boiled this down to, of course, is the age-old question, "Does the end justify the means?" The Communist can take the position that the end—the party's end—invariably justifies the means; but from the Christian point of view this can be true only in relation to particular ends and particular means. One can certainly not maintain that the end and means of lunch counter desegregation are everywhere the same. Integrating the drugstore counter in a Mississippi county seat town is not the same end as integrating Woolworth's in Knoxville, unless one is speaking in very theoretical fashion. And certainly the sit-in technique takes on different implications in the same two settings. For Christian ethics, is it not finally a question that must be left to the informed Christian conscience, guided by the community of faith?

If the end is important in reaching the decision on the method, at least equally important is the spirit in which the method is used. In our campaign we often fell short of loving the store managers; yet I think we never bore them ill will. Many times we said, "It is for their good as well as ours—the rights we seek are not for ourselves alone, but for all Americans." I think we really believed that. The utter pacifist would contend that it is not possible to strike a man while loving him. One Quaker woman here refused to join the economic withdrawal for this reason alone. But most Christians would affirm that it is possible to strike, even to kill, a man in the spirit and motive of love and that sometimes it is unfortunately most necessary. Perhaps in the consideration of "spirit with which" we have another mark that distinguishes the Negroes of Knoxville from the whites of Heywood County. Only the whites of Heywood County can say; but I, from my base in Christian ethics, can say this much: if they acted in love, it was a mistaken love.

The conscience continues to accuse. This time it objects to any kind of public demonstration or group pressure as a way of settling differences. "It is not the American way. It is not the method of mature and reasonable men." The internal objector contends that when a minority group resorts to a means other than persuasion or law to enforce its will on the majority, the very existence of democratic processes is threatened.

The answering voice asserts that of course public demonstrations have been used by groups hostile to democracy, but it would be wrong to condemn the method because of the people who have used it or the purposes for which it has been used. The difference, the voice maintains, again lies in the *end* and the *spirit*. "In this case the demonstration is being used to achieve that equality of citizenship which is the very essence of democracy. We do not seek to take anything away from anyone else, but only to achieve it for ourselves as well."

The answering voice may go on to argue that indeed it is better to use reason and the ballot when these can be effective, but that in the South today the public demonstration furnishes a voice for a group which often has no other way of making itself heard. It is the cry of anguish which says for the oppressed minority, "I am hurting! Please step off my toe!"

The answering voice speaks persuasively. It should be pointed out, however, that by its own logic, every possibility of quiet negotiation should be exhausted before public demonstration is resorted to.

Conscience stirs again. "You go in love, committed to a non-violent course, but your adversary has no such commitment. You go knowing that your action may evoke violence; therefore you cannot escape some of the responsibility for that violence!" (I thought of the baby struck by the salt-shaker and my own feeling of guilt because it was our presence that incited the hatred.)

The answering voice replies with a note of hesitance, "It is principally ourselves that we stand ready to sacrifice to appease the monster Hatred; if others must suffer, we would be deeply grieved, but we cannot feel that their sacrifice would be any less worthwhile than our own. We would rather hope, however, that some innocent bystander, observing that we do not return evil for evil, might be accidentally blessed."

At this latter remark, I thought of "Spraybomb" (real name, Sprayberry), the white heckler jailed with the Negro student demonstrators in Atlanta for spraying them with insecticide. When the students were told that they were to be released, their response was, "What about Spraybomb? We won't go unless he is released too!" After two days in the same jail with these good-willed students, "Spraybomb" told one of them, "I would have killed you the other day if that had been a real gun, but after seeing the way you've acted here in jail, I feel entirely different about it now."

Conscience is still not convinced. "But I tell you, you are indeed hurting the innocent along with the guilty. For did not every downtown merchant, even those who have been your best friends in the past, suffer from the general economic withdrawal, and not just those merchants with lunch counters?"

The voice answers this time with more assurance: "No man is an island. Our whole culture is guilty. Does anybody suppose that if J. C. Penney had a lunch counter, it would have been integrated all this time while all the others were segregated? Or that Hall's is less prone than Miller's to esteem profit above justice? It would be more accurate to say that if we did *not* make the boycott general, most of the guilty would be escaping scot-free, leaving the few who happen to have lunch counters to take the rap.

"But you have tricked me into arguing on the basis of your assumptions. For when you speak of the 'guilty' and the 'innocent,' you imply that our objective is to *punish*.[1] Not so. We are not withdrawing our business *because* something happened, but *in order to cause* something to happen. This requires that we face up to some very practical considerations: If we buy at The Knox

1. On this point I will have to take exception to Paul Ramsey's emphasis in his penetrating study, *Christian Ethics and the Sit-in* (New York: Association Press, 1961), pp. 99 ff., where he contends that only the "guilty" should be subject to economic sanctions, implying that a rather clear distinction can be made between the innocent and the guilty. The question is not "Who are the guilty who should be punished?" but "Who will respond to economic sanctions by effecting the desired change?" I do agree with Mr. Ramsey, however, that economic power should be used as "economically" (sparingly) as possible.

because we are boycotting Grant's, then The Knox is actually benefiting from the continuation of segregation. On the other hand, if we withdraw from the entire downtown area, Penney's and Hall's and The Knox will begin to use persuasion on Grant's and Miller's and Woolworth's—something which they could have done long ago had they been really concerned about justice but have apparently not done even during the long months of negotiation." Looking at it from hindsight, we can see that in this case the end *did* justify the means because the whole community—not just the offending stores—benefited by the removal of a social canker and the reconciliation of a group representing some 18 per cent of the potential retail market; the price paid for this in terms of economic loss was very small indeed.

There is no recourse, really, but to let the two voices battle on to a decision in the heart of every man.

The question of civil disobedience is one we never had to answer unequivocally in Knoxville. It is perhaps the most difficult of all for the conscience. When the General Assembly of the United Presbyterian Church declared that "some laws and customs requiring racial discrimination are, in our judgment, such serious violations of the law of God as to justify peaceable and orderly disobedience or disregard of these laws," the official board of one local church protested: ". . . when the 'disregard' or 'disobedience' of the laws . . . is openly supported, the words 'orderly' and 'peaceable' . . . become outright contradictions."

Surely one assumes a very grave responsibility when he elects to disobey the law. The Presbyterian Assembly recognized this when it went on to caution students to "continue to recognize the dangers to the civil order inherent in conflict with established authority." Nevertheless, does the Christian not accept the principle of civil disobedience when he asserts that God is above the state? The First Epistle of Peter admonishes, "Be subject for the Lord's sake to every human institution, whether it be to the emperor as supreme, or to governors as sent by him to punish those who do wrong and to praise those who do right" (2:13-14)—and yet the

Apostle Peter himself, after being strictly charged by the Sanhedrin not to preach Jesus anymore, was soon arrested again for doing exactly that (Acts 4:18 ff., 5:18 ff.). Nor can we suppose that it was for obedience to the law that Peter, according to firm early tradition, was put to death during the Neronian persecution. There were Christians in Nazi Germany who in defiance of law hid Jews and helped smuggle them from the country. Did they sin in so doing, or would it have been a greater sin not to do so? (Perhaps the answer to both questions is "yes.")

Is it not vital to the American political concept that the state exists to serve values greater than those of its own creation? If I believe that I have been "endowed by my *Creator* with certain inalienable rights" and that the state itself exists to protect these rights, then perhaps I ought to consider it a dereliction of duty *not* to resist when an arm of the state's power, in ignorance or perversion of its true purpose, tries to rob me of those rights.

Negroes are in a particularly sensitive position with regard to civil disobedience, since they must depend upon general respect for the law both for protection from violent extremists and for the gradual extension of integration through legal procedures. They know that civil disobedience can be used to prevent integration, as happened, for example, in the New Orleans school integration controversy. But the fact that federal law and the moral law as they conceive it coincide for them enables them to disobey state and local laws in the name of a higher *civil* law. This protects them from some of the onus that would otherwise be attached to "taking the law in their own hands."

Preservation of law and order is a high value. We cannot violate that responsibility lightly. Whether or not we will do so seems to depend upon how high we rate that other principle—religious or humanitarian—which has come into conflict with the demand of the state. The individual must decide for himself after repairing to the deepest recesses of his personal faith and the profoundest wisdom of the group in which he has his spiritual fellowship. But to deny the possibility of disobeying the law is to have another god before Him who is the source of both law and conscience.

In all the discussion about the sit-ins, I have never once heard the fundamental question raised which has been very much in my thoughts since my participation in the Knoxville struggle: Is an economic system *right* which places a higher value on personal profit than on human dignity and simple justice, which traps a man in such a way that it is almost impossible for him to live by his own noblest insights?

As a minister, I had preached for years the application of the Christian ethic to life in the business world, but I discovered in June, 1960, that I had not begun to comprehend the gap that exists between the mandates of religion and life in the business world. I am haunted by a statement reputedly made by one of the merchants to a minister member of the Mayor's Committee—"Your Christian ethics are fine down at the First Baptist Church on Sunday, but they won't work on Gay Street during the week!" We found our merchants to be decent men, most of them unprejudiced themselves. As a group, they responded much better to this social challenge than might have been expected. They went farther in relation to what could have been expected of them than the Knoxville ministers did in relation to what could have been expected of them. But they simply didn't consider morality a proper test to apply to business procedures. They are trained to make decisions on the basis of profit, either immediate or eventual. Some told us frankly that their jobs depended on it. Most of them have a high respect for the Christian faith; they retain both creeds only by making just the sort of dichotomy between their religious life and their business life which the merchant revealed in the comment to the minister.

It seems to me that Christians in the Western world must at last face the serious question whether there is not inherent in the capitalistic system an anti-Christian motive. Christ says man's first duty is to love God and his second duty to love his neighbor.

Capitalism as it is understood among us says man's first duty is to make money. Is it as simple as that? If it is, then Christianity's unqualified blessing on capitalism may be as great a sin as its unqualified blessing (in some parts) on segregation.

The defender of this type of capitalism reasons that in the long run it is for the good of everyone, that the business man automatically helps others by helping himself. But the Christian must ask two questions in reply: Would it fulfill my obligation to Christ to act selfishly, even though it would accidentally work for the good of my neighbor? And the second, *will* it work for the good of my neighbor?

If not capitalism, what? Certainly not Communism with its complete denial of freedom to the individual to make his own moral decision. Some other type of communal society? My enthusiasm is held in check by the frank recognition of the amazing rapidity with which an individualistic society was able to solve a problem (though, we reiterate, not on moral grounds). Had the stores been owned by the state of Tennessee, we no doubt would still be seeking for the office of the bureaucrat in charge of lunch counters, haunted by the shades of Calvin Coolidge: "There is no right to strike against the public welfare." If there is an answer, it would seem to lie in some modification of the free democratic society toward making it freer. The charter for the New Age must include a Fifth Freedom—the freedom to live morally.

The least that may be said is that the Church must find a way to get through to the businessman with the conviction that his religion imposes strict limitations on the extent to which he can make profit the guiding principle in the conduct of his business.

But if society is to learn anew that it exists to serve *God*, we must first have a Church leadership both deeply concerned that the sovereignty of God be acknowledged over all society and courageous enough to bear testimony with lips and with lives. A minister named Andrew Foreman leading his little girl by the hand to an integrated school in New Orleans, or the saintly layman from my Texas parish quietly living in love—these testify to the deep contribution of the Christian faith through converted individuals to the solution of the race problem. But I have no fear of making a false judgment when I say that the Church as a whole and as an institution has failed and is failing in its response to the challenge of racial discrimination. It was a young engineering professor at the University of Tennessee and a salesman who were discussing the lunch counter movement with me when one commented, "The Knoxville ministers have been a flat tire in the whole desegregation effort." The other agreed.

While God's own mills grind not so slowly, most of the white ministers of the South are waiting patiently for the will of man to permit the word of God to be spoken. I cannot help thinking again of the prophet Amos. This time he goes by appointment to ask Amaziah, the high priest, if he may be granted permission to preach in the temple court. Amos returns to his comrades (if we can picture Amos having any) and reports, "While I had no immediate success, at least the ground has been broken. I have made a valuable contact and perhaps set the old fellow thinking. Of course I did not mention any of the social evils directly; we must avoid any appearance of bringing pressure to bear on responsible public officials. About the preaching, I said that of course he was in the better position to judge its possible effect. I assured him that he had our prayers and asked if there was anything our band of prophets could do to help in his great responsibility. He was very cordial. He said, 'Tell them to tell the people to love the poor and make their sacrifices daily in the temple.' Old Amaziah, in spite of what some have said about him, is really a very devout man. We can thank God that we have such a man as our high priest in these critical times."

A half-naked beggar, who had by chance overheard the prophet's words, turned, retched from his empty innards, and bent his faltering steps toward the temple of Baal.

Afterword to the Second Edition

I HAD been sitting in front of the TV that morning, watching as the House of Representatives paid tribute to John Duncan, dead at sixty-nine after representing his eastern Tennessee district for twenty-four years in the U.S. Congress. Another evidence, I was thinking, that those dramatic events of the summer of 1960 have passed into history. For John Duncan was the far-sighted mayor who had taken two black college students to New York in a vain attempt to talk top management of the national dime store chains into desegregating their lunch counters in Knoxville. He was the mayor who also granted me an interview only to implore me not to publish *Diary of a Sit-In*, which he with a strange lapse of prescience thought would tarnish the reputation of his city.

That afternoon of the Duncan eulogy, I learned that *Diary of a Sit-In* was to be reprinted, twenty-eight years after the events it describes. So, then, what is history? Not the garbage dump of deeds forgotten, but the collective memory of events that have made us what we are. A full generation after the civil rights revolution, it has passed into oblivion as current event, but has begun to be respected as history by a generation of students who missed its excitement, but have a suspicion that it is important for them.

We knew that summer that we were participating in history. It was a glorious feeling that gave meaning to our lives then and still does. That is the kind of experience one is lucky to have once in a lifetime. The chance depends a lot on where you happen to be. I hope others may be inspired by this story of the sit-ins not to be afraid of the chance if it comes.

You will see from the book that in 1960 I was ashamed of the Christian community's failure to stand up against racism. Looking back on the civil rights movement now from a more objective position, I am more impressed with the fact that the movement itself was a dynamic expression of Christian values. It may be one of the rare examples in history of a successful mass movement to realize the ethical teachings of Jesus and Paul. This is not to minimize the influence of Gandhi on Martin Luther King, but the black church understood King in terms of its own faith.

The civil rights movement succeeded. It clinched its victory in a series of laws passed by Congress. But the essential victory was won in the marches, the sit-ins, the freedom rides, and the voter registration drives. Some few gave their lives, forever to be honored, but all in all it was a remarkably peaceable revolution.

One cannot escape the question: Why then has not nonviolent action been used to solve more of the world's problems? The answer seems to be that the requirements for its successful use are stringent. First, those who use it must be able to subject themselves to a discipline that it may not be possible to muster for purely strategic purposes, contrary as it is to our natural instinct to strike back when struck. I think successful nonviolent demonstration must grow out of a philosophy of life held in common by the group. Second, it has the prospect of success only where those who hold the ultimate power (in our case, the white electorate) share at some level the values being appealed to by the protestors. It is doubtful that nonviolent resistance would have worked for the Jews against the Nazis.

There is another perspective that will insist that nonviolent action can succeed only where economic factors support the change being advocated. But this does not tell us much, because what people are willing to pay for something *is* its economic value, and sometimes people are willing to pay a great deal to sustain their prejudices. The dominant group will always in the beginning see the proposed change as against its material self-interest. What Knoxville in the summer of

1960 did was confront the community with the cost of its prejudice in a way that required it to decide among conflicting values. Finally, we were able to pull off the lunch counter sit-ins with comparative ease because even those who counted least in American society had the right to assemble, to communicate, and to move about freely. Any society that precludes these essentials to nonviolent organization helps to assure that protest, when it comes, will be violent.

The glory of the American civil rights revolution is that it effected a social revolution without replacing one oppressor group with another. But that means that the original group has largely remained in power. The contention thirty years after the lunch counter sit-ins is a struggle on the part of those who remain on the receiving end to get some meaningful share in the power that makes the dispositions within our society.

MERRILL PROUDFOOT

Appendix

A Chronology of Negotiations Leading to Lunch Counter Desegregation in Knoxville, Tennessee

Preliminary Events

FEBRUARY 3. President Colston of Knoxville College meets with deans and counselors of the college to discuss the handling of a lunch counter movement if one should develop among the students. It is agreed to seek a "progressive and constructive" approach to the problem in Knoxville.

FEBRUARY 15. Knoxville College students, after having visited several merchants without receiving any promises to desegregate, plan a sit-in on February 17.

FEBRUARY 16. President Colston meets with the students and persuades them instead to negotiate so long as there is hope of reaching a settlement by these means. In the days that follow, students continue their visits to merchants and talk with Chamber of Commerce officials. In general, merchants commend the students for their intelligent approach to the problem, but feel that the merchants are not in a position to desegregate at the present time.

The Mayor's Committee

MARCH 1. At the invitation of Mayor John Duncan, some twenty-two persons meet in his office to constitute a biracial citizens' committee to work on the lunch counter problem. The committee, as ultimately composed, included the following persons: city officials, Mayor Duncan (who served as chairman) and City Councilman Max Friedman; Chamber of Commerce officials.

There is a general feeling on the part of committee members that the solution lies in the direction of desegregation, and that desegregation can be accomplished in Knoxville through negotiation. Chamber representatives agree to seek a meeting of the merchants concerned, to take place within the next several days.

MARCH 4. Downtown Restaurant Association, having been contacted by the chamber, asks for a joint meeting of merchants with the Mayor's Committee on March 7. The lunch counters in view at this time are those of the four variety stores and three department stores.

MARCH. A "file-through" by twenty to twenty-five Knoxville College (K.C.) students, walking past the lunch counters in several downtown stores, but not sitting down. Students say they did this to express their feeling that merchants' meeting is being unnecessarily delayed. Merchants say they had planned to meet this very day, but have been unable to do so because of the "file-through."

MARCH 14. Mayor's Committee meets, decides to work out a quiet, planned program for desegregation. A subcommittee is designated to work out details of the plan. It is reported that some merchants feel the time is wrong for desegregation due to the national attention being given to sit-ins.

Hostess Seating Proposed

MARCH 21. Mayor's Committee meets. The Committee has in mind to work toward announcing a desegregation plan jointly with Nashville and possibly Chattanooga. A written communication is sent to the merchants asking if they will consider desegregation using a hostess plan of controlled seating and provided evidence of broad community support is secured. (The Mayor's Committee, including its Negro members, is willing to accept controlled seating by a hostess in the initial stages.)

MARCH 22. Executive Committee of the Retail Merchants Division of the Chamber of Commerce meets, acts affirmatively on the communications received from Mayor's Committee, adding other conditions, however. The text of their statement:

> The Executive Committee of the Retail Merchants Division of the Chamber of Commerce announces acceptance of the recommendation of the Mayor's Joint Citizens Committee with the following stipulations:
> > That seven (7) of the principal stores serving food participate in the program and that a trial period of 60 days be used with the right to declare a moratorium in the event of difficulty. That this acceptance be subject to Home Office approval of any national chain involved.
> It was the decision of the Committee that this trial program be timed to coincide with a similar program from Nashville; that the announcement from both cities be simultaneous.

It is understood that the stipulated number of seven stores were party to this agreement provided the other conditions could be fulfilled.

MARCH 23. 11:30 A.M. President Colston, believing that an agreement has almost been reached in Nashville and understanding the merchants to feel that approval of their home office is largely a formality, discloses to K.C. students that he expects official notice of the merchants' agreement on March 24. He counsels students on how to cooperate with store managers to make the sixty-day trial successful.

8:00 P.M. K.C. students meet with faculty advisors to plan program to enhance success of sixty-day trial period. Plan to go into schools on March 25 and churches on March 27 to urge cooperation with merchants.

MARCH 24. Merchants inform mayor and President Colston that nothing can be done at this time. The home offices of chains feel that too much pressure is being exerted upon them by the national situation and that more locally owned stores should share in the responsibility. K.C. students meet at 5:30 P.M. to continue plans to make desegregation successful, but receive instead the news that the desegregation will not take place after all.

MARCH 29. Meeting of Mayor's Committee with merchants scheduled for 10:30 A.M., but merchants send word that they prefer to meet alone so they can decide "something concrete" to present to meeting of Mayor's Committee on May 30.

Community Support Sought

MARCH 30. Mayor's Committee meets. Chamber of Commerce President William Arnett reports from the merchant's meeting of March 29 the following five-part proposal:

1. Get support of influential community groups
2. Involve more local retail merchants to balance the chain stores
3. Controlled seating
4. Mayor's Committee accept responsibility to get approval of community groups and to enlist locally owned stores
5. Publicity should be of a general nature, pointing up the move as a community effort rather than focusing on individual stores

Two subcommittees are appointed, one to get endorsement of community groups and the other to solicit participation by local stores in the move.

(Five organizations gave endorsements. They are the Board of Directors of the Chamber of Commerce, the Downtown Knoxville Improvement Association, the Board of Directors of the Association of the Women's Clubs, the Central Labor Council, and the Knoxville Ministerial Association.) The identical resolution adopted by these groups reads as follows: "Believing that what is morally sound is good for our community, we support the principle that all food services of retail establishments be opened to all citizens alike, and that as a means of getting this program started, a plan of controlled seating be instituted initially, in the event the merchants deem it necessary."

In addition, the Knoxville Area Human Relations Council and the Union Presbytery of the United Presbyterian Church adopted resolutions calling for lunch counter desegregation.

APRIL 6. Knoxville College students in a written communication to Negro adult leaders express their displeasure with the lack of progress. They ask support of the Negro adult community in a withdrawal of trade from those who discriminate at lunch counters. Adult leaders persuade students instead to join them in a request to merchants and Mayor's Committee for definite action by April 13.

Seek Participation of Local Stores

APRIL 18. Subcommittee of Mayor's Committee meets with merchants for two and a quarter hours. Store managers say that since economic success of their stores, and even their own positions, depends on success of any step taken, they cannot move unless at least three downtown drugstores participate. (Subcommittee of Mayor's Committee has already contacted the drugstores and found that two refuse, while one would cooperate, but not without the others. Two drugstores outside the downtown area, one a multiple operation, have indicated willingness to go along with a downtown solution.)

APRIL 22. Mayor's Committee meets. The Mayor reports that it has proved impossible to broaden the base by the inclusion of several locally owned downtown stores as the merchants requested, so negotiations are back where they were in the beginning. He reports that the druggists, meeting today, decided they cannot go along as a body with the programs—that while they agree in principle, it would be economically disastrous for them to desegregate if other food stores (presumably restaurants and cafeterias) were not included. The Mayor proposes that he, two Chamber of Commerce officials, and the two student members of the Mayor's Committee go to New York to confer with the executives of the four variety store chains to try to persuade them that their stores should go ahead without additional local stores.

(Continuing visits were being made throughout this period by representatives of the Mayor's Committee to merchants. Reactions of the merchants varied, but most merchants made their participation dependent upon the participation of certain other stores, while there were several who never agreed to participate under any circumstances.)

Mayor, Chamber Officials Go to New York

MAY 6. Mayor Duncan, two Chamber officials, and two students make the trip to New York. Variety store executives refused to see the students on the ground that if they did, students would be coming from all over the country to petition them. The Mayor and Chamber officials conferred with the executives. No official report was made immediately of the trend of the conversation. Unofficial reports circulated that the talks were "disappointing."

MAY 12. Mayor tells President Colston that merchants are planning to meet the next day, and he thinks things "may be completely worked out." A few minutes later, the Mayor calls Colston to report that he has heard students are sitting in at two Cole's drugstores. Colston contacts student leader by phone at the store and receives his assurance that they have accomplished their limited objective and are coming back to the campus.

MAY 13. Students inform President Colston in early afternoon that they are preparing to sit-in in numbers at several stores that afternoon. Colston informs students what he has heard from the Mayor about the merchants' meeting. Student leaders reply, "They have said that so often. We don't believe it anymore." Since merchants have previously met at 3 P.M., students agree to withhold demonstration until 3:30. At 3:30 they call from downtown to ask if President Colston has heard anything more; he has not. Students say the managers are still in their stores; they think the report of the meeting was a ruse to prevent their sitting in. They proceed to sit-in at three variety stores and one drugstore. President Colston checks with Chamber official who verifies that merchants were planning to meet at 4 P.M., but it is too late to stop the sit-ins. Later, merchants say they were unable to attend a meeting because students were in their stores at the hour set.

MAY 16. 9:00 A.M. Negro adult leaders agree not to try to restrain students from demonstrating while negotiations proceed. They express concern that no report has been given of the conference in

New York and that no meeting of the Mayor's Committee has been held since April 22.

Early evening. A mass sit-in by K.C. students is attempted at downtown stores. A crowd of hecklers collects and police protect students' return to the campus.

MAY 17. Mayor's Committee meets. Decides to send subcommittees to each of the seven original stores' managers asking them to cooperate by opening immediately on a desegregated basis. The subcommittees report back to the Mayor that evening. All stores express a willingness to desegregate lunch counters except one variety store and one department store; these two stores were anticipating a change in management.

MAY 18. Morning. Merchants meet.

Afternoon. Mayor's Committee meets. Mayor reports on conference in New York. Mayor also reports that merchants have requested a ten-day "cooling-off period." Their written communication was as follows: "In view of the events occurring last Friday, the merchants want a 'cooling off' period of ten days during which there will be no sit-ins or other demonstrations. This—as evidence of good faith. At the end of ten days the merchants will consider implementing a plan similar to Nashville's." (Nashville had some weeks earlier desegregated the lunch counters of six downtown variety and department stores. The plan followed was that Negroes might come in small numbers during specified slack hours the first week, and beginning with the second week the counters would be completely desegregated.

Discussion arises as to what the merchants meant by "will consider implementing." The Mayor states that from his conversations with representative of the merchants, it is his understanding that the merchants intended actually to put the Nashville plan into effect at the end of ten days. While the committee continues meeting, he checks this by phone with one of the merchants and is assured this is the correct interpretation.

Wishing to make absolutely certain, however, the Mayor's Committee sends the following communication to the merchants: "We accept the proposal made by the merchants to the Mayor's Committee May 18th and interpret the good faith of the merchants to mean that a plan similar to the Nashville plan will be put into effect at the close of the ten day period, and request a report back to the Mayor's Committee if this is an inaccurate interpretation."

Evening. A subcommittee consisting of Mrs. Perry, Mr. Dempster, Rev. James, and Rev. Linsey meets with Knoxville College students to persuade them to accept the ten-day "cooling-off period" proposed by merchants. They assure students they are confident this is a bona fide offer and merchants will desegregate at the end of ten days. Since ten days would be the end of school, students ask for a five-day period instead.

MAY 19. Mrs. Perry confers with merchants asking if five days is acceptable. Merchants state that five days is acceptable if local stores can be persuaded to participate, otherwise the ten-day period would stand.

MAY 20. President Colston meets with merchants. Merchants express fear of losing business to stores located outside the downtown area if downtown stores desegregate. Colston asks merchants to help persuade other stores to go along, and they agree to do so. Agree to report back on May 23.

MAY 23. President Colston again meets with merchants. Report is that merchants and Mayor's Committee have been unable to secure cooperation of major locally owned drugstores, therefore the five-day compromise cannot be granted. Negotiations therefore revert to the ten-day "cooling-off" period. Merchants agree to indicate their intentions to Mr. Nash of the Chamber of Commerce by Saturday morning, May 28, the end of the ten-day period.

(Sometime during the course of the ten-day period, merchants reply in negative to communication from Mayor's Committee. Merchants state they did not commit themselves to desegregate at the end of ten days, but only to *consider* putting the Nashville plan into operation. This statement never reached the full Mayor's Committee, however, since the Committee never met again after May 18.)

MAY 28. End of ten-day "cooling-off" period. Five stores have registered their intention to desegregate if a total of seven would. Two abstaining stores did not report either yes or no to the Chamber. No official word is received from the merchants as to what they plan to do.

Subsequent Events

MAY 30. Knoxville College commencement. Students leave the campus not having heard that merchants stated Mayor's Committee misinterpreted their promise. Knowing only that counters are still segregated, students believe merchants deceived them with ten-day "cooling-off" period, aiming only to avoid sit-ins until students would be gone for the summer.

JUNE 7. Negro leaders, including students still in Knoxville, meet to plan further action. Present are virtually all Negroes who were members of the Mayor's Committee. None holds any hope for continued negotiations through the Mayor's Committee. All believe that the ten days which have elapsed since the end of the ten-day "cooling-off" period has given the merchants ample time to consider putting the Nashville plan into effect. Adult leaders recall their promises to students that if and when all hope vanished for reaching a solution through negotiations, they would join the students in demonstrations. The group decides that first a test should be made to see whether counters have been desegregated.

JUNE 8. Negroes go two by two to each of the ten establishments involved in the negotiations and are refused service in all except one place which served them ("by mistake" as they were later told).

The Associated Council for Full Citizenship formed to lead lunch counter movement. Rev. R. E. James elected chairman, Rev. W. T. Crutcher, co-chairman.

Sit-ins Begin

JUNE 9. Sit-ins in numbers commence at Rich's, Grant's, Sears, Todd & Armistead (downtown store). Public statement explains why sit-ins are necessary. Customers continue to patronize counters while they remain open, but as soon as several Negroes arrive, the counters are closed. Rich's has barricade around counter, guards to exclude Negroes; Negroes form protest line, counter is closed to avoid violence. (Sit-ins continue from this date through July 1, occurring Monday through Friday from 11 A.M. until about 2 P.M., sometimes longer. There is regular organized participation by white women and white men.)

JUNE 12. First mass meeting, Mt. Olive Baptist Church. Enlists sit-inners and previews as possible moves "Trade with Your Friends" and "Economic Withdrawal from Downtown."

JUNE 13. Kress's included in sit-ins (one day only). Miller's operates as usual with signs up: "For Employees Only."

JUNE 16. By this time, groups of white youths are collecting in stores and outside them to heckle and threaten sit-inners. Their efforts are directed mostly against white sit-inners. Grant's counter is now staying open during sit-ins; customers continue to come even though at times there are ten to twelve Negroes at counter.

JUNE 17. Large crowd, including many of the hecklers, gathers in Todd & Armistead to hear a harangue by white segregationist; the police are called. Rich's closes "for repairs," Sears "for two-week vacation," Todd & Armistead "for vacation and repairs." After University of Tennessee (U.T.) student roughed up on street and white K.C. professor followed and threatened, sit-inners adopt procedure of protecting white sit-inners as they leave stores.

JUNE 20. With three counters closed, sit-ins shifted to Cole's (next to Hamilton Bank) and Walgreen's; Grant's still included.

JUNE 21. Cole's ropes off counter in attempt to keep Negroes out. Demonstrators form standing protest line. Several demonstrators at Walgreen's sprayed with insecticide, which makes one white woman demonstrator ill. *News-Sentinel* reports Rich's counter is "closed permanently."

JUNE 22. Demonstrators go under the rope at Cole's after white customers are admitted.

JUNE 23. Two Negro women turned away from Rich's Laurel

Room. (On subsequent days, others go and are refused service.) Two Negro ministers refused admittance to Miller's counter, while whites are admitted. (A few days later, after more visits by Negroes, Miller's counter is closed, and the word given out privately that it will not be reopened.)

JUNE 24. Fifteen white and Negro ministers meet to discuss lunch counter situation, ask official meeting of Knoxville Ministerial Association. Negro leaders rally in increasing numbers to support the lunch counter movement. Handbills distributed throughout Negro residential areas urging "Trade with Your Friends."

JUNE 26. Second mass meeting, Mt. Olive Baptist Church. Crowd estimated at 1,400. Emphasis on "Trade with Your Friends" and demonstrations.

JUNE 27. All-day picketing of Rich's involving several hundred Negro and white picketers. The "news barrier" is broken, with fair newspaper, radio, and TV coverage and thousands driving by to watch. The Negro community is now fully aroused. Todd & Armistead reopens its counter.

JUNE 28. Meeting of Knoxville Ministerial Association adopts statement to merchants, Mayor, and Chamber of Commerce favoring opening counters to all and asks renewal of negotiations and the support by Christian people of merchants who desegregate. Sit-in (one day only) at McClellan's, Woolworth's, Kress's in addition to Grant's, Cole's, and Walgreen's. White U.T. student sitting-in at Cole's struck with fist three times by white youth.

Violence at Walgreen's

JUNE 29. Violence erupts at Walgreen's. Lunch counter employee throws lighted cigarette on white demonstrator, spills coffee and Coke (which had been purchased by white sympathizers and set before sit-inners) on two Negro demonstrators. White youths throw Coke over white Knoxville College professor sitting in booth with Negro man, then strike the professor on the face twice and try to pull him out of the booth. A white male customer restores order, since management has made no move to do so. Later, another white man who has been sitting in a booth throws a saltshaker at a Negro demonstrator, hits instead a white woman and her thirteen-day-old baby. He is arrested, ultimately fined $14.50 for disturbing the peace. The story of these incidents goes out through wire services to papers all over the country.

Mr. Judson K. Shults, owner of Todd & Armistead stores, gets an injunction from Chancery Court Judge Dawson against any member of the Associated Council, any Negro, or any sympathizer attempting to get service at the counter of Todd and Armistead store at Market and Clinch.

JUNE 30. White U.T. professor struck on head at Kress's, requires medical attention. Two Negro boys pulled from stools at Grant's. Four Negro men picket Todd & Armistead; one elderly picketer knocked to the ground by hecklers.

JULY 1. Eleven Negro boys, not sit-inners, arrested and charged with disorderly conduct and inciting to riot (latter a state charge). Is climax of a situation where gangs of youths of both races are roaming downtown streets, apparently looking for trouble.

City Safety Director Oglesby asks that sit-inners be limited to six per store. *News-Sentinel* editorializes against sit-ins. Handbills are distributed calling for a "Stay Away from Downtown" movement.

JULY 2. *News-Sentinel* runs another editorial with more positive tone, headed "Let's Start over Again" (that is, with negotiation). Executive Committee of Associated Council, hearing that merchants may meet soon, decides not to demonstrate at all through July 6, nor anytime when negotiations are going on. This also constitutes temporary reply to city safety director's request.

JULY 3. Third mass meeting, First AME Zion Church. Stresses "Stay Away from Downtown" movement. Those who had been demonstrating are put to work passing out handbills at bus stops and door to door in Negro areas.

JULY 7. Negotiating committee of the Associated Council meets with Mayor and Chamber officials. Merchants meet and report progress toward agreement. Two thousand five hundred handbills are passed out at U.T. explaining the movement for equality at lunch counters and asking for support. (Sit-ins not resumed, negotiations going on.)

JULY 8. Associated Council Negotiation Committee meets with merchants, who are now organized with a chairman. Agree on procedure. Five Gay Street stores have agreed to open counters to all, and the two suburban stores of one firm will be included.

JULY 10. A one-fourth-page ad paid for by the Associated Council appears in Sunday *News-Sentinel*. Headed, "An Appeal for Human Rights," it lists some sixteen areas in which Negroes are discriminated against. Fourth mass meeting, Mt. Zion Baptist Church, anticipates victory, but learns few details.

Desegregation Announced

JULY 12. A "Good Will Committee" of prominent white citizens meets at call of Mayor and Chamber. Committee requests desegregation. Merchants meet, reply in affirmative. Merchants issue statement which is published in afternoon paper. The merchants are presented with the statement signed by seventy-four ministers calling for desegregation, and send this together with the names of members of Good Will Committee to their home offices to show that desegregation comes by local request with local support.

JULY 17. Fifth mass meeting, Logan Temple AME Zion Church. Negroes learn terms of agreement with merchants: A ten-day "easing-in" period during which only two Negroes at a time would patronize a counter; the council to supply each store with a "host" or "hostess" during hours counter is open. White friends from churches and civic groups asked to patronize the counters. "Stay Away from Downtown" movement ended; Council reverts to "Trade with Your Friends" movement.

JULY 18. Counters of seven stores open to all. No incidents. Business appears as brisk as usual. Observers note a tour of the five Gay Street stores often finds no Negroes at any counter, though the total number during a day is appreciable.

JULY 24. Sixth mass meeting, Tabernacle Baptist Church. Report desegregation going well, no open opposition has appeared. Announced that two outlying stores have voluntarily desegregated and two other firms will do so soon. Continuing "Trade with Your Friends" emphasis. Other goals listed: opening U.T. undergraduate school, removing inequalities at Eastern State Hospital, increasing opportunities for Negroes in employment.

Derived from a chronology prepared in 1960 by a member of the Knoxville sit-in movement.